# The Subversion of Romance
# in the Novels of Barbara Pym

# The Subversion of Romance
# in the Novels of Barbara Pym

## Ellen M. Tsagaris

Bowling Green State University Popular Press
Bowling Green, OH 43403

Library of Congress Cataloging-in-Publication Data
Tsagaris, Ellen M.
 The subversion of romance in the novels of Barbara Pym/Ellen M.
Tsagaris.
  p. cm.
 Includes bibliographical references (p.     ).
 ISBN 0-87972-763-2 (cloth). -- ISBN 0-87972-764-0 (pbk.)
  1. Pym, Barbara--Criticism and interpretation.  2. Literature and society--
England--History--History--20th century.  3. Women and literature--
England--History--20th century.  4. Man-woman relationships in literature.
5. Manners and customs in literature.  6. Middle aged persons in literature.
7. Single women in literature.  I. Title.
PR6066.Y58Z88   1998
823'.914--DC21                                                    98-2630
                                                                      CIP

Cover design by Dumm Art

*For Dad with my thanks:*

*Doctor Johnson has nothing over you*

# Contents

# Introduction:
# "Something Very Barbara Pym"

About ten years ago, while I was teaching in a community college, I read a review in a Spanish magazine about a woman writer I had never heard of. As I would later discover, it was ironic that the magazine was one of the so-called women's magazines, geared primarily to female readers. That writer was Barbara Pym. Immediately, I became enamored of her cozy plots involving unmarried but independent women, and their eccentric friends and neighbors. Her characters seemed like real people, and the plots of her novels appeared to be biographical chronicles of their adventures, the more so because the same characters appeared and reappeared throughout the novels. For instance, the characters of *A Glass of Blessings* read a story written by Catherine Oliphant, the romance author of *Less Than Angels*. Pym's depictions of church life inspired me, her mouth-watering descriptions of food piqued my appetite. My friends and I would comment that, every time we read a Pym novel, we got strange cravings for poached eggs and Ovaltine.

Years later, when I was in my second year of graduate school, I took a seminar with Dr. Judy Little, herself a Pym expert. In class, we studied the works of Pym and Virginia Woolf. The rest, as the saying goes, is history. I read everything I could about Pym and her writing. Like her, I started reading cookbooks for their own sake, and I started thinking about romance novels and everyday life in ways I had not even dreamed of before. This book was the final product of my own fascination with Pym. But, as I read, studied, and reread *A Very Private Eye* and *A Lot to Ask,* the portrait of a savvy, very clever, and very creative writer emerged alongside that of the bubbling ingenue who loved to go parties and to fall in love. "Good books for a bad day," one critic called her novels, but though an apt description, this one statement does not adequately bring to life the complex, scholarly woman who "fought tenaciously and coura- geously to establish herself as a professional writer" (Holt xi). In fact, Holt points out that Pym took great pleasure at the reviews of her novels near the end of her life because these reviews gave recognition to the fact that she had achieved the status of a writer, which status was more important to her than anything else (x). To understand the elements of a Pym novel, one has to understand a little about Pym herself.

Barbara Mary Crampton Pym was the daughter of Frederic Crampton Pym and Irena Pym. Irena was a handsome, "tomboyish" woman with a good sense of humor. She was assistant organist at her church and much of her family's social life centered around the church calendar. Clergy were frequent guests in the Pym home, just as they are in Pym's novels. In *A Lot to Ask*, Hazel Holt, Pym's friend, colleague, and biographer, writes that Frederic's birth certificate, uncovered after the author's death, gave rise to suspicions that he was illegitimate (5). Holt observes that Pym died without knowing there had been a mystery about her father's birth, "which is a pity, since it would have been just the sort of investigation that she enjoyed so much" (5).

Frederic Pym grew to be a young lawyer in a firm of solicitors. He married Irena Thomas in 1911. Barbara, the younger of two daughters, was born in 1913, in the town of Oswestry, population about 10,000 during the 1920s (Holt 6). Oswestry is a small market town in Shropshire, near the Welsh border. Lately, the town has been in the news because it is the home of the late Princess Diana's bodyguard. The Pyms were not well-off, but the professional class they belonged to, which included lawyers and clergy, was more educated and thus appeared to be more cultured. According to Holt, the caste of professional folk that Pym's family belonged to was just below the Gentry (6). The Pyms, in short, belonged to a "microcosm of English provincial life, where the social classes were neatly stratified and people knew exactly where their place was in the scheme of things" (6).

Both parents loved music. The elder Pyms had a good sense of humor, and they loved to socialize with friends and family. Relatives and cousins on her mother's side made up an influential part of the scheme of things for Pym. Her mother's sister, Jany, was "dashing, full of ideas and initiative, with a passion for painting and a great flair for design" (Holt 10). Like Tom Mallow's old flame, Elaine, of *Less Than Angels,* Jany loved dogs. She was the first member of her family to drive a car and she was athletic. Aunt Jany also was very popular with her nieces, and knew "instinctively" what children liked (10). For the young Barbara, she was a "splendid example of how it was possible to be unmarried and still have a 'rich full life'" (10). In Holt's sketch of Jany, one is reminded a little of Vanessa Bell, the artist who was also the sister of Virginia Woolf.

Barbara had a friendly, easy-going relationship with her parents and made up nicknames for them and for other members of her family. Irena was "Links," and Frederic was "Dor" (Holt 10). Her sister Hilary was "Poopa," and Barbara herself was called "Buddy." Barbara's carefree mother with the ironic sense of fun and humor set the tone for the household. Years later, Barbara would remember Irena in her portrait of Jane Cleveland of *Jane and Prudence.* The Pyms' large, Edwardian house was home to Barbara for over 20 years.

Frederic's younger daughter attended Huyton College, Liverpool, a boarding school for upper middle-class girls. The headmistress of Huyton was Helène Le Jeune, a cheerful, eccentric woman who was the sister of C. A. Le Jeune, a well-known film critic of the time (13). Pym then attended St. Hilda's College, Oxford, and graduated in 1934, in English (Burkhart 2). It is significant to note that she was among the first young women to attend Oxford, as if in answer to Virginia Woolf's complaints in *A Room of One's Own,* written in 1928.

During World War II, Barbara found work as a censor, a job particularly fitting to her inquisitive personality. Later, she joined the Women's Royal Naval Service and went to Naples. In time, she would write about the WRNS in *Excellent Women,* and she would describe how Rocky Napier, a dashing character in the novel, had charmed lonely WRNS during his tour of duty. In 1948, she began work at the International African Institute as a research assistant. By 1958, she became an editorial secretary and eventually assistant editor of *Africa,* the institute's periodical. She worked there with Hazel Holt until failing health forced her to retire in 1974. Holt, the author of *A Lot to Ask,* a biography of Pym, also served as her editor and literary adviser. Today, Hazel Holt writes the "Mrs. Malory" mysteries, about a fiftyish widow, very much like a Barbara Pym character. In novels like *Mrs. Malory and the Festival Murder,* and *Mrs. Malory Wonders Why,* Holt gives lavish descriptions of good food, and features characters such as Enid Palgrave, who writes cookery books. In *Mrs. Malory Wonders Why,* an octogenarian gentlewoman is killed by cyanide put in her favorite almond tarts, a particularly uncivilized act, so that her flat can be sold at a profit. Holt's style is reminiscent of Pym in almost every way, so that the excellent woman continues to live on in English literature, this time as a true detective solving murders.

Her friends and biographers have called Pym a woman of stoicism, courage, and endurance, qualities she later gave to her heroines (Holt x). Like them, Pym was vulnerable; Hazel Holt has written that, even at the end of her life, her eyes were "those of an anxious girl" (x). Also like her heroines, Pym could make the best of things. Like them, she enjoyed most "small, blameless comforts" (x). Charles Burkhart, another Pym critic, says that Barbara was obsessed with curiosity, and he further observes that every Pym heroine is inquisitive in one way or another (10).

She had always "scribbled" and kept notebooks and diaries. Pym's notebooks remained important for her throughout her life. They were working journals, in which she jotted down appealing quotations, possible scenes for novels or plots, overheard bits of conversation, anything that interested her. Pym writes that keeping these notebooks was often "more of a pleasure than the actual writing" ("Finding a Voice" 386). For example, when she was very young, she was an avid golfer along with the rest of the Pyms. Barbara was particularly interested in Rex and Lister Hartley, two brothers who were famous golfers. She chronicled their careers and personal lives in great detail in her notebooks in an example of what Holt terms Barbara's passion for "finding out about people," and showing the thorough and organized way in which she went about it" (9). Later, she would engage in a similar exercise centering on author Denton Welch and his work. As Pym herself stated in her radio talk, "Finding a Voice," "I've been trying to write novels, with many ups and downs, over more than forty years. I started as a schoolgirl, when I used to contribute to the school magazine—mostly parodies, conscious even then of other people's styles" (382). Pym studied the styles of others because she felt it was important that she find her own writing voice, so that her work "would be immediately recognizable as having been written by [her] and by nobody else" ("Finding a Voice" 388). One of her critics, the distinguished Charles Burkhart, writes that Pym's tone of voice belonged to teatime, and that her conversation would be "well-bred, urbane, ironic, with a hovering sense of the absurd; it would never be contentious or dogmatic or impertinent" and he laments that "we can only meet her in the long teatime of her books" (70). He writes that there is "joy" in Pym's literary voice, and that it is the joy "of an artist entirely in command of her instrument" (72).

But Pym was not content to write only for herself. When pondering the question "Why write at all?" Pym agreed with Ivy Compton-Burnett, who often said she would write for a dozen people, but would not write for no one. Pym said, "This is what I feel myself—it is those dozen people that spur me on, even when it seems that I'm writing for myself alone" (386). She was inspired to become a writer full time when she read Aldous Huxley's *Crome Yellow* at the age of sixteen. After reading Huxley, Pym wrote her first attempts at a novel, *Young Men in Fancy Dress*. The experience of writing a long work taught Pym that she could write easily and fluently, so that as Holt says, Barbara's perception of herself as a writer grew (20). Later, Pym stated that she enjoyed the novels of "Elizabeth," who wrote "Elizabeth and Her German Garden" and novels like *The Enchanted April* and *The Pastor's Wife* ("Finding a Voice" 383). By this time, Pym was at Oxford, and she realized that, as she says in "Finding a Voice," these novels were to her a "revelation" (383). Pym was taken with their "dry, unsentimental treatment of the relationship between men and women" (383). The style of these novels, with their wit and "delicate irony," touched a "chord" in Pym herself, and she chose them as her literary models (383). What Barbara read often inspired her own books, so that when she read Gertrude Trevelyan's *Hothouse,* she wanted "desperately" to write an Oxford novel (41). She did so later when she penned *Crampton Hodnet.* Pym began *Some Tame Gazelle,* her first published novel, in Oswestry, but continued to work on it during her years at Oxford. Holt says that at this point, Pym "already saw herself as a professional writer" and was very disciplined about her craft (52). In fact, when she died in 1980 of cancer, she left behind notebooks and sketches for yet another novel. Even her stays in the hospital yielded creative material.

Myriad examples of Pym's love of trivia appear in her novels and notebooks, too. Pym enjoyed small pleasures best throughout her life, and was happy and comforted by a good meal, a decent cup of tea, or an interesting bit of gossip. The same obsession with detail and curiosity which prompted her to follow-up on people she admired prompted her to start collecting material on writer Denton Welch. On a trip to Portugal, Pym first read Welch's *Maiden Voyage.* As Hazel Holt writes, Barbara became "besotted" with the writer who died at age thirty-three (1972). Pym began to collect everything she could on Welch, and even obtained a copy of his will. Also, she took a trip to Greenwich to look at a house in which he once lived (173). Holt observes that Pym loved Welch "for his acute miniaturist observation and vibrant interest in everything he saw, focusing in on the smallest object or incident so that it became something brilliant and living" (172). Welch seemed to influence Pym the most in her own work because he, too, realized "the value of small comforts (of trivia) in an embattled life" (173). She found a kindred spirit in Welch, who was a complex and moody person. Like Pym, Welch showed that "littleness" can build up into something moving and universal in the right hands" (Holt 173).

Pym was at her creative best, though, when she wrote about love and romance. Her vivid imagination often swept away her own emotions, so that she was at times more in love with "being in love" than she was with another human being. Hazel Holt writes that Barbara liked the "preliminaries" in a love affair best. So much, that Barbara invented Barbara Bird, the young undergraduate in *Crampton Hodnet,* who is more in love with the idea of being seduced by an older man, than with the physical consummation itself. For Barbara Bird and Barbara Pym, true passion is cerebral, and romance embodies the idea of love, not just the physical act. Pym, who loved to play detective, enjoyed the speculation, and the "pursuit" of the love object, the "finding out" about the person, almost more than the affair itself (95). Because her style dictated a "dry and unsentimental" treatment of love, Pym was able to write about love in a "detached" manner ("Finding a Voice" 383). She herself has written that "The concept of 'detachment' reminds me of the methods of the anthropologist, who studies societies in this way. The joke definition of anthropology as 'the study of man embracing woman' might therefore seem peculiarly applicable to the novelist" ("Finding a Voice" 384).

The man who came and went as Barbara's steadiest love interest throughout her life was Henry Harvey, called "Lorenzo" by Barbara. Though Harvey married and divorced another woman, and moved to another country, he and Barbara remained close. After she died, Harvey called her a "triumphantly good person" (qtd. in Holt x). Their friendship began during their days in Oxford in 1932, and lasted until Barbara died; in fact, Henry was one of her last visitors. At this time, Holt describes Pym, saying that her manner was "a kind of overflowing vivacity which held an essential innocence, and he [Harvey] could have no inkling of the intricate web of romance and fantasy that Barbara had already begun to weave around him" (38). So intricate was this web, that Barbara was virtually seduced by her own creation, the Lorenzo persona she created for Harvey (49).

Yet many themes run through Pym's works, including themes involving loss, suffering, and desperation. Her unique view was comprised of examples from the well of her own experience, defined by Holt and other friends and critics as a view which included "ironic observation and deep feeling . . . frivolity and high spirits and a sensitive understanding of the unspoken happiness, the unformed wish that can never be fulfilled" (ix).

By 1977, three years before her death, Pym was enjoying some of the critical acclaim that had escaped her during the fourteen years the publishing world had ignored her. In January 1977, *The Times Literary Supplement* published a list of the most "under-rated writers of the century." The list was chosen by respected literary figures, and Philip Larkin and Lord David Cecil selected Barbara Pym, the only living writer on the list to be named by two people (*A Very Private Eye* 191). Also that year, Macmillan published *Quartet in Autumn,* and Jonathan Cape, her first publisher, reprinted her earlier books. In November 1977, the BBC produced a television program about Pym and her work, and *Quartet* was shortlisted for the Booker Prize. Macmillan published *The Sweet Dove Died* in 1978. After she finished the last draft of *A Few Green Leaves,* the cancer she had been suffering from for several years began to take its final toll on Pym (*A Very Private Eye* 291). By January

1980, Pym became gravely ill. She was admitted to a hospice and took with her a final notebook. Henry Harvey was one of her last visitors on January 8, and Hazel Holt comments, "It seemed, somehow, fitting that almost the last visitor Belinda had should be the Archdeacon" (*A Very Private Eye* 292). (Holt is making a reference to the two characters in *Some Tame Gazelle* who were based on Barbara and Harvey.) Pym died on January 11, 1980. Hazel Holt, her friend and editor, has written perhaps the most fitting epitaph anyone could about Pym: "Throughout her illness she had maintained a cheerful stoicism, very down-to-earth and practical, never self-pitying. She was sustained, certainly, by her strong faith, and still able, as she had been throughout her life, to draw comfort from small pleasures and ironies, and this is perhaps, the greatest gift she has bequeathed to all who read her" (*A Very Private Eye* 292).

# 1

# The History and Definition of Romance Fiction

Much has been written about Barbara Pym's love of the trivial and mundane. In fact, the plots of her novels center around afternoon tea, jumble sales, cafeteria meals, housework, and flower arranging. While it is true, as many critics have noted, that Pym found joy in the everyday occurrences of life, she also used the seemingly trivial elements of her stories to subvert the discourse of the romance novel. As Barbara Brothers writes in "Women Victimized by Fiction: Living and Loving in the Novels of Barbara Pym," Pym's art is subversive; her "gentle ironies mock the romantic paradigm and her characters' acceptance of it" (79). Brothers's thesis is that Pym wants to show that romance in fiction and romance in real life are not the same (69). Brothers uses the example of Pym's character Catherine Oliphant, the romance writer, who questions a scene in her story because she wonders if it is realistic. According to Brothers, Catherine, by finally choosing to use her own experience as a basis for her story, chooses an episode that actually reflects a woman's life (69). Brothers also argues that Pym controverts the idea that women's images of themselves are formed by poets, novelists, popular culture, and magazines (71).

Pym was influenced by earlier writers such as Austen and the Brontës, and knew romances as well. She borrows and rewrites the standard plots and characters of romance novels to create her own version of the heroine's quest for a meaningful life. Pym is especially fond of subverting the stock elements of romance. She uses descriptions of food and clothing for comic effect and for undermining the romance genre. Furthermore, Pym's comic reduction of the Byronic and aristocratic hero and her revision of the romance heroine redefine romantic love as it is presented in literature. Pym spoofs various forms of romance novels to answer the question of whether a human being, particularly a woman, can live a full life in a less-than-perfect world. Pym's subversive treatment of the romance genre usually answers the question positively; a single woman living in the dreary modern world is still capable of adventure and of living a meaningful life.

Pym was a member of the Romance Novelists Association which included Barbara Cartland and other romantic novelists, but she herself found writing according to the romance formula difficult, though she did publish one romantic magazine story (*A Very Private Eye* 280). Yet, she was fascinated by stories of romance, and often parodied her own unhappy love affairs in her diaries, and later in her books. Romance writers like Catherine Oliphant of *Less than Angels* and aficionados of the romance genre like Prudence Bates of *Jane and Prudence* are among her most interesting characters. Through irony, hyperbole, metaphor, and exaggeration, Pym often parodies the stock romantic plots of the "pot-boiler" romances.

For example, Pym takes the plot of the younger woman falling in love with a married, older man and subverts it through humor, and more important, through emphasizing the trivial and everyday. Pym also subverts romantic discourse by using food. Where novelists like Cartland and Victoria Holt use description in the extreme, describing either a feast or a famine, pauper's tatters or ball gowns, Pym cooks up for her heroines common meals of cafeteria food and baked beans on toast. In a Pym novel, food can serve as a means of self-expression, or as an indicator of class. Moreover, the discourse of eating may also be a metaphor for sex.

Pym's treatment of physical affection parodies romance as well. Where romance writers describe the main couple's first kiss as one that "takes one's breath away," and leaves the heroine "reeling with lusty passion," Pym's Leonora of *The Sweet Dove Died* is shocked and slightly sickened at her first passionate kiss. While sex is very much a part of Pym's work, it is often minimized through jokes and humorous situations. For some romance writers, however, graphic sex takes the part of centerpiece in their plots.

Pym's subversion of the discourse, however, is not just a parody, and it is on this last point that I differ from others writing about her work. Pym's characters, like Mildred Lathbury of *Excellent Women,* are people who lead believable, if not very glamorous lives. Pym's style is primarily realistic, and more in keeping with the styles of writers like Ivy Compton-Burnett, Elizabeth Taylor, and Margaret Drabble.

Because Pym's characters are basically realistic, her readers may see in them types of people that they know. In fact, Barbara Brothers calls Pym's heroines "those fiction has ignored" (79). Other critics call Pym's heroines "excellent women," thus borrowing the title of one of Pym's most famous novels. The origin of the phrase, however, dates to metaphysical poet John Donne. In his "Paradox XI: A Defence of Womens Inconstancy" of his *Dubia,* Donne writes, "In myne opynion such men are happie that women are *Inconstant* for soe they may chance to be beloved of some Excellent Woman (when it comes to their turne) out of their Inconstancy, and Mutability, though not out of their own desert" (Donne 54). Mildred Lathbury, the female protagonist of *Excellent Women,* is thirty and rather "mousy" when compared to heroines like Kathleen Winsor's buxom Amber, but like Amber, Mildred has been left orphaned and has serious concerns with what to do with the rest of her life. As an "excellent woman," she is called on to make tea in crises, organize jumble sales, and befriend clergymen and respectable "gentlewomen" of limited means. Mildred's dilemma is whether such is a "full life." Feeling resentment at having always to make tea, share bathrooms, and make meals is not one of the great heroic myths of Western culture, but to Mildred, feeling resentment is a serious problem.

Though Pym uses romantic discourse to inflate the events in Mildred's life, the reader understands that Mildred is not a caricature of a romance heroine. Perhaps Pym is making a point about the lives of women and the fact that they often inhabit different, more isolated worlds than men. Or, she may be saying that most people, male and female, dwell on trivialities (Brothers 74). For example, what men label trivial—housework, cooking, visiting, church work—is to women an entire network of connections. Others besides Pym have studied women's networks of connection.

Elaine Showalter's "Feminist Criticism in the Wilderness" uses the Ardener diagram to illustrate the separation in men's and women's lives. According to the husband and wife anthropologists who developed the diagram, some spheres of human experience are exclusively female and others exclusively male. Because of this exclusivity, members of one sphere do not necessarily understand those of the other. The "trivial" world of housework and cooking that Pym so often describes is generally part of the female sphere.

Perhaps Barbara Brothers puts it best when she writes that Pym rejects as romantic the fictional and historical idea that life is lived in pursuit of noble ends (77). One might see some similarity with views that Virginia Woolf holds in *Jacob's Room* and *The Waves.* In both, a young man dies by "defending" or by representing the British Empire; Jacob dies in war; Percival dies by falling off a horse in India. Both deaths seem pointless and less than noble. In the same way, Tom Mallow of Pym's *Less Than Angels,* another representative of the Empire, is accidentally shot in Africa because he is wearing native robes and someone mistakes him for a native.

Critics such as Janice Rossen in *Independent Women* and Anne Wyatt-Brown in *Barbara Pym: A Critical Biography* have touched on Pym's interest in romance and on her love of humor, and Lotus Snow in

*One Little Room* emphasizes that Pym loves the trivial to the point of obsession (Snow 9-10). One crucial point that critics who discuss Pym and romance miss is that romance writers *know* they are writing escapist fantasy; they do not claim to write realistic stories. Perhaps this is one reason they use detail differently and less often than Pym. As Jayne Ann Krentz, Daphne Clair, Doreen Owens Malek, Angela Wells, and other romance writers (who are also literary critics) write in their essays and letters, romances are related to ancient myths and fairy tales; they are meant to be illusions. In any case, no critic to date has approached Pym as this study will, by focusing on her use and subversion of romantic discourse to achieve comic effect.

Catherine Oliphant of *Less Than Angels* is a sort of paradigm of Pym's technique. She is a romance writer and heroine who, according to Janice Rossen in *The World of Barbara Pym,* writes in a parody of Pym's own literary style because she, too, liberally sprinkles her work with literary epigraphs and quotations (142). Rossen further discusses Pym's subtlety in creating the Tom/Catherine liaison. For example, it is not at all clear that Catherine has any physical relationship with Tom, and she claims that Pym is reticent on the subject of sex (57). Instead, Rossen argues that Catherine, like Pym, is able to stand apart and view life with detachment in the manner of an artist. Because she is an artist, she is able to use her own disappointments in love and write about them in a removed, professional manner, a trait she shares with her creator (129). As Margaret Chittenden writes in "Writing the Romantic Novel You'd Like to Read," one advantage in writing romantic novels is that a person can draw on her own experience (268).

Still, Pym's heroines who are keen observers are also artists in their own right; they collect and use observations to interpret their surroundings. Rossen notes that Pym's artist heroines gain insight into love, and do not succumb to the chronic infatuation which plagues some of her other female characters (129). Perhaps at this point Rossen is thinking of Leonora from *The Sweet Dove Died* and Wilmet from *A Glass of Blessings.* Rossen is also among the first of Pym's critics to note that she subverts the conventional happy ending to her love stories by having the heroine reject marriage with the hero, as occurs between Jessie Morrow and Mr. Latimer in *Crampton Hodnet.*

In *Something to Love: Barbara Pym's Novels,* Diana Benet focuses on Pym's powers of observation and how she uses them when she writes novels. Benet also says that Catherine is a realist, despite her romantic fiction. In fact, Catherine uses the ingredients of romance to "make life palatable," perhaps because she observes the same unhappiness in others that she herself suffers (65). Unlike Rossen, however, Benet claims that

Catherine's detachment is not deliberate but rather subconscious on her part (66).

The ingredients of romance fiction vary. Janice Radway writes in *Reading the Romance* that romances are open-ended stories about different heroines who undergo various experiences that change their lives and cause them to grow or change emotionally (17). Radway argues that romance authors use the conventions of the realistic novel. She describes the realistic novel as the "yet uncompleted story of a singular individual" (17).

One may read Catherine Oliphant's own life in *Less Than Angels* as the uncompleted story of a singular individual. At the novel's end, she has come to terms with her former lover's death and is apparently courting Alaric Lydgate. We do not know, however, whether the two marry, though there is every indication that they might. In any case, Catherine looks as if she will have a very full life at the close of the novel. Robert Liddell, though, reads Catherine another way; he calls her "poor Catherine," and argues that she lives the romantic magazine stories she writes (101).

Liddell's assessment of "poor Catherine" living her stories is typical of criticism aimed at women who read and write romance. Several critics and romance authors counter assessments like this. Janice Radway argues that the romance does more than perform a social function by imposing an alien ideology on unsuspecting readers (8). In particular, Radway does not like to see romance readers characterized as "passive" receptacles (6). She points out that when asked why they read romances, women do not restrict themselves to textual reasons (9). Like all readers, romance readers interpret the text according to experiences in their own lives that they compare and contrast with the text (8). Yet, Radway writes that because women who read romances have been stigmatized and accused of "living their stories;" both authors and readers are on the defensive, and tend to develop coherent explanations or apologia with which to answer their critics (14).

Not all male critics see Pym's Catherine Oliphant as a passive victim of her own fiction. In Charles Burkhart's *The Pleasures of Miss Pym* the author calls Catherine "skeptical," and says her fiction is a contrast to her "generous and sharp sensibilities" (39). Burkhart sees her as a liberating force for Lydgate, her love interest, and comments on her strength of character.

Strength of character and keen sensibility are qualities that Catherine shares with heroines of romance novels. Because Catherine exhibits these qualities, Pym focuses on Catherine's emotions throughout *Less Than Angels,* just as romance authors highlight their heroines' emotions in their novels. In fact, Kristin Ramsdell writes in *Happily Ever After: A*

*Guide to Reading Interests in Romance Fiction* that the definition of a romance novel centers on the development of the love relationship between the hero and heroine (3). Therefore, the emotions of the hero and heroine are important. Pym generally records the emotions of the male/female protagonists in her novels, but she details different kinds of emotions than does the romance novelist. The passionate emotions Pym records have their origin in the intellect, not the physical senses. Barbara Bird's discourse of romance in *Crampton Hodnet* is a prime example. For the pretty undergraduate Barbara, romance is made up of two intelligent people who love each other despite the fact that one is married (132). Her ideas are noble to the point of being platonic, for she has no experience of physical love. Like any romantic heroine, Barbara is ready for whatever might be in store for her, but she finds kisses unpleasant (103). In an amusing passage which takes place at the library, Barbara feels "hopeless and frustrated and there was a sick feeling at the pit of her stomach, which she did not recognize as a craving for her lunch" (133). There is both sarcasm and good humor in this passage; Pym deflates the idea of a passionate embrace by making kisses unpleasant to her heroine and by identifying the feeling of faintness as a response to hunger, a bodily function.

The kiss is described in a far different matter, however, in a romance novel. The following is the standard description of a kiss in Angela Wells's *Rash Contract,* a Harlequin novel about an English heroine living in Greece:

Faced with the inevitable, Karis put as brave a face as possible on it, closing her eyes and lifting her cheek for Nik's peck. Instead it was her soft mouth he sought with his warm lips, brushing their surface with a slow, sensuous movement as different from their previous assault as it was possible to be. (86)

Wells describes the kiss itself, where Pym merely describes the heroine's reaction after the kiss has occurred.

While romances include descriptions of kisses and other types of love-making, they differ among themselves in other ways. All, however, have some sort of love interest central to their plots. Kristin Ramsdell, in *Happily Ever After: A Guide to Reading Interests in Romance Fiction,* defines a romance novel as "a love story in which the central focus is the development of the love relationship between the two main characters, written in such a way as to provide the reader with some degree of vicarious emotional participation in the courtship process" (4). Furthermore, Harlequin author Angela Wells has written that the love in a romance novel may be unrequited. Wells also says that a romance plot requires an emotional response toward another, where an emotional/physical relationship, most commonly called "love" is involved" (Wells, letter to the author, 5 March 1994). Part of the individual's emotional response is analysis of the heroine or hero in relation to the love interest.

Readers of romances apparently share Wells's opinion. Jane Finch, owner of The Bookkeeper in Rock Island, Illinois, is an avid romance reader as well as an expert. According to Finch, the object of the heroine's love can be a fantasy, or can even be deceased (Personal Interview, 14 March 1994).

Many of Pym's novels do satisfy the love interest requirements of the romance genre, at least on the surface. Belinda Bede of *Some Tame Gazelle* may not lament her fate, but she spends thirty years knitting sweaters as an expression of the love she feels for an unresponsive archdeacon. Wilmet of *A Glass of Blessings* cherishes a fantasy about Piers and emotionally rejects her practical, ordinary husband until she learns that Piers is gay. As Wells notes, a romance may be "sweet, sensual or raunchy," but should contain an element of love, even if "the heroine's emotions remain unfulfilled" (Wells, letter to the author, 5 March 1994). In contrast, Lori Herter, a writer for Silhouette Romances, argues that a happy ending is a must for a romance (Herter, letter to the author, 1 March 1994).

Romance novels have traditionally been considered women's fiction. Peter Conrad, among other writers, theorizes that reading fiction became "consecrated to the private and the secret life," and that this private life was female, so that the novel "announced a feminization of literature" (560). Romance novelist Lori Herter defines women's fiction as fiction written solely for women (Herter, Letter to the Author, 1 March 1994). British writer Angela Wells writes that "Women's fiction suggests . . . books written by women for women. I don't care much for the title because it is ambiguous. It seems to suggest that women are limited to the kind of freedom they can appreciate, whereas the opposite is true" (Wells, letter to the author, 5 March 1994). Another writer, Antonia Fraser, never uses the term "women's fiction" to refer to her own versatile writing (Fraser, letter to the author, 21 February 1994).

Some authors may be reluctant to use the term "women's fiction" because, from the very beginning, female novelists who wrote for women were scoffed at as uneducated or immoral, comments aimed at many romance novelists even today. English author Rumer Godden has recently written that she supposes the phrase "women's fiction" is derogatory (Godden, letter to the author, 25 June 1994). Still, a few male authors such as the Marquis de Sade have defended women novelists. In "Reflections on the Novel," de Sade writes of "gracious women who held sway in this kind of writing, wherefrom the men could learn most excellent lessons" (104).

The Marquis, however, stands alone in his praise. Daphne Clair notes, "Men scoffed at stories of love and marriage even while they insisted that love and marriage and housekeeping were the proper province, and the only proper province, of women" (62). Perhaps the most famous and notorious male critic of women writers was Nathaniel Hawthorne, himself author of such books as *The Blithedale Romance* and *The Scarlet Letter* that are often classified as romances. In January 1855, Hawthorne wrote to William D. Ticknor, his friend and publisher, the now infamous complaint about "that damned mob of scribbling women." The entire, devastating comment reads as follows:

America is now wholly given over to a damned mob of scribbling women, and I should have no chance of success while the public taste is occupied with their trash—and should be ashamed of myself if I did succeed. What is the mystery of these innumerable editions of the "lamplighter," and other books neither better nor worse?—worse they could not be, and better they need not be, when they sell by the 100,000. (qtd. in Mott 122)

To a certain extent, one can read Hawthorne's comments as sour grapes from Rappaccini's garden, yet his comments about women authors are typical even today. As Peter Conrad has written in *The Everyman History of English Literature,* men of letters are the enemies of novels written by women (394).[1] In discussing Hawthorne's comment, Nina Baym notes in "Melodramas of Beset Manhood: How Theories of American Fiction Exclude Women Authors," that male academics and literary figures were biased against women authors and women's fiction because it was so different from their own (64).

After studying the romance genre, one realizes that there are as many types of romance novels as there are romance authors. Pym herself writes in *A Very Private Eye* that romances "are extremely varied in type—some historical, others more purely 'romantic' in a modern setting" (280). Kristin Ramsdell traces the use of the term "romance" to the Middle Ages, though she notes that love stories as a genre go back to the Bible or the Greek myths (5). Peter Conrad in his *Everyman History of English Literature* says that myths no longer understood are repeated as fiction (18). Annette Townsend in "Historical Overview" for Eileen Fallon's *Words of Love: A Complete Guide to Romance Fiction* describes Heliodorus's *Aethiopica,* a romance that involves an abandoned princess and the hero who saves her, thus tracing the ancestors of the romance novel to the fourth century A. D.[2]

Other characteristics of the romance include a "battle of the sexes aspect" in which the heroine usually wins the battle by taming the man to some extent. (Herter, letter to the author, 1 March 1994). The ancestors of these heroines include Shakespeare's Kate from *The Taming of the Shrew* and Chaucer's Wife of Bath. Also, romance novelist Barbara Cartland indicates in *The History of Barbara Cartland and How I Wish to Be Remembered* that she had in mind the independent female characters of Shakespeare when, with a stroke of her pen, she created her romance mavens (26).[3]

New Zealand romance author Daphne Clair has written an excellent history of the romance novel in "Sweet Subversions" from *Dangerous Men: Adventurous Women,* which discusses in depth the ancestry of the modern romance heroine. Clair believes that these early independent women of fiction are the "vanguard of the feminist movement" (62). She traces the romance genre to Aphra Behn's novel *Orinoco; or the History of the Royal Slave* (1688).[4] Because this and other pieces by Behn advocated sexual equality for women, her heroines are among the first independent protagonists who later populate romance novels (62). She is also, perhaps, the first woman to write for money, so that she joins the ranks of those women described in Woolf's *A Room of One's Own,* as well as contemporary novelists like Barbara Cartland. Cartland indicates in *How I Wish to Be Remembered* that she began writing as a single mother who needed to support her children (9-14).

Kristen Ramsdell has written that *Pamela* is the direct antecedent of today's romances, partly because of its classic seduction plot where, as Ramsdell says, "a young servant girl resists repeated attempts on her virtue" and as a result, ends up marrying her seducer (5).[5] With varied endings, the plot of master or superior seducing the servant has occurred in George Eliot's *Adam Bede,* Daniel Defoe's *Moll Flanders,* Kathleen Winsor's *Forever Amber,* Jennifer Wilde's *Love's Tender Fury,* and other novels. Pym uses this theme differently. In Pym's novels, the paid companion may marry a man of independent means, but he is not her master or seducer. For example, a paid companion of limited means, Jessie Morrow, marries the well-off widower, Fabian Driver, in Pym's *Jane and Prudence,* but it is she who attracts his attention and encourages the relationship. Jessie is not dishonored or lured into sin.

According to Daphne Clair, another type of novel written during this time employed the theme that "love conquers all" (62). Clair argues that these novels represent pure escapism for women whom society forced into conventional, often unfulfilling marriages to strangers that resulted in virtual servitude (62). For different reasons, romance novels continue to be escapist literature for many women today. Carol Thurston deals with this theme in *The Romance Revolution* as does Jayne Ann Krentz in her Introduction to *Dangerous Men: Adventurous Women.*

The gothic romance, with its elements of the supernatural and its often historically remote or geographically far away setting, became a peculiarly feminine genre due to the work of Ann Radcliffe, whom Clair says "changed the course of women's fiction" (63). Radcliffe's *The Mysteries of Udolpho* influenced novels like those of the Brontës as well as Daphne du Maurier's *Rebecca* and Victoria Holt's *Mistress of Mellyn* (Clair 63). Jane Austen alludes to *Udolpho* repeatedly in *Northanger Abbey.* Radcliffe also influenced the modern gothics of Anne Rice. In a particularly appropriate remark, Clair notes that "Mrs. Radcliffe put into print women's deepest fears: the fear of being trapped and imprisoned in the house to which all women were supposed to confine their lives; the fear of male sexuality, male power, and male duplicity; and, not least, the fear of losing their own identity" (64). American writer Charlotte Perkins Gilman plays out this fear in her novella *The Yellow Wallpaper.* Radcliffe has also influenced the modern gothic romance or "potboiler" where heroines are commonly orphaned, earn a small inheritance, travel to foreign countries, and are kidnapped or employed by dark, ruthless Lords of the Manor (64). Philippa Gregory's *Wideacre* is an example of this plot. (Philippa Gregory is one of the pseudonyms for English writer Eleanor Buford Hibbert, a.k.a. Victoria Holt).

Another work that deals with the theme of the heroine being "captured" by a dark, mysterious lord is Anne Rice's story "The Master of Rampling Gate." In Rice's short story, Julie and her brother return to the fictitious English village of Rampling to visit their ancestral home. Their father has just died, and on his deathbed asked that the mansion be razed. Upon their arrival, they soon discover that the old house has a tenant, an early lord of the manor who has been immortalized as a vampire. Like many gothic heroines, and like many of Pym's heroines, Julie becomes mesmerized by the dark lord, and falls under his spell. At first Julie is angry with the Master of Rampling Gate, but she soon succumbs to him saying, "The core of my being opened to him without a struggle or a sound" (196).

Rice's story makes a good comparison for Pym's *A Few Green Leaves,* because both deal with life in a quiet English Village. Each village has a secret, but the secrets differ. Where Rampling harbors the supernatural secret of the vampire lord and deals with "large themes" like damnation and death, Pym's villages harbor secrets of a smaller, more intimate scale. In *A Glass of Blessings,* a curate occasionally steals his superior's Fabergé egg then returns it. In *A Few Green Leaves,* a young woman anthropologist studies the village in its more trivial aspects, what people wear, what they eat, etc., in order to uncover their true nature. Also, Rice and the other gothic authors write a serious, heavy-handed prose. Pym's discourse is light-hearted and filled with humor. As she herself complained after she served as a judge for the annual awards of the Romantic Novelist's Association, "The one thing they lack is humour or irony—and of course one does miss that" (*A Very Private Eye* 280). Pym also contemplated writing gothic or historical novels during the fourteen-year "literary excommunication" she suffered (Weld 168). At one point, she wrote a story entitled "A Painted Heart," which was written in the gothic mode. Weld writes that Pym was "seduced by melodramatic language" when she wrote the story, and created a Hungarian hero who is also guilty of murder (159). The heroine narrowly misses becoming his next victim, but she is still enthralled with him (159). The setting is full of skulls and graveyards, and the dark, mysterious hero is at least a distant cousin to Stoker's seductive Count Dracula.

During the 1960s, gothic romances became popular again. Romances with windswept cliffs and "dark, saturnine heroes with hooded eyes" were published in great numbers (Kristin Ramsdell 8). These novels were labeled Romantic Suspense and were written by such authors as Victoria Holt, Phyllis Whitney, Dorothy Eden, Marilyn Ross, a.k.a. Dan Ross, and Mary Stewart (8). Vestiges of these novels exist in Mary Higgins Clark's books today, as well as in the serial novels of John Saul titled as a group, *The Blackstone Chronicles*. Clark and Saul feature heroes with dark secrets, and often use remote settings like a mad artist's studio buried in the woods or an abandoned insane asylum.

At about the same time that the early gothics were being written, Jane Austen was writing as well. Several critics consider *Pride and Prejudice* to be a romance. For example, Daphne Clair in "Sweet Subversions" discusses Jane Austen and argues that her books are also romances (65). She is not alone in this judgment. Peter Conrad writes that Austen is "an unabashed romantic" (393), while Lori Herter believes *Pride and Prejudice* is a romance because "the main plotline has to do with the developing love between Elizabeth and Mr. Darcy and it has a happy ending" (Herter, letter to the author, 1 March 1994). Kristin Ramsdell writes in *Happily Ever After* that Austen wrote the contemporary romances of her day (21). Ramsdell also observes that Austen's novels, like many romances written today, deal with the theme of a woman seeking financial and emotional success (21).

The Austen novel most similar to Pym's plots is *Northanger Abbey*, the story of Catherine Morland, the girl "no one" would have supposed to have been born a heroine (329). In many ways, Catherine Morland is like a Pym woman, for she leads an ordinary life. She is a clergyman's daughter, but not a poor one. All ten children in her family survive to adulthood and are happy, and her mother is a woman of "useful plain sense, with a good temper" (329). Catherine, like many a Pym excellent woman, is not particularly beautiful, either. As Austen writes, she has "a thin awkward figure, a sallow skin without colour, dark lank hair, and strong features; so much for her person" (329). Yet, Catherine is heroic because she prefers boys' pastimes, and is not in the least interested in female occupations like gardening, embroidery, or doll-play. She is not tempestuous, but has "neither a bad heart nor a bad temper" (330). Austen, like Pym, parodies the romance heroines of her time, by creating an ordinary, good-natured girl who aspires to be a tempestuous romance heroine. Catherine trains herself for the job by reading "all such works as heroines must read to supply their memories" including Gray and Shakespeare (331).

More appropriate than any description of a heroine in *Northanger Abbey* is the narrator's vigorous defense of novels. The narrator says that the novel is "only some work in which the greatest powers of the mind are displayed, in which the most thorough knowledge of human nature, the happiest delineation of its varieties, the liveliest effusions of wit and humour are conveyed to the world in the best-chosen language" (349). It might have been Pym defending her favorite literary genre.

In *Barbara Pym and the Novel of Manners,* Annette Weld writes that "Pym was aware of her debt to Austen but was never willing to allow a comparison of their skills" (160). In the preface to *A Very Private Eye,* Hazel Holt observes that, while Pym was aware that she was often compared to Jane Austen, she considered the comparison "mildly blasphemous" (xv). Pym herself writes in her diary on 11 August 1969 that during a visit to Austen's house, she put her "hand down on Jane's desk and [brought] it up covered with dust" (*A Very Private Eye* 250). Pym then laments, "Oh that some of her genius might rub off on me" (250). Earlier, in 1952, Pym writes that she is reading "some of Jane Austen's last chapters [to] find out how she manages all the loose ends" (188). While Pym was willing to admit to Austen's influence, she was not willing to be compared to her.

From Austen, Clair moves to a discussion of the Brontës, saying that they voiced what Radcliffe intimated, that what "women most loved, and most feared, was that dangerous, fascinating creature, Man" (65). She notes that in *Wuthering Heights,* Emily Brontë fused the character of hero and villain into Heathcliff, the "Byronic figure whose literary descendants still stalk glowering through the pages of many modern romances" (65). Though less diabolic, Charlotte Brontë's Mr. Rochester from *Jane Eyre* is "something of a bully" who tries to trap the naive ingenue, Jane, into a bigamous marriage (66). Jane, like the typical romance heroine, ultimately stands up to him and only marries him later, on her terms, when he is blind and maimed (66).[6]

Mr. Rochester haunts the pages of Pym's novels in characters like Alaric Lydgate of *Less Than Angels* and Everard Bone of *Excellent Women*. In fact, Anne Wyatt-Brown, in *Barbara Pym: A Critical Biography*, writes that Pym seems haunted by *Jane Eyre*, but that there is no reunion with Mr. Rochester in Pym's novels, with the possible exception of the Catherine and Lydgate liaison in *Less Than Angels* (6). She also notes that Pym had a "youthful obsession" with Charlotte Brontë and Charlotte Yonge (6). Later, Wyatt-Brown points out that Pym mentions governesses or paid companions in twenty-seven of her manuscripts (162). Finally, Pym herself contemplated writing a novel that was an updated *Jane Eyre* or *Villette* during the years her books were not being published (Weld 167). In fact, Leonora's last name in *The Sweet Dove Died* is Eyre. In her books, though, Pym is somewhat uncomfortable with the comparison. In *Excellent Women*, Mildred explains "I am not at all like Jane Eyre" (7), and Pym tends to mock the themes of love, loss, and reunion that Brontë treats with such grandeur (Janice Rossen 14-15).

It was during the 1950s, when Pym wrote *Less Than Angels,* that Harlequin of Canada began to publish (8). By way of contrast, Wyatt-Brown, who discusses Pym in terms of novelists contemporary with her and those who preceded her, sees similarities between Pym and other pre-1960s and 1960s writers. Wyatt-Brown says that:

Pym's fiction has much in common with that of a small band of contemporary novelists—Elizabeth Taylor, Penelope Mortimer, Molly Keane, Elizabeth Jolley, and Anita Brookner. They were all born in the first third of the twentieth century, and their fiction reflects slightly old-fashioned attitudes toward gender relations. In fact, Jolley, Brookner, and Keane owe some of their current popularity and the ease with which they find an international market to the rediscovery of Pym. (1)

Furthermore, by the 1970s, "heroines no longer hid their inner strength but gloried in it" (Clair 68). Some of these heroines had characteristics in common with Pym's Jane Cleveland and Catherine Oliphant, in that they were truer to themselves than to society's expectations for them. Moreover, Kay Mussell writes that there are two types of romance heroines, those who conform to traditional sex roles, and the others who do not conform, but who fail in traditional areas of female influence like motherhood and domesticity (84-85). So, it is no accident that Kathleen

Woodiwiss's heroine Shanna loathes sewing or that Jude Deveraux's heroine in *Twin of Fire* is a physician. This failure at housework is especially characteristic of heroines in romances that are both gothics and bodice busters, also called historical romances.

Historical romances began to enjoy a renaissance during the 1970s, but Kristin Ramsdell notes that they differed from their predecessors because of the graphic sex scenes included, hence the name "bodice rippers" or "bodice busters" often attributed to them. Wild, distant settings, isolated castles, and remote historical epochs relate them to the gothic romances. In the "bodice rippers" or "sweet savage romances" of the late 1970s, spirited heroines fought "tooth and nail" but were constantly being ravished by "handsome, virile, often angry men who finally repent of their sins and settle down to wedded bliss" (Clair 69). In *The Romance Revolution,* Carol Thurston notes that the heroines must be "feisty," and sexy, and the word "juicy" is used often (67). By the mid-1970s, when historical romances and bodice busters enjoyed their greatest popularity and when Pym was not publishing, Thurston says, the heroines began to outgrow their submissive, traditional female roles and became rebellious (67).

Feminists are outraged by the bodice buster genre, and even writers like Cartland, who says she is a "moral" writer, deplore them (Cartland, *History* 26). Clair and others argue, though, that these novels do not encourage their readers to condone rape; instead, they show women taking control of situations which horrify the average reader. As Clair notes, they face one of their greatest fears, rape, and conquer it safely between the pages of a book (69). Clair points out in "Sweet Subversions" that if we assume that women engage in "rape fantasy" when they read graphic romances, then "We might assume . . . that men enjoy being beaten up, tortured, shot, stabbed, dragged by galloping horses, and thrown out of moving vehicles" because they read westerns or spy novels (69). These sexually explicit novels by authors like Rosemary Rogers, Jackie Collins, and Kathleen Woodiwiss also explored women's sexuality with a new freedom (69). Clair says that in an age when women had so few writers, their sexuality was their strongest weapon, so that Miss Milner of Mrs. Inchbald's *A Simple Story* (1791), will not yield sexually to her lover until he acknowledges her equality (63).

Furthermore, according to Carol Thurston in *The Romance Revolution,* the bodice ripper women outgrow the submissive, childlike heroines of the Regency Romances (loosely based on Austen's novels). They are "obstreperous and rebellious" women, playing the role of pirates and outlaws, and are generally "mistresses" of their own fates. For example, Morgan Llewellyn's *Grania* is the story of Grace O'Malley, a legendary female pirate of the Elizabethan Era. In fact, it is fair to say that these women are the female version of the Horatio Alger and T. E. Lawrence figures so popular in male adventure stories. Jean Auel's romances about Cro-Magnon people feature a heroine who is a hunter and who breaks prehistoric codes prescribed for women, as well as the so-called feminine mystique, which Betty Friedan argues enslaved women in their own homes during the 1950s and early 1960s. Pauline Gedge and Lynne Barrette in *The Eagle and the Raven* and *Defy the Eagle* have written romances about Boudicca, and thus have created a romance heroine who is not only independent but who leads entire armies in revolt against Rome. Linda Wolfe's *Boudicca* portrays the fearless queen as a "tempestuous woman" who is untamed by any man.

On a cozier, smaller scale, Pym's independent heroines are also mistresses of their own fate. Pym heroines Jessie Morrow and Catherine Oliphant are sisters to the independent romance heroines; they, too, are somewhat daring and adventurous, and live independently, taking fate into their own hands.

Bodice buster heroines also define their own identities, though they may find it difficult to stress their individuality when faced with fathers and husbands who view them as possessions and not as human beings. As one heroine of Jocelyn Carew's *Golden Sovereigns* laments, "None of the men she knew—from her father on down to Howard Vickery— had looked on her as a person" (qtd. in Thurston 70). Similarly, the younger anthropologists and other characters of *Less Than Angels* do not see Catherine as a person; rather they view her as a potential typist and help meet to Tom Mallow. By the 1980s, American romances began to follow and challenge the British tradition, so that "feisty" heroines battle with heroes and conquer them, with the American strong-minded career woman replacing the independent women of the British novel (Thurston 70). As the 1990s draw to a close, the heroines of many romances, and novels that play heavily with the elements of romance, are slowly moving from being career women to "rogue heroines." For example, the gorgeous heroine of Nora Roberts's *Honest Illusions* is a magician and part of a family of thieves who steal from the rich and give to the poor. Dr. Kay Scarpetta of Patricia Cornwell's mysteries is a passionate woman, embroiled in at least one love affair per book. But she is also a brilliant coroner, attorney, and Chief Medical Examiner for the State of Virginia. Kay is also sort of a "demon" or rival woman, for her boyfriends are sometimes married. Diane Mott Davidson's loveable Goldy Bear is a caterer who attracts men as honey does flies. She is a successful businesswoman who likes to solve mysteries, and her stories always include recipes in their text.

While there are many types of romance novels, the same types of heroines populate all their pages. In "The Gentle Doubters," Susan Gorsky describes the types of heroines that appear in romance novels. These are the ingenue, the independent woman, the romp, and the demon (Gorsky 38-45). The ingenue is generally a sheltered young woman in her late teens who seldom leaves her drawing-room (38). The ingenue will generally develop and mature by the story's end, but she gladly "exchanges her father's arm for her husband's with no perceptible change in herself" (38). Gorsky calls her "innocent, uninformed, and naive, often self-effacing and unsure . . . at the mercy of the adults— especially the men who enter her life" (38). One is reminded of Henry James's Pansy Osmond from *Portrait of a Lady*. Isabel Archer is another type of ingenue, for she marries Osmond without really knowing him, and thus becomes a pawn in the plans of the sinister Madame Merle and Osmond himself. The ingenue's complete trust in men usually leads to some disaster in her life, including a bigamous or "false marriage" (Gorsky 38-39). On some level, Jane Eyre is such an ingenue during her early days at Thornfield because she is nearly duped into a secret marriage with Rochester. Her disastrous discovery of Rochester's duplicity leads her to wander in the countryside, starving and alone. Other ingenues include Hardy's Tess and DuMaurier's unnamed narrator in *Rebecca*. In the 1996 British PBS version of DuMaurier's novel, the young heroine is dressed in "little girl" dresses and looks more like Maxim DeWinter's granddaughter than his wife.

In Barbara Pym's novel *Less Than Angels,* young Deirdre is an ingenue, completely trusting the older, more experienced Tom Mallow. Through Pym's comic subversion of the ingenue plot, Deirdre is saved from disastrous marriage because Tom, a sort of reluctant T. E. Lawrence figure, is killed in Africa. Yet Pym is also playing a joke on her readers, for the telling of Deirdre's story is a retelling of the Old Irish myth, "Deirdre of the Sorrows." Though a much deflated heroine, Pym's heroine, like her ancient role model, affects the fates of three men.

The independent woman differs from the ingenue in that she is not quite as young or naive (Gorsky 40). For example, some heroines must accept responsibility for orphaned brothers or sisters because of the death of one or both parents. An example of this type of heroine is Barbara Cartland's Erlina from *Look with the Heart*. Erlina is in her late teens, and her brother Gerry is twelve. They are orphans and the last of a once great family, left destitute after their shabby estate, Sherwood House, accidentally burns to the ground (1-3). Erlina is then left with the responsibility of finding a home and financial means for herself and her brother. Her task is most difficult because her village is dying, abandoned by the Lord of Meldon Hall, the Marquis of Meldon, the man Erlina will later marry. Erlina proves her competence as an independent woman by serving as housekeeper for Meldon Hall, as nurse for the blinded Marquis, as healer for the sick inhabitants of the village, and as detective who uncovers a plot to murder the Marquis.

Other plots involving the independent woman focus on antagonism between marriage and career because the hero assumes the heroine will graciously give up her own goals and aspirations to be his wife (Gorsky 41). So, in Annie Edwards's *A Girton Girl,* the heroine tells the hero that she needs "no other life, no other wisdom, no other ambition than" her husband's, thus proving "herself a very wild woman after all" (qtd. in Gorsky 41). In Amanda Quick's *Ravished,* a female paleontologist of the Regency period fights the advances of the hero and risks her reputation in order to continue her studies and write papers for the archaeological society. As Jayne Ann Krentz (who is the real name behind the pseudonym of Amanda Quick) writes in her introduction to *Dangerous Men and Adventurous Women: Romance Writers on the Appeal of Romance,* the woman usually emerges victorious in these male-female struggles (Krentz 5). Another contemporary author who is also an attorney, Doreen Owens Malek, notes that one reason romance novels are so popular with women is that the woman emerges victorious against an obdurate hero who is brought to his knees. The hero ultimately succumbs to the heroine's professional goals and personal aspirations (75). He "capitulates because he simply must have her" (75).

In Pym's novels, the hero loses out because the heroine will not give up her own independence or lifestyle to marry him. For example, romance writer Catherine Oliphant in *Less Than Angels* is not a perfect companion to Tom because she is too independent to fawn over him the way he would like. Jessie Morrow of *Crampton Hodnet* will not marry the vicar, Mr. Latimer, in part because she does not want to give up what little financial independence she has as a paid companion to marry a man who does not love her. The most common examples of independent women are governesses, most of whom have their roots in *Jane Eyre,* and paid companions to wealthy women, like the unnamed narrator of *Rebecca.*

The romp flouts the codes of behavior for women in her time by climbing trees, playing with boys, "scandalizing the neighborhood gossips . . . and breaking men's hearts everywhere" (Gorsky 41). She acts as a coquette, flirt, and in her worst form, becomes a sort of sexually promiscuous "bad woman" (44). Because she does what she pleases in defiance of conventional codes, the romp is also a type of independent woman. Pym's Prudence Bates, who flirts with married men and attracts all types of other men, is a kind of romp. So is Frances Hodgson Burnett's heroine in *A Lady of Quality.* Contemporary novelist Patricia Matthews creates one heroine who is a jockey. Some of Hemingway's "tomboy heroines" like Brett Ashley of *The Sun Also Rises* owe their heritage to the romp. In fact, British author Mary Hillier considers some of Hemingway's writing to be romantic (Hillier, letter to the author, 1 March 1994). If the romp is not careful, her scandalous behavior can ruin her reputation. She will then become the last type of heroine Gorsky discusses, the demon. Mollie Hardwick creates a good portrait of a romp in her historical novel *Blood Royal,* which is about the life of Anne Boleyn. Anne's sister Mary is a romp at the French court, and loses her reputation after she sleeps with the French king and his courtiers.

According to Gorsky, the demon, another romance type, is both a schemer and "woman" (45).[7] The demon is an archetypal figure who comes to life in a variety of characters including the match-making mother, the girl who wants a husband at any cost, the unfaithful wife, and the wicked stepmother (45). Several of Joyce's characters from *Dubliners* fit this category. An example of the matchmaking mother might be Mrs. Mooney of "The Boarding House," who with her daughter Polly, ensnares Mr. Doran into marriage with Polly. Polly herself may typify the girl who wants a husband at any cost. In Joyce's *Ulysses,* Molly Bloom is an example of the unfaithful wife because of her exploits with her manager.

Gorsky writes that Rosamund Lydgate of George Eliot's *Middlemarch* is a demon because she plots against her husband, and Lady Culmore in Breame's *Married in Haste* is one because she is willing to commit murder for her husband (46). In *Jane Eyre,* Bertha Mason, the mad, murderous wife of Rochester, is portrayed as a demonic figure, while in Cartland's *Look with the Heart,* Lady Isabel Fisher, former lover of the Marquis of Meldon, is a demon because she turns on the Marquis and plots his murder. Gorsky notes, however, that the various types of demons do not set out to earn their reputations. Many are stigmatized by society for their independence or for their sexual freedom (46). Pym characters who share some qualities with the demon include the scheming Allegra Gray of *Excellent Women* and, to a certain extent, Leonora of *The Sweet Dove Died.* Leonora, however, is more reflective than some of the other heroines mentioned. She also has more of a conscience than Allegra Gray.

Novelist Penelope Lively discusses Pym women in terms that could classify them as hybrids of the demon/romp classifications. In "The World of Barbara Pym," Lively calls Pym women an "army of beady-eyed, vulnerable, frequently romantic, often exploited . . . women" (45).

Examples of the "frequently romantic/often exploited" heroines include Belinda Bede, Mildred Lathbury, Jane Cleveland, Dulcie Mainwaring, and Emma Howick (45). Another type of Pym woman that Lively identifies is similar to what Gorsky calls a romp (44). Gorsky writes that the romp is a "tomboy" or a "daring girl" who "breaks the minor conventions" (44). According to Lively, Pym women who are romps are the women who rush "headlong into the sexual struggle, starry-eyed [and] doomed to humiliation" (45). Ultimately they are less susceptible to being hurt because they are "all too well aware" that they are being exploited as part of a sexual game (45). Prudence Bates, and Jessie Morrow of *Jane and Prudence* fit this type. Robert Liddell implies in "Two Friends" that Pym aligned herself with this last group of women who rushed headlong into the sexual struggle because she herself had the qualities of a romance heroine (59). In fact, as Liddell and others note, Pym referred to herself as "Sandra" in her letters and early journals because she thought that this was a more romantic name (59).

While Janice Rossen's *The World of Barbara Pym* is more concerned with discussing literary tradition as a "counterpart" for Pym's fiction (7), Rossen does give some insight on the Pym heroine. Rossen touches on the romantic aspects of the heroine's personality and implies that Prudence, at least, is conscious of her role as romance heroine because she is continuously becoming involved with attached or unsuitable men. She "craves the trappings of romance" (34) by favoring red velvet robes and lacquered nails and she is skilled at "creating new fictions from old patterns" (36).

Many of the unsuitable men that romance heroines fall in love with and marry are patterned after the Byronic hero. Germaine Greer writes in *The Female Eunuch* that Rochester, Heathcliff, Mr. Darcy, and Byron are the originals of this type of hero (183). William Rose Benet argues in *The Reader's Encyclopedia* that Lord Byron, "in both his works and his life . . . created the 'Byronic hero'—a defiant melancholy young man, brooding on some mysterious, unforgivable sin in his past" (152).

Mr. Rochester of *Jane Eyre* certainly broods on his past throughout the novel. Mrs. Fairfax, housekeeper of Rochester's home, Thornfield, is the first to describe him. She answers Jane's inquiries by saying Rochester's "character is unimpeachable," but that he "is rather peculiar . . . nothing striking, but you feel it when he speaks to you" (92). Jane gives the first physical description of Rochester saying, "His figure was enveloped in a riding cloak, fur collared and steel clasped. . . . He had a dark face with stern features and a heavy brow, his eyes and gathered eyebrows looked ireful and thwarted . . . he was past youth, but had not reached middle age, perhaps he might be thirty-five" (99). (It is interesting to compare Jane's impressions of Rochester with those of Antoinette in *Wide Sargasso Sea* by Jean Rhys. Also, Woolf's *Orlando* includes a parallel to the Jane-Rochester meeting when Orlando meets Shelmardine. In Woolf's book, however, the hero is not Byronic.)

Even more mysterious than Rochester is Heathcliff of *Wuthering Heights*. Emily Brontë's description of the adult Heathcliff reads as follows: "He is a dark-skinned gypsy in aspect, in dress and manners a gentleman . . . he has an erect and handsome figure, and [is] rather morose" (*Wuthering Heights* 11). The words "gypsy," "fortune teller," and "devil" are often used in the novel to describe Heathcliff. Like Lord Saxton of Kathleen Woodiwiss's *A Rose in Winter* and Rochester, Heathcliff keeps mean, snarling dogs. In short, he is a far cry from Pym's heroes who are Byronically handsome, but love soap animals, darned socks, and homegrown vegetables.

In a *Romantic Times* magazine article entitled "Dangerous Men," romance author Anne Stuart writes that women readers are sometimes drawn to "darker, more problematic men"—the Byronic heroes who are "mad, bad, and dangerous to know" (12). She gives the following as examples of the modern Byronic hero: the vampire, the burned out CIA agent, the beast, and the lost soul (12). The appeal of the Byronic hero is that the heroine is willing to risk her own soul to help him reform and attain his soul's salvation (13). Carol Lee, in discussing Angela Carter's "The Company of Wolves," writes in *The Blind Side of Eden* that the man's salvation in the Carter story lies in the woman's "befriending him and letting him know that the monstrous edifice he has created can indeed be transformed by affection" (181). Ann Rosalind Jones writes in "Mills and Boon Meets Feminism" that current romance heroines are fulfilled not by the brutality of the hero, but by his transformation (200). According to Jones, the romantic novel's turning point "is often a moment of collapse through which power relations are reversed" (200). For example, if the heroine collapses, the hero becomes a nurturer (200). While she is predominantly known as a Renaissance scholar, Jones is also knowledgeable in the field of romance because she once worked as an editor for Dauntless Books, which published *Revealing Romances* (195).

In another article for *Romantic Times,* "Heroes of the 90's," Stella Cameron writes that heroes now come "in every shape, size, age and race" (12). Cameron, too, finds the wild, arrogant hero attractive because he can be "tough and tender" (13). While he is "untameable," he will sheath his claws for the woman he comes to love (13). The happy ending many romance writers believe is crucial to romance often develops because the heroine manages to "tame" or change the hero in some way.

Jayne Ann Krentz and Linda Barlow, critics and romance writers, claim in their essay "Beneath the Surface" that this is one of the stories that is part of women's culture; women all over the world love to tell stories about love to each other (27).

Although Barbara Pym was not a romance writer, she was aware of the many types of romance novels and of women's tradition of story-telling. She even knew some romance authors and judged romance novel competitions. While she criticized what she considered to be the short-comings of the romance, e.g., heavy-handed prose and lack of humor, she borrowed from this genre to enhance her own work. Many of her heroines are actually types of traditional romance heroines, but they live life on a much humbler, cozier scale than the displaced princesses and bold wantons who populate the pages of the pulp romance.

Barbara Brothers notes that Pym often mocks the romantic para-digm (79). I agree with Brothers on this point. I also agree that Pym wants to show that fictional romance and real life romance are not the same.

Pym does not deal with fantasy in the same way that romance writ-ers do. She focuses on the trivial and on the woman's point of view, and makes heroines out of unlikely middle-aged and older single women to emphasize that their lives, too, are "full" and important, and that, even for them (because Pym women are unlikely heroines), there are opportu-nities for change. Like the romance writers, she is aware of literary his-tory, as her allusions and quotes indicate. Unlike them, however, she uses her trivia to recreate the cozy but interesting worlds of her everyday heroines.

Romance novels are often criticized for bad writing and sexist por-trayals of women. Writers like Tania Modleski, Beatrice Faust, and Ger-maine Greer find them harmful to their female readers and have little to say that is positive about their authors. Yet, literary critics Peter Conrad, Kristin Ramsdell, Carol Thurston, and Annette Townsend find a link between romance novels and other types of literature, including the medieval epic, chivalric romance, early English novels, gothic novels, and nineteenth-century works by women. They argue that *Pamela, Pride and Prejudice, Northanger Abbey, Wuthering Heights,* and *Jane Eyre* are sisters to romance novels like *Rebecca, The Flame and the Flower, Golden Mistress,* and *A Dynasty of Love.*

Pym, a well-educated and avid reader, was aware of the legacies of Austen, Radcliffe, Richardson, the Brontës, and other writers to the genre of romance. The work she did for the Romance Novelists Associa-tion inspired her fertile imagination with ingredients for her novels, just as her other life experiences did. With *Some Tame Gazelle,* Pym began to use her recipe for a successful novel. It was in this amusing portrait of two middle-aged unmarried sisters and their quirky friends and acquaintances that Pym began to explore the question of whether single women could live full lives. It was also in this novel that Pym began to subvert some of the basic plots of romance novels, including the Cinderella story, where Prince Charming arrives to save the heroine from a life sweeping a sooty hearth. The Bede sisters of *Some Tame Gazelle* decide that they prefer their own independent lives and sweeping their own hearth. Harriet and Belinda Bede decide that they prefer to remain devoted to each other and the simple pleasures of their cozy lives, than to accept the proposals of their own Prince Charmings.

# 2

# The Virtue of a Single Woman

Pym began writing her novel of two middle-aged sisters, *Some Tame Gazelle,* on September 1, 1934 (*A Very Private Eye* 44). On October 4 of the same year, she noted in her diary that she was "writing a novel of real people" (44). *Some Tame Gazelle* illustrates one of the themes that pervade Pym's fiction, that single women can live full lives. Part of the plot of the novel defines what the term "full-life" means. The novel's two heroines are not the young, nubile women who populate romance novels, but fiftyish spinster sisters. Both refuse "Prince Charming" and offers of marriage at the end to stay together and to resume their comfortable household. As a result of choosing what makes them happy over what society might expect for them, Harriet and Belinda Bede remain true to each other and to themselves.

The Bede sisters are loosely patterned on Barbara and Hilary Pym, and the other characters, according to Charles Burkhart, are based on people Pym knew in her university days (31). Both sisters are middle-aged and live comfortably. Belinda, the more reserved sister, has been in love with Archdeacon Hoccleve for more than thirty years. Among the trials she has had to bear are the catty comments and superior attitude of Agatha Hoccleve, the archdeacon's wife. Harriet, the other sister, is plump and flamboyantly dressed. She lacks Belinda's shyness, and enjoys entertaining young curates to the point of flirtation. Harriet is attractive, and is repeatedly proposed to by a displaced Italian nobleman, Count Ricardo Bianco. Bianco is a gentle soul with a name Burkhart says sounds like "an aperitif" (30). The climax of the novel, if climax it can be called, occurs when both sisters are proposed to by a clergyman and a librarian. Mr. Nathaniel Mold, the librarian and the Bishop of Mbawawa in Africa, and Theodore Grote, the clergyman, are somewhat aged, unappetizing examples of Prince Charming, which both sisters refuse in favor of their comfortable, happy life together. In *Some Tame Gazelle,* romance is subverted precisely because Prince Charming is a threat to the heroine's living happily ever after.

Like Harriet and Belinda, Pym's spinsters often choose not to be married, yet are not left outcasts from "life's feast," a phrase Joyce uses in "A Painful Case" (117). By constantly having men propose to Belinda and Harriet Bede, Pym makes her characters desirable, romantic women interested in how they look and in living well. Harriet Bede, in particular, is an attractive, flirtatious, well-fed and well-dressed middle-aged woman who defies stereotypes of frumpy old maids. Part of living well is having good food to eat, and meals are lovingly described in the novel. Feminine activities like knitting and sewing are also discussed in detail.

Another theme in this and other Barbara Pym novels is love. Diana Benet in *Something to Love: Barbara Pym's Novels* identifies five love subjects in Pym. These are "the need for love, the definition of emotional purpose from the needs of others, [the idea of] observation versus participation, the impact of the imagination on the emotional life, and [the achievement] of unsuitable attachments or [discovery of] love objects" (11). Pym explores these different types of love through careful portrayals of her heroes and heroines. These portrayals also subvert the romantic characterization of hero and heroine.

Benet argues that Pym "turns the staples of the romantic novel upside down" by using heroines and heroes who are middle-aged (16). Middle-aged love "is rarely anguished or even unsettling" (16). More important, marriage is not "the glorious conclusion to the heroine's story, though she is given the option; and marriage itself is not the supreme love-inspired choice by which a man supposedly validates a woman's singularity or worth" (16). Benet writes that Pym "dislocates" romantic convention in *Some Tame Gazelle* by featuring two single heroines in their fifties (16). Yet, as Benet notes, some Pym characters are in love with images of their own creation and the image of the self is reflected in their lovers's eyes (13). In this, the Pym characters are a little like romance authors: they are creating characters for their own enjoyment, as well as a discourse of what love means to them. For Belinda, love's discourse includes hearing Henry Hoccleve read T. S. Eliot aloud. It does not matter to her that he does so inappropriately as part of his sermon. The fact that Hoccleve quotes Eliot is significant to at least one critic. Michael Cotsell argues in *Barbara Pym* that the author is contrasting modernism and Hoccleve's taste for Eliot with Belinda's preference for simpler and more nostalgic poetic quotations. According to Cotsell, Belinda prefers poetry with a "homely application" (24). Cotsell says that Belinda prefers literature that expresses sentiments to which everyone can respond (24). In other words, she prefers smatterings of often quoted lines that are familiar to ordinary people, not just to learned archdeacons and academics.

Besides dealing with modernism, Pym deals with and alters the conventions of the romance novel in *Some Tame Gazelle*. When Belinda pines for Archdeacon Hoccleve, she knits a jumper or a pair of socks. She does not throw herself from a cliff or write wild letters of her burning, impassioned love. Her cheeks do not flame, nor does her long, golden mane of hair stream behind her in the manner of a typical bodice buster heroine. Yet, as Mason Cooley notes, a belief in Belinda's thirty-year unrequited love for the archdeacon "is the sort of thing only a devoted reader of romantic literature would be capable of" (51). (Pym herself often took Yeastivite tablets as a cure for love sickness.)

Robert Liddell, Pym's long-time friend as well as one of her biographers, has written that *Some Tame Gazelle* is "an Oxford novel written away from Oxford" because its characters are all "Oxonian" (16). Pym, an undergraduate at Oxford, read often in the Oxford Bodleian English Reading Room, particularly during the summer of 1932 (11). At this time, her diaries show that she had an active social life and was familiar with the people and landmarks of Oxford (12). The often comic characters of the novel are based on personalities she actually knew (11).

Cotsell, however, might disagree with Liddell. Cotsell does not believe Oxford was the model for the village in *Some Tame Gazelle*. He writes that the model for Belinda's and Harriet's village is Pym's own Oswestry (9). In Pym's novels as a whole, European countries like France and Germany represent the world of romance (9).

Yet, even in the less romantic English world, love becomes important. Each heroine will use romantic love to help create the needed love object for herself. Though romantic love is important, it does not appear in Pym's novels in its more traditional forms. That is to say, not all love relationships end happily in marriage and not all marriages in Pym novels are happy. While Pym may use the traditional trappings of the romance novel, she often subverts these trappings to achieve comic effect. Pym also subverts the romantic tales she spins to make a point, that real love is not like romantic fantasy. Pym uses in her novels such elements popular with romance writers as food and clothing descriptions, heroine descriptions, Byronic heroes, and marriage. Through subversive means, however, she makes these elements unrecognizable. Only a very well-read romance novel aficionado might recognize the romantic ancestry of food, clothes, etc., in Pym's books.

Pym's heroines, Belinda and Harriet, have traits in common with typical romance heroines, but they are uniquely different as well. Mason Cooley has said that in Belinda, Pym creates a new heroine, "neither beautiful or rich" (4). Robert J. Graham writes in "Cumbered with Much Serving: Barbara Pym's Excellent Women," that Pym's women desire love and romance, although precious little of the latter exists in the male-female relations Pym dramatizes (150). According to Lotus Snow in *One Little Room an Everywhere,* Pym's women "are transitional figures, caught in history between the Victorian ideal of womanliness and the liberation moment of the mid and late twentieth century. Rebels in their thoughts, they are loyalists in their actions" (65).

Belinda of *Some Tame Gazelle* is a gentlewoman, "living at the shabby lower end of gentility" (4). Worst of all, writes Cooley, "[Belinda] is not rescued by Prince Charming, but is likely to remain drab and unmated" (4). Cooley is correct on this point, but in many ways, his analysis of Pym's work is not accurate. At least Cooley is right that remaining drab and unmated would be Belinda's sad fate in a Harlequin or other romance novel. In Pym's world, however, the "happy ending" so crucial to romance is subverted because it does not necessarily involve marriage to the hero or "Prince." The ending in *Some Tame Gazelle* is happy precisely because the sisters refuse their suitors. For them, the desire to remain in the home they have built together is stronger than the social pressure to find husbands. Robert J. Graham would explain the sisters' decision as "overt love displacement," where feelings of love are linked to home and garden (150). In his essay "Cumbered with Much Serving," Graham summarizes recent research about the importance of home for never married women by claiming that, to single women, home represents control over their environment (150). Moreover, Graham argues that ritualized housework provides affirmation of unmarried women's single householder status and a "substitute for social exchange and intimacy" (150).

Yet the fact that Belinda and Harriet refuse their suitors does not mean that they are not interested in love. On the contrary, the sisters are interested in all types of love and love affairs. Diana Benet writes in *Something to Love: Barbara Pym's Novels* that many types of love are represented as the major "quest" of Pym's characters (1). Benet calls Belinda Bede a "refinedly repressed" spinster and claims that she identifies the need that all of Pym's major characters share. In other words, all of the major characters, male or female, gay or straight, are looking for something to love (1).

Still, Benet writes, though Pym's major characters seek fulfillment through romantic love, their author treats them unromantically, for there are "no hearts throbbing as one" amid the pages of her books (9). In this, Pym differs from romance writers. For example, in Maggie Shayne's *Twilight Fantasies,* Eric Marquand regards his lover Tamara impatiently as "the fire inside him burned out of control" (164). Eric notes the heroine's "luscious body" and he wants to "devour" every "succulent inch" of her (164). Shayne uses words like "ravage" and "sweet nectar" to describe the lovers' tryst (164-65). As Benet notes, however, passion is not so urgent in Pym's novels. There are false starts, errors, and failures that surround romantic love (9). According to Benet, "Pym's novels make us conclude that those who desire romance can have it only through relationships removed from everyday reality, like Belinda Bede's, or through serial affections and flirtations," like Harriet's (10).

Another Pym critic writes that love for Pym's single women is more theoretical than actual (Graham 150). As a result, Pym heroines find other outlets for their love, such as Church, a woman friend, a few relatives, or a pet (150). Graham notes that Belinda throws herself into parish duties for this reason (150). Therefore, for Pym's characters, loving *something* is necessary if they are to live full lives. It does not matter if their love remains unrequited or if it finds fruition in marriage. Mild infatuations for curates or others which inspire the imagination can also provide something to love. Finally, there is love of home and garden, of friends, of pets, of charity and Church for those whom human romantic love eludes. Where a romance writer may restrict herself to describing love in its human romantic form, Pym describes other types of love. Pym also describes other aspects of her characters' lives, like their everyday meals and clothing.

Though romance novelists like to write in detail about physical and emotional passion, clothes that characters wear, and interiors of grand houses, they seem to balk when it comes to describing their characters' meals. Food is described only in terms of feast or famine. Margaret Ann Jensen addresses how food is presented in Harlequin romances in *Love's Sweet Return: The Harlequin Story*. According to Jensen, older Harlequins focused more on women living in the domestic sphere. Neither the older nor the newer books, however, "pay specific attention to women's actual work in the home" (109). Pym, however, does pay attention to housework. Moreover, Jensen writes that Harlequin romances "emphasize consumption, a more enjoyable preoccupation than the production and maintenance of everyday necessities" (109).

Jensen argues that the Harlequin authors "are able simultaneously to draw on women's interest in personal and household goods and to avoid reminding women of their tedious role in connection with these goods" by emphasizing consumption (109). When, therefore, Harlequin heroines are faced with cooking, they are "never faced with the three-times-a-day inevitability of meal preparation, serving and cleaning up" (109). Instead, Jensen points out, heroines eat in restaurants or have others cook for them (109). Having heroines eat out and having others cook are two of the ways Jensen claims that

Harlequins "glamorize women's work in the home and gloss over the drawbacks" (108).

Sometimes, though, food is described in "luscious" detail, similar to Pym's technique. Here is one example Jensen quotes from Essie Summers's *Through All the Years:*

> But the dinner was heavenly . . . the steak and mushrooms were perfectly grilled, the baked jacket potatoes artistically cupped in slit foil, the vegetables obviously home-grown and flavoury. The pavlova was all a pavlova should be, crisply sugary on the outside, marshmallow-soft inside, filled with a delectable mixture of fruit and cream and tangy with the passion-fruit pulp. (qtd. in Jensen 109)

As Jensen says, the "abundant use of adjectives glamorizes the meal" (109). Words like "passion-fruit," "pulp," "artistically," "heavenly," and "pavlova" lend a sexy, sophisticated, even exotic character to an otherwise ordinary steak and potatoes dinner. The usually female reader will not realize that this meal may well be the product of a woman laboring in the home without pay (109).

Roland Barthes addresses the same point in "Ornamental Cookery." Barthes uses the French magazine *Elle* as an example. According to Barthes, the structure or core influencing the magazine determines how food is presented. The recipes in the magazine provide for elaborate sauces and garnishes for common, familiar, inexpensive foods like chicken in order to appeal to the expensive tastes but low incomes of *Elle*'s predominantly lower-middle-class readers (Barthes 145). In the spirit of *Elle*, Barbara Cartland wrote *The Romance of Food* with the intent of glamorizing it. Her biographer, Gwen Robyns, describes how Cartland selected expensive china from her own collection for the book's illustrations to make the food's appearance more romantic (204).

Pym, however, does not glamorize food in this way. In *Some Tame Gazelle*, Hoccleve remarks to Belinda that he thinks women enjoy missing meals and "making martyrs of themselves" (39). Belinda answers that women often miss meals because they have no time to eat. In discussing missed meals with Hoccleve, Belinda says, "We may [miss meals], but I think we can leave the enjoyment . . . to the men" (39).[8]

When romance writers do not want to stress food consumption, we do not read scrumptious, painstaking details. In contrast, Pym includes delicious details about simple meals like afternoon tea, or about snacks and light suppers like baked beans on toast or cauliflower cheese. For instance, when the maid is out, Pym bothers to tell us that Harriet and Belinda have sardine eggs for dinner (63). There is even a *Barbara Pym*

*Cookbook* edited by Hilary Pym and Honor Wyatt. The cookbook is arranged by courses and meals, e.g., one chapter is entitled "Starters and Soups," another is called "Main Dishes." Described are recipes for shepherd's pie, steak and kidney pudding, and Miss Prior's cauliflower cheese (10). There are also recipes for tea cakes and for French dishes that Pym enjoyed (10).

Where Pym describes how to make tea cakes and baked beans on toast, romance novelists will only describe food eaten on drastic occasions, or they will describe it when it is somehow tied into the hero's and heroine's sexual foreplay. In Kathleen Woodiwiss's *Shanna,* references to "juicy meat" are really sexual innuendoes. In one scene, Shanna uses a food metaphor to describe herself. She says to Ruark, her husband, "your eyes deceive you. You have fasted long and would relish plain porridge for a dainty dish" (575). In other words, the heroine is a passive dish of porridge that waits to be "devoured" by the hero.

One should mention that Pym is capable of such sexual references, too. For example, in *Some Tame Gazelle,* she reminds us that a man needs a woman to "cook his meat." In the same novel we learn that "Harriet's appetite was just as rapacious in her fifties as it had been in her teens" (16). Pym refers to the dinner of boiled chicken smothered in white sauce that the sisters will serve Mr. Latimer, visiting curate, but the reader understands that Harriet is also "hungry" for young curates, if only for their company. Yet, unlike many of her romance counterparts, Pym does not make a sexual allusion every time she mentions food.

Food in Pym's novels plays a variety of roles. As Penelope Lively points out, food in Pym's novels has a rich, subtle language of its own (49). In fact, Pym uses food to criticize her characters' skills as hosts and housekeepers. For example, though she is a bishop's daughter, Agatha Hoccleve is said to keep a mean house. When Miss Prior, the touchy seamstress goes to visit her, Agatha gives her only "a dried-up scrap of cheese" and sometimes no sweet (48). It is plain to Miss Prior that Agatha gives her scraps because she considers her beneath her in class. In this instance, food becomes a social marker. In "Well-Fed or Well-Loved?—Patterns of Cooking and Eating in the Novels of Barbara Pym," Mary Anne Schofield quotes from Claude Lévi-Strauss's *The Raw and the Cooked* for the proposition that converting raw ingredients to cooked food marks the "transition from 'nature' to 'culture'" (qtd. in Schofield 1).

Class is part of any discussion of culture. Pym addresses class in *Some Tame Gazelle* by discussing food. Even when there are caterpillars in the cauliflower cheese, Miss Prior prefers to eat at Harriet's and Belinda's house because they give her what they eat (52). Belinda tiptoes around the seamstress, and gives her meals on a tray because if she asks her to eat with her and Harriet, Miss Prior, as a hireling, may take umbrage at the "patronage" (45-46). As the narrator says, Miss Prior was "very nearly a gentlewoman" and "was so touchy, so conscious of her position, so quick to detect the slightest suspicion of patronage that one had to be *very* careful" (46). Earlier, Belinda argues with Harriet that Miss Prior could not be served just cauliflower cheese, Harriet's choice, because dinner that night would be duck, in honor of Mr. Donne. Belinda protests, "You know how she enjoys her meals and we always give her meat of some kind" (45). Harriet hopes that Belinda is not suggesting they serve Miss Prior the duck, but Belinda says, "Well, I don't know, really . . . Would it matter if we gave Mr. Donne cauliflower cheese?" (45). Belinda argues her case by pointing out that they had a similar meal when Edith Liversidge came to dinner, and that Edith only provided baked beans (45). Harriet, however, listens to Belinda's protests in "stony silence," for it is inconceivable that a man should have "women's food" of cauliflower cheese and no meat (45). Throughout the meal, it is clear that Belinda is working in the kitchen, because, unlike a Harlequin heroine, she is piling plates and "scraping fish bones from one to another" (45).

Whether or not one provides a "sweet" with a meal is a sign of how good a hostess she is. Margaret Visser in *Much Depends on Dinner* writes, "Dessert ends the meal with a high note for . . . we are Romantics still, determined to end our works of art with a climax, in spite of the classical centrality of the main course" (19). Edith Liversidge, who is a bad housekeeper, gives Belinda baked beans on toast for dinner, enhanced by ashes from her ever-present cigarette, and no sweet (45). Belinda emphasizes to Harriet that cauliflower cheese and good coffee with a sweet would make a very nice meal for Mr. Donne (45).

Pym's single heroines sometimes use food to attract the attention of the opposite sex. Single women apparently outnumber men in the world of Pym's novels, so Pym spinsters who want to attract men's attention have several ways of doing so. Their methods are often a means of expressing love. Food gifts in *Some Tame Gazelle* often are given with love, especially when presented to curates and clergymen (66). One of the only "safe" ways Belinda has to express her love for Henry Hoccleve is to bake for him. At one point, she ponders making rich cakes for him (66). When Harriet takes a basket to Mr. Donne, she includes apple jelly and a cake, besides "some very special late plums which she had been guarding jealously for the last few weeks" (54). Harriet's plums become "love tokens," because she "guards them jealously" (54). They are also symbolic of Harriet herself, like her, they are "mature" fruit, ripening in the autumn, the latter part of the year. As a middle-aged heroine, Harriet, too, is ripening and plump, pleasing and round like the plums.

In Pym's world, men accept food, while women cook it (79). Pym's men simply do not consider the work that goes into meals, work Pym emphasizes with her detailed description of how Belinda makes ravioli. After ten minutes of kneading and rolling the sticky pasta dough, Belinda finds she needs to rest and that her back aches (219). The narrator informs us that kneading "was exhausting work, and the paste was nowhere near the desired consistency yet" (219).

The ravioli is a metaphor for the difficulties Belinda faces as a single woman who must run her own home and for the difficult situation she will have to deal with in her life. It is also an example of Pym's use of imagery. Different foods in Pym are representations for other things. For example, while the sisters discuss various foods, the conversation begins to focus on salt. Belinda immediately thinks of Lot's wife, imagining it would be restful to become a pillar of salt and "to have no feelings or emotions" (80). Belinda also says, "Or perhaps . . . it would have been simpler to have been born like Milton's first wife, an image of earth and phlegm" (80).

The images of a salt figure and an earth figure are poignant ones for Belinda. Belinda's comments imply that having feelings and emotions involves suffering. That she is thinking of Hoccleve is revealed in her next statement about Milton's first wife because Hoccleve often read Milton to her while they were courting. In fact, Pym notes in *A Very Private Eye* that she and Harvey, Hoccleve's prototype, were caught in bed, "with nothing on," reading *Samson Agonistes* (40). So, for both Pym and Belinda, Milton and his writings are linked with romantic love, however unpalatable or unhappy.

Just as the reference to a pillar of salt implies emotional numbness, the allusion to an inanimate figure of earth and phlegm implies something insensible or unfeeling, a sort of Golem, waiting to come to life under the hands of its creator. Yet, like the pillar of salt, the image of earth and phlegm cannot feel pain. The allusion Belinda makes comes from Milton's treatise on divorce, which questions why a man should be forced to stay in a bad marriage with an incompatible wife. In many ways, Milton's arguments remind one of Mr. Rochester's justifications for shutting Bertha Mason in the attic. Though Mr. Rochester is fictional, both are men known for their bad marriages and apparent mistreatment of wives. For instance, William Rose Benet notes in *The Reader's Encyclopedia* that Milton treated his wives and daughters deplorably (671). While he may not be as impossible as Milton, Hoccleve is often peevish and demanding of the women in his life, including Belinda, who is infinitely patient.

Besides using food to describe Belinda's emotional state, Pym uses it to describe the respective personalities of Edith Liversidge and Connie Aspinall. At one point, Harriet and Belinda contemplate possible meals for the pair and decide on a tin of tongue, potato salad, macaroni cheese, and bottled fruit and coffee (89). The tongue might be a joke about Edith's outspokenness, the bottled fruit an image for the often cowed and repressed Connie.

Food, then, is also a discourse some of the characters use to express themselves. For example, Harriet keeps a diary of what she serves curates for dinner (101). The fact that Harriet is the sister more concerned with food and its social ramifications is one of Pym's touches of humor, for Harriet is the plumper of the two sisters, who often uses meals as an occasion to flirt with younger men, including curates. Curates may seem an interesting choice for a love object. Critic Charles Burkhart has noted, "There are women, there are men, there are clergymen" (92), but lascivious vicars have long played their part in romances. Daphne du Maurier writes about a brutal vicar in *Jamaica Inn* while George Eliot laments in "Silly Novels by Lady Novelists" that many a silly novel contains a salacious vicar as a hero (530). Finally, Molly Hardwick, author of romances and mysteries, has created Rodney Chelmarsh, country vicar and loving husband to Doran Fairweather, amateur detective of the Doran Fairweather mystery series of novels.

In a not-so-subtle metaphor involving the word "appetite" that is typical of a romance writer, Pym tells us that Belinda is writing a letter to the absent Agatha Hoccleve in an uneasy, but sisterly fashion. She writes that the archdeacon "is looking well and has a good appetite" (140). Because, however, Belinda is constantly worried about impropriety, she wonders, "Was this last sentence perhaps a little presumptuous? Ought an archdeacon to be looking well and eating with a good appetite when his wife was away? And ought Belinda to write as if she knew about his appetite?" (140). As a result of her thoughts, Belinda adds "as far as I know" to the sentence about appetite (141).

The word "appetite" has a double meaning in this passage. On the one hand, Belinda does not want to be too familiar or imply that she eats frequently with Hoccleve, or that she cooks for him, thereby usurping Agatha's place as his wife. On the other hand, the word's other meaning describes sexual appetite, and Belinda does not want to intimate that she is an expert in that area of the archdeacon's life, especially after Agatha has implied that it would be improper for Belinda to see him in his bath. Later, Belinda actually has dinner with Hoccleve. At home drinking Ovaltine with Harriet that night, she wonders if she has done the wrong thing, though the evening has left her feeling romantic. In Pym, Ovaltine and tea often take the place of wine in romantic novels. To Belinda, who is eager to confide her "racy" evening, the Ovaltine "loosens" her tongue. Yet, though Belinda may like something stronger, she sticks with Ovaltine, and the narrator says that to Belinda "it seemed an unromantic end to the evening" (155).

In another passage with Mr. Parnell, food again becomes the basis of emotional expression. After the distasteful Mr. Mold's marriage proposal to her, Harriet indignantly tells Parnell that the only thing she and Mr. Mold have in common "is a love of good food"; therefore, she could never marry him. Dr. Parnell replies, "But surely liking the same things for dinner is one of the deepest and most lasting things you could possibly have in common with anyone." Dr. Parnell continues, "After all, the emotions of the heart are very transitory, or so I believe; I should think it makes one much happier to be well-fed than well-loved" (145). Another fictional character expresses similar sentiment. Dorothy Eden's *Voice of the Dolls* is a romance written during Pym's lifetime. In the novel, an obese mother-in-law tells the young governess-heroine that her "stomach's far more faithful to [her] than men will ever be" (26).

In *Some Tame Gazelle,* Belinda does not contradict the statement that it is better to be well-fed than well-loved, "romantic and sentimental though she [is]," because she is happy to be relieved of the possibility of the unappetizing Mr. Mold as brother-in-law (145). Mr. Mold's very name is distasteful; it implies rotten food or decay, and is an unlikely name for someone who loves good food. Since mold is a sort of parasite, the joke Pym is making may be that Mr. Mold, too, is a parasite because he loves other people's good cooking.

In any case, food and love are clearly linked. Food is the superior interest; passion wanes, but a love of good cooking does not, and can bring an aging couple closer together. Mr. Parnell's conviction that he is right about being well-fed is most emphatic, just as romance heroes and heroines are emphatic about their physical passions.

The Bede sisters apparently also believe that their guests should be well-fed. At one point in the novel, Pym describes in detail a Sunday supper Belinda and Harriet host after Evensong. The archdeacon, Parnell, Mr. Mold, and other guests are present. The menu consists of cold chicken, ham, tongue, various salads, trifles, jellies, fruit, and Stilton cheese (*Some Tame Gazelle* 114).

Pym's food and menu descriptions are typical of a special, middle-class meal. When romance writers describe special meals, they are often lavish concoctions that feature expensive food. For example, when Angela Wells's heroine Catia is "not hungry," she has the following in an Italian open air restaurant: "cold lobster salad followed by strawberries and ice-cream, washed down by the omnipresent aqua minerale and a bottle of Gambellara" (101). Typical lunch for Catia and the husband she is beginning to resent because he married her without loving her is

*risotto primavera,* a rice dish served with minced fresh vegetables, followed by Adriatic sole in a sweet and sour sauce served with white asparagus and wild mushrooms and then a creamy trifle of custard and liqueur sponge cake, with a light Italian vanilla ice-cream to round the meal off and cleanse the palate. Nicolo had requested mineral water and a bottle of Soave to accompany the meal, both bottles reaching the table in an ice-bucket, their sides misted and dewed. (88)

They also have Amaretto and rich dark coffee (88).

Meals in *Sultana,* by Prince Michael of Greece, are even more exotic. The heroine of Prince Michael's novel is a cousin of Josephine Bonaparte who has been kidnapped and taken to a harem, where everything is larger than life. This is her description of the slavewomen's kitchen:

There my companions made all sorts of confections and delicacies I loved: dry cakes powdered with sugar, syrup or honey cakes, baklavas, kadaifis, galacto bouizikos, not to mention the so aptly named rahat loukhoums, literally "throat soothers," in varied pastel colors. We also prepared the national sherberts in many different flavors, conserved in ice brought from Mount Olympus in Bithynia, and the "spoon sweets" made from fruit—lemons, Chinese oranges, kumquats, nuts, figs—half candied and half stewed, served in a spoon with a glass of water. (75)

They eat at ten o'clock and five o'clock. The cooks feed five thousand people each day. The heroine is surprised by the frugality of the dishes after the French menus she is used to (75).

While Prince Michael writes about the ordinary habits of a harem, Barbara Cartland writes about "Sunday Dinner" at a witch's coven in *The Flame Is Love.* In the film version of Cartland's novel, the squeamish heroine, Vada, is served dishes of animals' heads and whole animals served on platters. Many of the heads have sharp tusks that reflect the even sharper knives of the table setting. Cartland writes that Vada attends the dinner adorned in a simple white dress that makes her look very young. Her host is a sinister Marquis (129). In contrast, the other guests, only four of whom are women, are richly dressed. The table is set with gold and silver goblets and the food is served on gold plates (131). Still, there is something very gloomy about the dining room and the curtains are blood-red (130). Vada notices that the courses are of "unusual ingredients," and she finds some of them inedible (131). Vada eats little, but notices that the other guests gorge themselves on the exotic food and drink. Finally, Vada is drugged and laid out naked on the altar for the Black Mass (140). When she regains consciousness in this horrific situation, she realizes that, all along, she was supposed to be the main course. The reader soon learns all the gruesome details of the Black Mass, and is informed that Satanists eat and drink to excess before their mass because Christians traditionally fast before theirs. Thus, the feast Vada attends is "a gesture of defiance of all that [is] Holy" (147).

In contrast to Cartland's demonic use of a dinner party, the sisters of *Some Tame Gazelle* use food to impress others and to express their hospitality as well. For one Sunday dinner, they serve roast beef, celery, roast potatoes, plum tart, boiled chickens, trifles, and jellies. The leftovers serve as Harriet's and Belinda's supper (103). This elaborate meal is a far cry from the sardine eggs or baked beans on toast that the women have when dining alone on the maid's day out. The courses from the various food groups and the various fowl, tarts, and jellies have Victorian and Edwardian overtones; they imply someone important is coming and that extra help is needed. They also imply that the hosts are comfortably well-off, and can afford extra help. In Victorian and Edwardian middle-class households, a woman's social standing depended on how many servants she employed (Berriedale-Johnson 7). For example, the single women who host the Twelfth Night Feast in James Joyce's "The Dead" need the help of Lily, "the caretakers daughter," who is "literally run off her feet," to help serve the elaborate annual meal (175). Joyce describes a meal that includes goose, spiced beef, elaborate table settings, jellies, fruits, and nuts. The meal as Joyce presents it is an example of Irish hospitality at its best, despite the fact that the Morkans may be struggling financially. As the narrator says, the sisters' life is modest (176).

Though many of her menus are modest, Pym, too, often emphasizes hospitality and prosperity when she writes about food. The dinner Belinda and Harriet serve Mr. Donne in *Some Tame Gazelle* is a typical Sunday dinner for two well-off single women like the Bede sisters. In *Much Depends on Dinner,* Margaret Visser describes the history of a typical chicken dinner consisting of the following: corn with salt and butter, chicken with rice, lettuce with olive oil and lemon juice, ice cream (14). The first time Mr. Donne comes to dinner in *Some Tame Gazelle,* the sisters serve chicken, and Mr. Donne gets the best portion (13). Visser writes that this chicken dinner is "almost totally female in connotation" (18). Corn, writes Visser, is "the American Indian 'mother and nourisher'" (19). Chicken is a typically female choice because it is pale meat with no red blood and little fat, so it is in Western culture a "typically female choice" (19). Romance writer Lori Herter would agree. In *The Willow File,* the heroine has chicken at her first dinner with the hero, and she barely picks at that (86).

That "real women" don't eat meat and don't have big appetites is evident in Anne Stevenson's controversial biography of Sylvia Plath, *Bitter Fame.* Stevenson writes that Sylvia Plath's British in-laws implicitly criticized Sylvia for preferring steak for dinner and for her large appetite. A friend of the Hughes's, Dido Merwin, criticizes Plath for "grimly downing the . . . *foie gras* for all the world as though it were Aunt Dot's meat loaf" (341).

Chicken is also "traditionally festive in overtone" according to Margaret Visser, who also mentions Pym's novels. In *Much Depends on Dinner,* she writes that Barbara Pym's novels are full of sly insights into culinary anthropology. Visser also says that, in Pym's novels, chicken is for when clergymen are invited for dinner. It is an elevated dish, not too fleshy (19).

Pym also uses food to define the men in her novels. Ricardo, the Italian count in *Some Tame Gazelle,* is a sort of vegetation god, he grows prize vegetables in a garden and is often associated with vegetation images (58). He grows corn and is thus linked with the Harvest Festival (75). Ricardo reads Tacitus and Dante and broods over letters of his deceased friend, John Akenside, in preparation for a biography he wants to write. These gentle habits and the association with vegetation make him seem more like a female figure, or a heroine.

Pym uses Ricardo's pastimes to subvert, in part, the image of the romance hero he resembles. Like Dracula, that other mysterious count of the gothic romance genre, Ricardo settled in the village "for some unexplained reason" (23). He is Italian and is thus associated with Dante and other poets who wrote about love. Like any good romance hero, he goes after his lady and constantly proposes to Harriet, who in turn, constantly refuses him. We know from the narrator's description of his gentle nature, however, that whatever mystery surrounds Ricardo is not nearly as macabre and gruesome as that which surrounds the notorious but charismatic Dracula.[9]

While the emphasis in contemporary romances may be on the development of the relationship between lovers and on the hero's ability to change his personality for his beloved, Pym's heroes resemble more the heroes of older romances. Barbara Pym may prefer working with the traditional Byronic model because it is easy for her to subvert. For instance, Pym heroes have touches of Byronism in their makeup, but they are often made ridiculous because of personal quirks, eccentricities, or mistaken conjectures about their sexuality. As Snow points out, Pym women are aware of their men's shortcomings but love them all the same. In "'For the Ovaltine Had Loosened Her Tongue': Failures of Speech in Barbara Pym's *Less than Angels*," Jill Rubinstein writes that Pym's males are "generally exploitive, although not intentionally cruel, almost always egotistical, frequently pompous, insensitive, and patronizing . . . hardly ever as smart . . . as the women who endure them and love them" (573). Spoofing her heroes's eccentricities is one way Pym displays their vulnerability. Jones writes that in a romance novel, the heroine wants not necessarily the safety of marriage, "but the certainty that the hero is as vulnerable as [she is]" (213). So Pym changes the vulnerable hero through humor. Even though a Pym heroine may realize her hero is as guileless as she is, she also may find the hero less desirable, even ridiculous, because of his eccentricities.

Rubinstein notes that Pym's women "display considerably greater intelligence" than Pym's men (573). She also claims that the male characters "exercise their imagination only upon themselves, whereas the women use imagination to transfigure their worlds, including, of course, their men" (573). Pym's women's are literary heirs to some of the female characters of Aldous Huxley's *Crome Yellow*. Anne, one of the characters of Huxley's novel, deflates the romantic ideal of the hero by saying "I should like to see myself believing that men are the highway to divinity" (42). The implication is that though she would like to believe so, she cannot. Still, romance writers like Stella Cameron and Maggie Shayne insist on creating malleable male characters who are changed and molded through love to be more considerate of their women.

In *Women in England: 1870-1950*, Jane Lewis quotes an American historian who writes that women redefine the male-dominated world in their own terms (xii). Their goal in doing so is to create a women's culture (xii). For instance, Belinda knows Henry is narcissistic, yet she continually takes the blame when he is insensitive or rude. In one instance, the pouring of sherry is delayed because guests to her dinner party are late. Instead of being angry at the absent guest, Belinda apologizes to Mr. Mold, to the bishop of Mbawawa, and to Hoccleve for her bad manners in offering sherry so late (119). She does so because it "was so obvious that women should take the blame. It was both the better and the easier part" (119). As Snow so aptly states, "Belinda opts for self-immolation on the altar of Archdeacon Hoccleve's arrogance" (57).

As an unmarried woman, Belinda is especially used to taking the blame. Throughout the book, she must endure the repeated snubs of Agatha who is often rude and unfeeling. Agatha often tries to ostracize or snub Belinda because Agatha is married to Belinda's former lover and

Belinda is single. Lewis writes that spinsters were ostracized because marriage "remained the normative expectation of women," particularly before World War I (3). As Lewis notes, "Spinsterhood was often referred to as 'failure in business' in middle-class households" (3). In creating Maria, the spinster heroine of "Clay," James Joyce portrays the type of single woman Lewis describes. Maria is "very small" with a long nose and chin that make her look like a witch (79). Appropriately, the story takes place on Halloween. Joyce uses both humor and pathos to show how others make fun of Maria and ostracize her for her ugliness and her single state.

Despite social ostracism, however, many single women still chose not to marry. Around 1880, many women consciously chose to remain single, according to Jane Lewis (76). Lewis claims this was because more middle-class women began to be interested in careers and activities outside the home. Marriage, with its responsibilities of running large households and raising large families, often condemned women to be virtual prisoners in their own homes. For example, articulate women successfully argued against their critics that "charitable work" represented an "acceptable extension of women's domestic work" (76). Wives and spinsters alike profited from this idea. Many single women in particular, like Florence Nightingale, were driven to remain single by "a strong commitment to a cause or ideal" (76). These women did not want to give up their causes to become wives. As late as 1922, Huxley in *Crome Yellow* pokes fun at women who embrace causes. Mary is described as a woman whose "eyes shone with the indignation of a convinced birth controller" (490).

Even in 1970, however, Germaine Greer writes that society believes the single woman must have missed her chance; she lost her boy in the war or she hesitated and was lost (209). In fact, British novelist Miss Read (Dora Jessie Saint) has written a book entitled *Miss Clare Remembers* about a single heroine who did indeed lose her "boy" in the war. The book is not, however, a romance. Ann Rosalind Jones wonders whether romance ever questions "the [heroine's belief in the] ultimate value of marriage" (214). If romance novelists do not question it, the single heroines in Pym's books who choose to remain single certainly do question marriage's ultimate value, and most consciously seek alternative roles for themselves.

Another way single women question marriage's ultimate value in Pym's books is by expressing themselves and developing their own style. Pym links meal time with personal expression in *Some Tame Gazelle,* for the narrator tells us that Harriet usually wants to look nicer on Sunday when curates come to dinner, than on other days of the week

(103). So, mealtime is often a dress-up occasion. From a "plump woman" on weekdays, Harriet becomes an "elegant creature" on Sundays (103). Pym often describes Harriet in animalistic terms like "creature." In one place, she splashes like a porpoise in her bath (115). Pym is not above writing about lavatories, that part of the bathroom not discussed in polite literature. In this, she shares a technique with Lord Byron, who makes allusions to chamber pots in *Don Juan*. In fact, Pym mentions in *A Very Private Eye* that she read *Don Juan* (68-70).

Harriet's wild and animal-influenced clothing is also a means of expression for her. Harriet's dresses are often jungle prints, or wild tropical designs, implying that there is something wild and untamed in the otherwise respectable Harriet. One dress is a savage jungle pattern and "flowers [riot] over her plump body" when she wears it (11). This link with the tropics is one Harriet shares with bodice buster heroines like Woodiwiss's *Shanna*, as well as with heroines by romance author Johanna Lindsey. These heroines often find themselves making love in tropical settings, or like Shanna, they were born on Caribbean islands. Harriet also wears exotic capes of white fur and gold lamé and is fond of wearing them to evening church affairs (40). Fashions in the 1930s often incorporated feathers and animal prints. If anything, Harriet's clothes reflect the current style, for in 1939, "picturesque," impractical fancy dress clothes were being shown on Paris runways (Garland, *Fashion 1900-1939*). Only a few years before Pym wrote *Some Tame Gazelle,* fur trim was very popular (7). In 1938, designers like Schiaparelli were showing short jackets decorated with circus elephants and embroidered with images of Medusa and other monsters (16).

Barbara Pym, like a romance novelist, pays particular attention to clothes (*A Very Private Eye* 21). Pym, however, differs from the romance authors because she manages to turn Harriet's wild wardrobe into a vehicle of humor, not of seduction. A romance author would use exotic prints and jungle materials to glamorize her heroine even further and to make her into some tropical Eve. Jensen writes that Harlequin authors glamorize items of personal adornment like clothes, makeup, and jewelry because women are "traditionally believed to be preoccupied with their appearance" (110). Furthermore, women are preoccupied with their appearance so that they can "present themselves in the best possible light" (110). As a result, Harlequins pay close attention to dress, hair, perfume, and makeup.

Greer writes in *The Female Eunuch* that all romantic novels have a "preoccupation with clothes" and "every sexual advance is made with clothing as an attractive barrier" (188). She quotes extensively from romance authors Lucy Walker, Barbara Cartland, and Georgette Heyer to prove her point. Cartland does pay attention to clothes and to their colors. In fact, she often dresses her heroines in colors like pink and scarab blue because they inspire her (*History* 46). Cartland herself prefers pink and has made it her signature color because she believes it has a positive effect on the human personality (46).

Romance author Margaret Heys plays out Greer's "attractive barrier" theory in her romance about Henry VIII's second queen, *Anne Boleyn*. Heys describes Anne's costume in one chapter as a fairy gown of pale green silk (144). The narrator informs the reader that Anne has a "flair" for clothes and is a wonderful designer. Her green silk gown "billows" like a "cobweb cloud" in a seductive manner (143). Anne's cloak is also elegant. It is made of richly embroidered black velvet, lined with iridescent taffeta. Her jewels and belt are emeralds (144). Anne dances before the king in her graceful dress until he is overcome with passion and he removes it from her body (145).

It takes skill and interest in fashion to know how to dress well. Harriet, too, is interested in clothes and in presenting herself in the best light. The difference is that she is fifty and plump; not the typical Harlequin heroine. Belinda, though more sober, is fond of nice clothes, too, and is attractive, though not flamboyant like her sister. In one episode, Belinda is self-conscious about wearing dowdy shoes (32). At the dinner party for Hoccleve and the curate, Belinda wears a blue chiffon dress and crystal beads and earrings "that went quite well with it" (*Some Tame Gazelle* 115). She also wears a little rouge, and "the whole effect was rather pleasing" (115). Pym, in *A Very Private Eye*, describes a similar outfit that she wore (31). Belinda dislikes sloppy dressing and is quick to criticize Edith for having dog hairs everywhere, and notes her brogues and unfashionable tweeds (*Some Tame Gazelle* 19). Pym herself was interested in clothes, and often dressed to achieve a "sexy effect." Lingerie, in particular, intrigued Pym. In January 1934, she describes a peach colored vest and "trollies" to match "with insertions" of lace that she bought, acknowledging that she bought underwear expecting it to be seen (*A Very Private Eye* 33).

*Crampton Hodnet* is another Pym novel that contains romantic elements. Much of the novel is told from the viewpoint of Jessie Morrow. Jessie is a companion to the bossy Miss Doggett, but she is far different from the scheming, sardonic Jessie of *Jane and Prudence*. This Jessie is a closet romantic with a sense of humor. She philosophizes on her life as a paid companion, but never gives up the belief that life, even for her in her single state, has great possibilities. She is proved correct, for a handsome curate, Mr. Latimer, proposes to her, albeit to escape the unwanted attentions of other women. Jessie refuses his hilarious proposal, where he calls her "Janie," but gently explains she cannot marry someone she does not love. She then recommends Ovaltine to Latimer. The novel basically explores various kinds of love relationships in its plot. Young love is studied and parodied in the Simon-Anthea romance. More typical middle-aged marriage and its crises are portrayed in the marriage of the Clevelands. The younger, "other woman"-older man liaison appears in the halfhearted, misunderstood affair between the young undergraduate Barbara Bird and Francis Cleveland. Pym uses her knowledge of academia and literature to parody love and romance in her fictional village set in North Oxford. In fact, the novel gives a good history of Oxford at this time.

Michael Cotsell implies in *Barbara Pym* that the history Pym is interested in representing is Victorian (36). He writes that *Crampton Hodnet* represents nostalgia for the safety of the Victorian age and that the North Oxford presented in the novel is full of nineteenth-century homes (37). These houses are gloomily opulent, and reflect their owners' social standing (36-37). The village is, in short, a place of secrets with occasional hints of racy scandal. For example, Cotsell notes provocative touches like a glimpse of feminine lace curtains that seem like the edge of a petticoat showing at a window (36-37). This image implies lingerie, and all the "sexy" connotations associated with it. The novel is subtler than *Some Tame Gazelle;* there is no outspoken Harriet Bede to hastily and uproariously stuff her corset under a cushion.

According to Cotsell, in *Crampton Hodnet* Pym treats romantic love as "unreliable, incongruous, [and] embarrassing" (40). Of the love stories in the book, Francis Cleveland's is the richest in these qualities. He is a milder brother of Derek Hawke of Jennifer Wilde's *Love's Tender Fury* and a host of other romance heroes caught by their wives and lovers in compromising situations.[10]

Mason Cooley argues that *Crampton Hodnet* contains the elements of romantic farce because lovers hide in bushes and are discovered, characters engage in uneasy romantic embraces, and gay young men dance together (16). According to Cooley, the concern of romantic comedy is the struggle of lovers against their elders. He also says that *Crampton Hodnet* is both a "romantic comedy and a laughing satire on the conventions of romantic comedy" (25). The hero, or as Cooley calls Mr. Latimer, "Prince Charming," is motivated to propose to Cinderella, as played by Jessie, because he wants to escape the unwanted attentions of other women (25). Heroines are also "caught" or inhibited in *Crampton Hodnet,* but for different reasons than heroes. Jessie Morrow, a poor gentlewoman, is the paid companion variety of heroine discussed in Chapter 1.

Gentlewomen were often poor and lived off their father's small inheritance. Homes for elderly, financially distressed gentlewomen were popular causes; 1950s British magazines often contain pictorial ads for such places. If gentlewomen worked, they worked as governesses or paid companions. The narrator says that Jessie "is introduced as an afterthought." As Miss Doggett says "Ah, Miss Morrow, I didn't notice you" (17). In fact, she replies to Miss Doggett by saying in part, "A companion is looked upon as a piece of furniture. She is hardly a person at all" (17). As if to confirm her statement, none of the others answer her. Instead, they all walk to the Cleveland's dining room where Francis is about to carve cold-beef on the sideboard (17). Jessie recognizes that she is ignored, but she is not offended; she often thinks inanimate objects, like one's bed, are nicer than people (31). Jessie's entire discourse throughout the novel seems to involve not being noticed, sometimes to avoid scandal. For example, she and the curate Mr. Latimer concoct an elaborate explanation for why they have emerged from the toolshed together (115). What would be a place for a romantic tryst in a romance becomes nothing more than shelter from the rain where Jessie and Latimer discuss cars.

Despite her dependent status as Miss Doggett's companion, Jessie manages to achieve distance from her situation and is capable of commenting on the other characters. Michael Cotsell writes in *Barbara Pym* that from her neutral position, Jessie surveys the romantic follies of the other characters (39). Cotsell notes that her personality is incongruous with Miss Doggett's. According to that formidable woman, women who dress well and use cosmetics are "attractive and significant" (39). Jessie, with her drab clothes and plain appearance, is no more than a household fixture to Miss Doggett, who is later shocked when Jessie dons her best dress and makeup.

Pym calls Jessie a "used-up" woman in her thirties (2). Like Catherine of *Less Than Angels,* however, Jessie is an artist because she is "able to look upon herself and her surroundings with detachment" and to interpret what she sees (2). For example, she is able to view the new curate, Mr. Latimer, with "dispassionate interest" (30). Like Catherine and Barbara Pym herself, Jessie's gift is the writer's power of observation. Cooley writes in *The Comic Art of Barbara Pym* that Jessie Morrow is descended from Jane Eyre (30). For one thing, like Jane, she will not marry a man who does not love her. Cooley writes on this point that Mr. Latimer's proposal to Jessie is a "spoof of very convention of a proposal scene." He notes that Jessie is "romantic enough" to prefer where she is to "rescue" by a man who does not love her (31). Unlike many romance heroines, Jessie does not express rage, humiliation, or a desire to escape. He claims she is resigned to her inferior position. Jessie is not like Kathleen Winsor's romance heroine Amber, who, in *Forever Amber,* constantly seeks to elevate her position as illegitimate daughter of a noble-man by entering into love affairs with important gentlemen. The description of Jessie as dowdy spinster is, however, not in keeping with her personality. Her name, Jessica, is itself romantic. She is a "closet" romantic who turns up the radio when love songs play because they give her "warmth and sinful brightness" (2-3). As she listens, Jessie thinks the program is "Chocolates," a radio show meant for lovers. Like the music, the ads on the wireless are meant for women and are focused on "attracting [their] man" or "getting the washing done" (3). Jessie is not immune to media ads aimed at women. She reads women's maga-zines and tries rouge she reads about in ads (20). She may be a virtuous spinster, but she is not repressed or bitter. Jessie continues to hope for romantic love in some form.

The romance between Anthea Cleveland and Simon is, according to Cooley, Pym's effort at telling the story of an adolescent romance (33). He notes she made no more attempts because the comedy of youthful love was written too often to interest Pym. He argues that their first kiss has "none of the privacy, secrecy or surprise of romance." (34). The adoles-cent first kiss in Pym is a social occasion, like a tea party. In fact, Simon takes note that he is the "only one of his set to have a young girl in love with him" (39). Thus, his kiss with Anthea becomes a rite of passage.

Anthea as a heroine has the "standard attributes of the attractive girl": she is tall, slender, and blonde, and her face is "gentle" and "not too intelligent" (Cooley 35). Simon is tall, dark, and thin. They are a conventionally matched "perfect couple," which does not interest Pym because their romance is socially approved (36).

If, as Cooley claims, Simon and Anthea do not interest Pym that much, it is interesting that she takes the time to describe them in roman-tic discourse. Pym sets the scene by placing Simon and Anthea in a room "dark except for the glow of the fire, for Simon understood the nature of a romantic atmosphere" (38). Through humor, Pym subverts the roman-tic discourse. Instead of love songs, the Salvation Army band plays hymns in the background (38). The statement that Simon understands the nature of romantic atmosphere is ironic; he really has no idea of what Anthea would find romantic. Germaine Greer writes that men typically do not understand the discourse of romance because they do not read romance novels (181). She argues that romantic discourse is defined in romance novels that women, not men, read (181). Yet, Carol Lee writes in *The Blind Side of Eden* that British men are brought up to be heroes and that women are glad that they are (1). These authors imply that both men and women are fed on romantic fantasy, and that reality is often dif-ferent, if not disappointing.

The reality of the scene between Simon and Anthea also subverts the romance. This is not the exotic atmosphere of Keats' poem "The Eve of St. Agnes." While she is being wooed, Anthea can see the *Sunday Times* lying on the floor. A leaping flame in the fireplace illuminates not her eyes as it would in a romance, but a headline about His Majesty's foreign policy. Still, like all good lovers, Simon and Anthea walk hand-in-hand and look in each other's eyes often, "completely unconscious that there [are] other people on the pavement" (39). When the love affair fizzles, Anthea looks for consolation in women's magazines and defines her discourse of women and beauty from them (210). While Anthea wants to show Simon her intelligence by discussing foreign policy, she finds a romantic novel more sympathetic (49).

Margaret Cleveland is another of the heroines in *Crampton Hodnet.* Her husband is one of Pym's "defective" heroes because he is a seventeenth-century scholar and lecturer who cannot seem to finish a book on his ancestor, the poet John Cleveland. His wife was once interested in his work and in seventeenth-century love lyrics, but she no longer has time for either (15). Looking after Francis and keeping him out of trouble is a full-time job. If Margaret has any hobby, it is letting Francis work alone on his book "because she fear[s] that with her help it might quite easily be finished before one of them died, and then where would they be?" (15).

Pym subverts romantic discourse through Margaret. The relationship between the Clevelands lost its sexual appeal long ago. Pym's portrayal of the couple might be the sequel to the romantic novel where the hero and heroine have reached middle age and now have nothing in common but a desire to keep out of each other's way. While Pym's treatment may be a parody, it is also the realistic fate of many married couples. Like Catherine in *Less Than Angels,* Margaret will learn of her man's infidelities in a restaurant, though she will not view them firsthand as Catherine does. Having the heroine catch the hero in the act of being unfaithful to her is a standard device in romance novels. Usually, the heroine and hero reconcile, but sometimes they do not. In Angela Wells's *Golden Mistress,* Catia learns second hand that her husband is having dinner with the "other woman" (108). She later goes to meet her husband, but finds him with the woman she thinks is her rival (127).

In Pym's *Crampton Hodnet* the rival woman becomes a heroine in the character of Barbara Bird, the undergraduate who becomes infatuated with her professor, Francis Cleveland. Bird may be a portrait of the early Pym in her Oxford days. In *A Very Private Eye,* Pym writes that she wants to put herself in her novels (53). While at Oxford, she often took the name "Sandra" to emphasize her more daring, romantic side and details her racier exploits in her diaries. For example, Pym is very fond of romantic items of costume like black velvet dresses and fur coats (*A Very Private Eye* 32, 17).

Barbara Bird is introduced as a student of Professor Francis Cleveland, who is also the husband of Margaret Cleveland. Barbara, we are told, has written "a remarkably fine essay on the love poems of John Donne" (27). She is about to take part in the standard romantic plot of the younger woman student falling for the older, more experienced male professor. Miss Bird is pretty, and wears a wine-red suit under her scholar's gown (32). Her wine-red ensemble indicates her passionate, even scarlet nature, but the color is not as brazen as the traditional bright red associated with "other women." The deeper tone indicates Miss Bird is more refined. In fact, Barbara is a sort of "other woman" heroine, based on characters from romance novels. Barbara is related to the variety of heroine that Susan Gorsky calls a "romp" in her essay "Gentle Doubters," described in chapter 1. Barbara is also the "other woman" in *Crampton Hodnet,* but her inexperience in the role makes her "the most laughable 'other woman' imaginable," according to Diana Benet (31).

Barbara's discourse of romance differs from that of the romance heroine, however. She does not base her relationships on physical desire. Mason Cooley even says that Barbara likes romance, not sex (26). For example, when Barbara sees the "enormous double bed" in the hotel where she and Francis check in, she panics (40). Instead, her discourse of romance involves intelligent people who love each other despite marriage. She thinks Margaret is the wrong wife for Francis because she cannot imagine them reading poetry together (32). Perhaps in her youthful inexperience she misreads Margaret, because when they were young, Margaret and Francis did indeed read together (32). Yet, like a romance heroine, Barbara is ready for anything in store for her. Diana Benet agrees with Cooley; she writes in *Something to Love* that Barbara's response to Francis is lukewarm, at best. At one point, Benet even calls Barbara an "idealistic cold fish" (32).

Ironically, however, Barbara misreads Francis as well. Benet writes that this is because each has a different definition of romance, and "the idea of precisely what romance involves differs for a man in his fifties and a girl of twenty" (32). In one episode, Barbara reads her essay to Francis. She thinks they have a good discussion afterwards because they have so much in common. In reality, however, Francis forgot what she read, and he is taken aback at how Barbara fawns on him and looks at him (35). Pym seems to take issue with the philosophy of romances like *Jane Eyre* and *Rebecca* where heroines marry out of their class to men with whom they have not much in common but their mutual passion. Pym seems to imply that having common interests is what holds lovers together, not passion. At least one romance author would agree with her. Kathleen Woodiwiss's heroine in *Shanna* is relieved to discover that her husband belongs to the same class she does. Also, part of the tragedy in *Wuthering Heights* occurs because Cathy tells Nelly Dean it would "degrade" her to marry Heathcliff. Significantly, Linn Haire-Sergeant's *Heathcliff* tells the story of how Heathcliff improved himself to be worthy of Cathy.

Through Barbara Bird, Pym spoofs the language of romance novels. In one example, the narrator says of Barbara, "She felt helpless and frustrated and there was a sick feeling at the pit of her stomach, which she did not recognize as a craving for lunch" (133). Normally, romance heroines feel helpless and have sick feelings in the pits of their stomachs when they are denied the physical presence of their lovers, or when they do not know how to attract their man's attention. For example, Cathy pines away for Heathcliff to the point of death.

Moreover, Pym uses food to subvert romantic discourse in *Crampton Hodnet,* just as she does in *Some Tame Gazelle.* Once again, love is related to a bodily function, or to some sort of physical inconvenience. In making fun of the loss of appetite lovers suffer in romance novels, Anthea Cleveland, teenaged daughter of Francis and Margaret, thinks of her beau Simon in the following way:

He had a way of suddenly taking hold of your hand when you were eating, and kissing your fingers or saying something so sweet that you went on chasing food aimlessly round your plate because you couldn't do anything or even think when his eyes were on you. Oh, the lovely food that had been wasted in The Randolph when two people in love had lunch together. A detached onlooker would have seen the funny side of those intimate meals—the abandoned fish, with the spiky bones peeping forlornly through the uneaten flesh, the wings of chicken lying desolate and untouched in their cold gravy, the chocolate mousse, the peaches, the expensive cigarettes thrown into the fire before they were half-smoked. (137)

Instead of being swept up in the lover's passion, the reader is lamenting the good food wasted and the expensive cigarettes that are thrown away. She also sympathizes with the heroine's annoyance. It is very difficult, after all, to eat when someone is holding one's hand. Yet again, the parody lies in the realistic portrayal of the scene. The unappetizing fish bones and cold gravy put a damper on the flame of passion, just as the expensive cigarettes are extinguished before they can be enjoyed.

This passage is also a good example of Pym's use of trivial details to make a point. As the mystery writer character of the television drama

*Murder, She Wrote* might say, "details make the story." A romance writer tends to glamorize food, according to Margaret Ann Jensen (109). Details like spiky fish bones and congealed gravy are left out of romance novels because they spoil the mood. As Caroline Moore has written in "Where are the Trollies of Yesteryear?" a review of Hazel Holt's biography of Pym, *A Lot to Ask*, "This book will not be enjoyed by those who believe themselves to be above gossip, or trivia: these will, I suspect, be chiefly men, who like to imagine that such things are a female preserve; although the best gossips, like the best chefs, are often male" (45).

The details and surroundings of everyday life were for Barbara Pym artistic fodder from which she created imaginary worlds like those of *Some Tame Gazelle* and *Crampton Hodnet*. Pym's fertile imagination allowed her to bring to life heroines and heroes like Belinda Bede and Francis Cleveland who, in one form or another, would populate her later novels. Like many a romance writer, Pym wrote of love and lovers and of all the accoutrements involved therein. Yet, unlike her romance colleagues, Pym used the elements of the romance to subvert the genre so that her love stories are not melancholy melodrama, but romantic comedy that, at its best, reaches a truly sublime, if not acerbic absurdity. Furthermore, Pym's comic reduction of the Byronic and aristocratic hero and her revision of the romance heroine redefine romantic love as it is presented in literature. Pym spoofs various forms of romance novels to answer the question of whether a human being, particularly a woman, can live a full life in a less-than-perfect world. Pym's subversive treatment of the romance genre usually answers the question positively: a single woman living in the dreary modern world is still capable of living a full life. Pym continues to answer this question and to undermine romance with *Excellent Women* and *Jane and Prudence*, two novels that many critics consider to be her best. As with *Some Tame Gazelle* and *Crampton Hodnet*, however, the reader will shed tears, but they will be tears of laughter, not of bittersweet sadness brought on by love gone awry.

# 3

# The Excellent Cinderella

If *Some Tame Gazelle* and *Crampton Hodnet* showcase some of the pleasures and virtues of being a single woman, *Excellent Women* showcases some of the pitfalls and loneliness of not being married. In a way, *Excellent Women* and *Jane and Prudence* are studies of the plight of single English women in the last half of the twentieth century. The heroine of *Excellent Women,* Mildred Lathbury, is thirtyish, plain, and single. She lives in a flat where she shares a bathroom with handsome Rocky Napier and his sloppy but beautiful wife, Helena, who is an anthropologist. The plot revolves around Mildred's interactions with her single and married friends, especially her attempts to run interference between the feuding Napiers and anthropologist Everard Bone. By the end of the novel, Mildred emerges as a witty, if sardonic narrator who considers a life with Bone for its interesting possibilities.

Another single woman over thirty, Jessie Morrow, is featured in *Jane and Prudence.* A woman named Jessie Morrow, also a paid companion, appears in *Crampton Hodnet.* That Jessie, however, is not the same woman who appears in *Jane and Prudence.* Jessie Morrow of *Jane and Prudence* is kin to the refined but somewhat unpleasant Allegra Gray of *Excellent Women* because, like Allegra, she schemes for a husband. Jessie, however, is more matter-of-fact in her pursuit. She has no illusions about the kind of marriage she will have with Fabian Driver; she only knows that it will save her from the humdrum life of being the formidable Miss Doggett's companion. Jessie is disliked by many who see her as a heartless user. Yet, these critics fail to understand the plight of women like her. Jessie and other distressed gentlewomen would be forced to be unhappy, lonely dependents at the mercy of their employers, living boring lives on severely limited incomes. For example, Radclyffe Hall's story "Fraülein Schwarz" is a study of a middle-aged, impoverished German spinster who is living in England in Pimlico (Mildred's neighborhood) at the outbreak of World War I. In many ways, Fraülein Schwarz resembles Pym's excellent women. As the narrator says, "Fraülein Schwartz was the friend of all the world, a fact which naturally made her feel lonely, since the world had no time for Fraülein Schwartz, nor had it expressed the least wish for her friendship" (740). Single women like Jessie and Hall's Fraülein Schwarz could look forward to virtually no financial security in old age and little chance for professional improvement as paid companions. In *A Chapter of Governesses,* Katharine West notes that by the time of World War II when Pym was doing much of her writing, the paid companion or governess had become a "period type" to be found only in literature (237).

Still, the paid companions and governesses of literature are independent women who on a small, cozy scale are mistresses of their own fate. They share qualities with independent heroines in romance novels who have outgrown submissive roles society has defined for women. Many romance heroines are pirates, outlaws, military figures, even magicians. What they share with Pym's women is their independence. These independent heroines are similar to heroes in male adventure stories. Katharine West discusses Angela Thirkell's *Miss Bunting* as an example of a novel where a governess or paid companion becomes a heroine in her own right. There, Miss Bunting becomes a trusted confidante of her mistress, who is so outraged by Nazism that she wants to take on Hitler personally (234). The heroine of Elizabeth Taylor's *Angel* chooses to be a romance writer instead of a paid companion because she will not demean herself "doing for a useless half-wit of a girl what she could perfectly do for herself" (46).

While there are no paid companions in *Excellent Women,* there are unmarried women over thirty who earn meager livings and whose prospects for marriage seem dim. The married women and widows in the novel form a different category altogether. They are rivals for male affection, professionals who are inept housewives, or schemers who will stop at nothing for the security of marriage. For example, the lovely but conniving Allegra Gray of *Excellent Women* thinks nothing of displacing the hero's devoted spinster sister from her home so that she, Allegra, can marry the hero.

First published in 1952, *Excellent Women* was reviewed by Sir John Betjeman, one of Pym's favorite poets. Betjeman, who wrote *The English Town in the Last Hundred Years* in 1956, claims that associations connected with places and buildings "can be turned to good advantage when they are literary" (5). Given the importance of home and of Mildred's neighborhood to the plot of *Excellent Women,* Betjeman might have been thinking of Pym. Betjeman believes, like Pym, that enjoying architecture and its surroundings gives one pleasure because of the associations connected with the buildings (5). Betjeman writes that certain authors' phrases conjure for him whole districts and buildings. For example, he says that "a single paragraph or lyric by Hardy conjures up at once the brown stone and gold thatch, the ominous silence, the horse-drawn slowness, the sweet baking smells, the brewing smells, the gorse smells, and the wood-smoke of Victorian Dorset" (7). Betjeman notes that Hardy fills his writing with a sense of place (7). In the same way, Pym fills her novels with what she saw when she wrote, so that she brings to life an entire parish as well as its inhabitants.

In a different way from many male authors, Pym also brings life to England of 1940. As a homefront novel, *Excellent Women* is similar to work like E. M. Delafield's *The Provincial Lady* and Angela Thirkell's *Cheerfulness Breaks In.* (Actually, Pym left an unfinished fragment for a book, tentatively titled *The Homefront Novel,* which discussed taking in refugee children and making sacrifices for the war effort.) According to Hazel Holt in *A Lot to Ask,* these novels tell the story from the point of view of comfortable middle-class village women who have a "calm ironic eye" for observation (96). Pym's younger male friend, Richard Roberts, found *Excellent Women* sad but witty. Pym found herself wondering at this point why men found her books sad (*A Very Private Eye* 223). There are those who find Pym's books sad because many of the heroines prefer to observe others rather than to participate in many of life's activities. Some readers may feel these women do so because they feel they are outsiders and must live vicariously. In reality, many Pym women who observe others are just being curious. For example, like many Pym heroines, Mildred Lathbury of *Excellent Women* is a keen observer. Pym's heroines who are keen observers are artists in their own right; they collect and use observations to interpret their surroundings.

Perhaps because they are such keen observers of other people and their habits, Pym women are also good at using the fruits of their observation to express themselves. That is, just as artists and writers use their observations of everyday life to create works of art that express their opinions, Pym women analyze everyday elements of life like cooking food and shopping for clothes to wear to create their own, non-verbal discourse. So, a character like Mildred Lathbury is able to express herself through the food she eats or the clothes she wears. In using her observations to fuel her own discourse, Mildred is like Pym, who describes and analyzes her heroes and heroines, as well as their marriages and relationships, by using a discourse that is rich in descriptions of food and clothing. Food was a favorite topic with Pym, who loved eating out and cooking. Holt writes that food was "a great subject of conversation" between her and Pym (31). In "The Novelist in the Field," Hazel Holt writes that if she or Pym had been out to dinner the night before, the first question asked in the morning was "what did you have?"

(31). Pym herself writes, "It takes so little to make us happy—just liver and bacon and a seat on the banquette" (qtd. in Holt 31). She was referring to dining at one of her favorite restaurants (31). One of these, Lyons Corner House, appears in *Excellent Women*. Mildred has dinner with Dora in an Edwardian room with white columns. The menu includes items like scrambled eggs and curried whale (104).

As with *Some Tame Gazelle* and *Crampton Hodnet,* Pym does not glamorize food the way a romance novelist might, but Mildred does like to eat out. Dining out "Mildred-style" creates imagery ranging from the ludicrous to the ceremonial. Once, when he invites Mildred to dinner, Everard Bone, the hero, has had someone else prepare the meal, but Mildred must check on the casserole and serve it. Even when someone else cooks for Mildred, the meal is not glamorous, and she is faced with playing waitress and serving her man. In fact, Rossen writes that Pym heroines are often found preparing meals or washing up (45). In her dissertation *The Novels of Barbara Pym,* Marlene San Miguel Groner finds it significant that Bone provides a meal for Mildred. Groner writes that Everard will use Mildred, but he will also cook for her (125). As Janice Rossen writes in "On Not Being Jane Eyre," Bone may take Mildred for granted, but he won't crush her spirit, either (148). Mildred has been indoctrinated with the notion that good wives cook for their husbands. She is mildly shocked that Rocky Napier does the cooking for she wonders, "Surely wives shouldn't be too busy to cook for their husbands?" (*Excellent Women* 9). Mildred finally decides Rocky may like cooking and she acknowledges that men act more out of their own selfish reasons than women because "men did not usually do things unless they liked doing them" (9).

Another instance where Mildred does not cook for herself occurs when she eats a cafeteria meal with Miss Bonner. The two have stopped to eat before the lunchtime church service. Mildred's lunch out is anything but glamorous in this example. She notes that her tray rattles along on the conveyer belt with "terrifying speed" (76-77). One is reminded of Chaplin's hilarious but efficient meal in his film *Modern Times.* Though the food is plentiful and cheap, Mildred experiences a "helpless kind of feeling" in the cafeteria line (78). She is not like Lady Selvedge of Pym's *An Unsuitable Attachment* who charges to the front of a cafeteria line at "one of those ubiquitous tea-shops which cater for the multitudes of office workers and others who want a cheap meal at any time of the day" (57). As Lady Selvedge's lunch partner observes, "The dishes get rather confused when they're all together on the table" (58). Like Chaplin's character, Mildred feels as if she were a cog in some machine, and she observes that there is an order to how the food is served, roll—

saucer—hot dish, roll—saucer—hot dish (77). Mildred's role is merely to move the tray along and keep the assembly line going.

Mildred, however, plays another role as a solitary female diner in a restaurant. Janice Rossen writes that Mildred and single women like her who eat by themselves in restaurants are both alone and performers surrounded by an audience. Rossen says, "Meals are by definition (or at least by strong Victorian tradition) a social time, and the absence of fellow diners stresses the aloneness of single women" (46). Every social occasion in *Excellent Women* involves serving some type of food, rationing notwithstanding. Because of the prevalence of food, the anthropologists in *Excellent Women* who study everyone realize the importance of food to social occasions. In their discourse, they refer to the refreshments at their meetings as "spoils." (88). "Spoils" is a curiously apt term considering that rationing is occurring. Even Mildred has been known to indulge herself in an extravagant lunch (44). Other Pym heroines indulge in infatuation of inaccessible men as they might otherwise indulge in forbidden sweets (44).

If food can be a sort of "forbidden sweet," it can also be part of a ceremony or ritual. For example, at one point, Mildred experiences a lovely day, and wants as a lunch companion someone, "a splendid romantic person" to dine with (66). Lunch for Mildred can be a sort of ritual or ceremony to celebrate the day's loveliness, with mimosa decorating the table the way flowers decorate the church altar. In fact, Claude Lévi-Strauss writes in *The Raw and the Cooked* that cooking itself and serving food are ways in which human beings distinguish themselves from animals. He writes, "The conjunction of a member of the social group with nature must be 'mediatized' through the intervention of cooking fire" (336). Lévi-Strauss discusses a variety of rituals where various tribes subject their members, particularly women, to symbolic ovens and cooking fires as a rite of passage or socialization. For example, in Cambodia, a woman who had just had a baby was "laid on a bed or a raised grill under which there burned a slow fire" (335). Evidently, since the woman has performed a natural function, she must be re-socialized by symbolic "cooking" because cooking represents culturalization while raw food does not.

The study of cooking also occupies a good deal of the anthropologist's time. In "Food and Power: Homer, Carroll, Atwood and Others," Mervyn Nicholson writes that anthropology could be defined as the study of how human beings acquire, share, and eat food (38). Nicholson argues that food is as "basic to socialization and social relations as it is to bodily existence" (38). The anthropologists in *Excellent Women* also refer to meals as the "ceremonial devouring of the flesh" (93).

Mildred's lunch with William is so ceremonial that it takes on characteristics of a meal at King Arthur's Round Table. For example, the wine, Nuits St. George, conjures England's patron saint who slew dragons and whose name is invoked when one is knighted. The Arthurian names, including Julian's last name of Malory, underscore the romantic theme of the novel, according to Robert Emmett Long (50). (Romance author Kimberly Cates also plays on the Arthurian legends. Her hero in *The Raider's Bride* is an eighteenth-century spy who adopts as his code name Pendragon, the surname of King Arthur.) Mildred admits that the wine conjures romantic images for her. In imagining romantic images, Mildred is a sort of romance writer glamorizing food. Also, Pym appears to be borrowing from romance authors because in this example, she does not describe the meal past the wine.

Perhaps Pym makes the allusions to Arthurian romance and legend to show that, like Pound and Eliot, she "deifies" the masters of the past, as Janice Rossen writes (9). Ritual meals like those held by the knights of the Round Table survive in Pym's works as somewhat comic allusions of once potent beliefs that have been reduced to fairy tales. In *The Uses of Enchantment,* Bruno Bettelheim writes, "Most fairy tales originated in periods when religion was a most important part of life; thus they deal, directly or by inference with religious themes" (13). According to Bettelheim, our cultural heritage is still expressed in fairy tales and folk tales. Thus, Pym, through Mildred, might use the tales of King Arthur and his knights, who are British heroes, as ways to find meaning in life. In place of King Arthur and Guinevere presiding at the Round Table, however, we have the plain, self-effacing Mildred and the "old maidish" William as the only guests. Yet, in a rather offhand allusion to Guinevere's unfaithfulness, Mildred finds herself thinking of Rocky, her own version of Sir Lancelot, not William, her companion. In place of the company of the Round Table are the anonymous, scattered guests and employees of the restaurant.

Other myths besides the Arthurian legends are corrupted, as well. Columns that once decorated ancient places of worship like the Acropolis now decorate restaurants like the one where Mildred and Dora dine in *Excellent Women* (104). Food and decor serve as connection for a once glorious, mythical past that has been reduced and degraded. In *The Picara: From Hera to Fantasy Heroine,* Anne K. Kaler makes a similar connection between food and ritual, using *Great Expectations* as an example. Kaler calls Miss Havisham, the jilted, mad, and aging would-be bride of the novel, a "death-in-life" figure. The moldering wedding cake is the ritual food that links her to the marriage ceremony (105). Vestiges of ritual more likely than not belong to the world of romance.

Other members of Mildred's group may even see her as a Miss Havisham. In another episode that occurs after Julian Malory's engagement to Allegra Gray is announced, Mildred once again makes do with plain fare. This time, her meal is fish with no sauce or relish. Mildred has attended the usual weekday service where Julian presides, only to discover that the congregation, and Julian himself, consider her to be the "rejected one." That is, they believe Mildred has been rejected in favor of Allegra (134). Later, Mildred says she went home and cooked her cod, sardonically commenting that it seemed a "suitable dish for a rejected one" (134). As a result, she eats it "humbly without any kind of sauce or relish" (134). It is as though her meal would be an appropriate one for Cinderella to eat amidst her ashes. Yet, just in time, Rocky arrives, a sort of prince, to save Mildred from her boring meal. Deserted by Helena in favor of a memorial service, Rocky invites himself in for coffee (134).

Certainly, modern ritual is practiced through elements belonging to the trivial world. Pym was aware that literature acknowledged the vestiges of once important rituals.

Robert Long notes in *Barbara Pym* that the collection of stuffed birds in the Bone household reflects the family's adventurous, romantic days (54). It is also a symbol of Mrs. Bone's eccentricity. Mrs. Bone keeps the birds as trophies of a war she has been waging against her feathered enemies. She would fit comfortably into Daphne du Maurier's short story "The Birds," and she declares ruthlessly to Mildred that she eats as many birds as possible (*Excellent Women* 149). This is a very effective way for Mrs. Bone to conquer enemies. Mervyn Nicholson writes in "Food and Power" that eating "divides humans from subhumans" (39). Nicholson claims that meat, in particular, dramatizes human superiority over animals. He writes, "Eating meat is often associated only with ruling strata. . . . It is prestige food" (39). Therefore, argues Nicholson, "[T]he creatures man eats must be weaker than he is. They are overcome by man's superior power" (39).

Yet, in Pym's novel, the ritual connected with eating may also be joyous. Mildred speaks rapturously of an extravagant lunch consisting of the remains of some soup, two scrambled eggs, soup, cheese, biscuits, and an apple (217). Perhaps the fact that she eats more than she usually would is a sign that she is taking control of her emotional life and coping with being alone. Mervyn Nicholson writes that overeating is a sign of power (40-41). Or, perhaps the meal seems extravagant to Mildred because she has two eggs at a time when rationing is still in effect. Or maybe the size of the meal, with its soup appetizer and fruit, cheese and biscuit dessert, is more festive than what a spinster usually eats. In any case, the meal is a ceremonial one for Mildred, for she has just learned that Julian has broken his engagement with the scheming Allegra. Mildred is triumphant, yet not selfish. Always an "excellent woman," she considers whether it might be her duty to marry Julian anyway to save him from being too well protected.

What is curious in this passage is that Mildred, like Prudence Bates of *Jane and Prudence,* thinks enough of herself in this instance to prepare a good meal. The fact that her lunch consists of several simple, but ample courses even makes it a little luxurious. Still, Mildred is mindful that she is a woman dining alone. She is glad she is not "a man, or the kind of man who looked upon a meal alone as a good opportunity to cook a small plover, though [she] should have been glad to have somebody else to cook it" (*Excellent Women* 217). The implication is the same one that occurs in *Jane and Prudence;* a man must have his bird or meat (30). If there is no woman present, a capable man will cook for himself. Unlike Joyce in "A Painful Case," Pym seems to say that single men can and do live full lives, while single women live meager ones. Yet, Mildred identifies enough with men who are waited on to admit she would like a plover if someone else would cook it for her (217). At another point in the novel, Mildred enjoys preparing her solitary breakfast and thinks that it is pleasant to live alone (19). In this instance, eating alone is a sign of independence.[11]

Wearing certain types of clothing may also indicate independence. In *The Picara: From Hera to Fantasy Heroine,* Anne K. Kaler writes that clothes in literature often become symbols of character as well as status. Characters in *Excellent Women* are often defined by how they are dressed. For example, anyone who reads Pym knows that gentlewomen, particularly church women, dress tastefully but not too elegantly. They are modern Jane Eyres in their gray silks and good wool dresses. Allegra Gray is a clergyman's widow who has entered Julian's congregation. After awhile, she and Julian become engaged and she plans to move into the rectory. What Julian and his sister Winifred do not realize is that the selfish Allegra is planning to evict Winifred from both her home and her role as Julian's housekeeper. Allegra is very much like Gorsky's scheming women because she is purely self-centered and does not care whom she hurts in order to achieve her goals. In this instance, Allegra wants to marry Julian and force Winifred to live elsewhere, preferably with Mildred Lathbury.

Appropriately, the cunning Allegra wears silver fox, judged to be too rich for a clergyman's wife (57). Yet, silver is a more subtle color for the clever Allegra than red fox. Allegra considers herself important and would never condescend to playing the role of distressed gentlewoman. Unlike Winifred Malory, the woman she tries to displace from Julian

Malory's household, she would never wear castoff clothing. Still, Allegra is a sort of castoff, because she is an outsider to Julian's congregation. She has no way to talk to the other excellent women and finds herself an outsider at the flower arranging. Like Gorsky's demons, Allegra has no respect for tradition; she does not care that there have always been lilies on the altar and she chides Winifred for always being so conventional (117). While she may win the battle of usurping Winifred's place at decorating the altar, the other women of the congregation resent her. She will never be one of them.

Mildred is not cunning like Allegra, and does not own furs. Mildred's clothing is so drab that she does not describe her underwear, not because she is modest, but because it is dull and depressing to her (85). Thus, Mildred's wardrobe is indicative of her feelings, including resentment at having drab underwear. Mildred hangs her "dreary looking underwear" in the kitchen, a rather symbolic place (*Excellent Women* 105-06). Where Mildred is embarrassed by her underwear, her friend Dora Caldicote is not. Dora brazenly hangs her graying drawers to dry on a line in Mildred's kitchen where Rocky Napier eventually sees them. Diana Benet writes that Mildred is upset by Dora's drab drawers and that she would like to believe that she is not a woman like Dora who wears boring lingerie (38). Mildred surveys the "lines of depressing-looking underwear—fawn locknit knickers and petticoats of the same material" and decides that it is even drearier than her own (*Excellent Women* 106). The choice of words is interesting in this passage. "Locknit" implies that spinsters' lives are repressed as well as dreary; as Mildred says, they cannot do anything about their feelings.[12] Patricia Meyer Spacks writes in *The Female Imagination* that during the eighteenth and nineteenth centuries women often concealed their emotions (103). If so, then Mildred carries the earlier tradition into the twentieth century and imitates her author's self-concealment. As she says, "I must not allow myself to have feelings, but must only observe the effect of other peoples'" (76). Maybe like Fay Weldon's Ruth of *The Life and Loves of a She-Devil,* another plain woman, Mildred can "harden [her] skin against perpetual humiliation" (6).

Pym gives no filmy descriptions of provocative garments like those in romance novels, where even single women wear undergarments frothed in lace. For example, in Bertrice Small's *The Kadin,* Janet, the unmarried fifteenth-century heroine, wears a gauzy harem costume of "diaphanous fabric" of pale gold (32). On the other hand, Pym's spinsters wear plain underwear, just as they eat plain food. The irony is, of course, that Rocky, the romantic interest, does see the drab underwear because he blunders into the kitchen seeking coffee and he manages to charm Dora amid the forest of dripping knickers (106). Unlike Dora, Mildred is not "cheerfully dowdy," and she is embarrassed that Rocky sees the drab garments (*Excellent Women* 106).

Like many unmarried women of the time period, Mildred has to cope with her emotions alone. Perhaps the allusion to feelings addresses the fact that in the years immediately following World War II, single women did not openly discuss their sexual passions and frustrations, just as they did not in the Victorian Era (Lewis, *Women in England* 127). They probably would not have had any discourse for it. As Groner argues in *The Novels of Barbara Pym,* Mildred may have been denied the full recourse of language because she has no vocabulary with which to describe her feelings (120). The lack of discourse for Mildred may be one reason that Mildred states that if she were to write a book, she would write a stream of consciousness novel (*Excellent Women* 161). Mildred could use the artifice of the technique of stream of consciousness to create a character that would indirectly speak for her. The reader would be engaging in the fiction of observing the character's thoughts in the order in which they occur in her head.

Married women do have their own discourse, however, and speak or express themselves as they wish. Married women like Helena Napier wear glamorous outfits. Helena Napier, Rocky's wife, is never embarrassed by *her* clothes. Helena, the married woman, is a far more exotic figure; she dresses in black and does not have to look like the dowdy stereotype of a female anthropologist (86). Part of her dogma is to keep herself looking attractive for men. In *Reading in Detail,* critic Naomi Schor makes several remarks that pertain to Helena. She paraphrases Viennese architect Adolf Loos on why women dress as they do. According to Loos, if a woman wears rich clothes, cosmetics, and ornaments, it is because "she must attract and keep a 'big strong man' if she is to hold her own in the 'battle of the sexes.'" Loos continues that a woman must "fetishize" herself because of the "inherent perversion of male desire" (qtd. in Schor 52).

In *Excellent Women,* however, men, too, take an interest in clothes, particularly in cloaks. Rocky comments that Julian looks good in his cloak. Rocky fancies he, too, would look good in one (106). Romantic heroes from Count Dracula to Ian Blackheath of *Raider's Bride* wear sweeping cloaks. Ian's cloak is like the wings of a fallen angel and makes him seem even more Byronic (Cates 110). The first glimpse Jane Eyre gives us of Mr. Rochester also involves a description of his cloak. Jane says, "His figure was enveloped in a riding cloak, fur collared and steel clasped (99). As seen earlier, allusions to Rochester often occur in Pym's novels.

Charles Burkhart writes in *The Pleasures of Miss Pym* that Pym differs from romance writers because she does not write in clichés; she writes about them and satirizes them (79). While Mildred is a spinster, she is not stereotypical. Mildred's powers of observation and her ability to create a fantasy triggered from personal memories make her into a kind of artist. She is the epitome of virtues that Pym herself believed in, including the values of humility, community, and what Joan Gordon calls in "Cozy Heroines: Quotidian Bravery in Barbara Pym's Novels," the ordinary miracle (224). As Gordon points out, however, Mildred and other Pym heroines like her "seem to learn enough to invest their lives with integrity and meaning," though she has not committed "unpardonable sins, travelled up the congo, studied natives, or witnessed uprisings" (224).

If Mildred Lathbury had had these adventures, she might be categorized as a cliché romance heroine like the heroine of Bertrice Small's *The Kadin* who is kidnapped and sold to a harem, or Angelique of the series by the same name written by Sergeanne Golon. Angelique, too, has spent time in a harem in *Angelique in Barbary* and has been married to a pirate in *Angelique and the Ghosts.* Scarlett O'Hara commits murder when the need arises in *Gone with the Wind,* and Amber steals and spends time in Newgate prison in *Forever Amber.* Perhaps, as Joan Gordon observes, the difference between these romance heroines and Pym's heroines lies in the fact that Pym describes real women, not characters in fiction (226). Gordon says, "Barbara Pym's goal is to write about people, not characters. And who are most likely to behave simply as people, not imposing the grand gestures that might transform them into characters? Why, just the unassuming modest, detached cozy women who are Barbara Pym's heroines" (226).

Women like Helena Napier and Prudence Bates are more glamorous than Mildred, but they too are described as people, not characters. Helena Napier is a new kind of woman, well-dressed, glamorous, but sloppy and completely human. She is a disastrous housekeeper who drops ash on the carpet, but unlike frumpy Edith Liversidge of *Some Tame Gazelle* who also drops ashes on things, Helena is stylish. She rejects housewifery in pursuit of a career, even at the risk of social alienation. She is like the beautiful heroine of Mollie Hardwick's *The Duchess of Duke Street* who only agrees to marriage and to becoming Edward VII's mistress because the rich gifts she will receive will help to finance her catering and restaurant business. These women are independent because they risk social ostracism by living as they choose. They do what pleases them, and do not marry to devote themselves to their husbands.

Like Mildred, who likes to read cookbooks and worries about toilet paper, Helena cultivates her own quirks and is often thought eccentric by more conventional married women and their husbands. Helena is not the only literary figure, however, who has a slight tendency toward eccentricity. Heroes of romance novels also tend to be eccentric and are patterned after the Byronic hero.

The Byronic hero is deflated in *Excellent Women* in a passage that features Byron, the ultimate romantic hero. According to Eileen Fallon in *Words of Love,* which is a history of the romance genre, Byron is "pale of skin, dark of hair, brooding and alone, a man of action, and a poet" (93). She argues that Byron the man lent these qualities to the Byronic hero, and that he is one of many writers whose life is as fascinating as his literary creations (93-94). Mildred Lathbury, however, is not swept off her feet by Byron or Byronic heroes, no matter how "pale of skin" and "dark of hair" they might be. After the jumble sale where Mildred and Winifred Malory have just met Allegra Gray, Winifred, with shining eyes, talks to Mildred about Allegra. Mildred wonders if Allegra is her real name, or if she has adopted it to replace a more conventional one (64). Mildred takes the romance out of Allegra's name, and out of the myth of Byron as romantic hero by stating, "Wasn't Allegra the name of Byron's natural daughter?" (64). Mildred's comment is loaded, to say the least. Allegra, too, turns out to be a "bastard" in another sense of the word for she attempts to usurp Winifred's place at home and to entrap Julian into marriage. Mildred's observation is a humorous way of foreshadowing these events. Her comment about Allegra is also ironic for there is a play on words with "natural." Besides meaning illegitimate, the word means without artifice. The reader knows from the first that there is nothing natural about Allegra; she wears makeup and is subtly manipulative, creating a sort of mask or persona to hide her actions.

Mildred continues to pierce the myth of the Byronic hero with Byron himself. When Winifred exclaims that Byron was a "splendid romantic person" Mildred is critical. She asks, "Doesn't one look for other qualities in people?" (64). Later, Mildred defines the qualities a man needs to be splendid and romantic. Good looks and charm appear to be requisite (64). She decides there is nothing romantic about Everard, but he may be "just a little splendid" (65).

There is, however, something both splendid and romantic about Rocky Napier. Rocky, a sort of romantic slayer of dragons, has also been linked by Robert Emmet Long to *Alice in Wonderland* (50). In *Barbara Pym,* Long observes that once Mildred meets Rocky Napier, the narrator begins to allude to *Alice in Wonderland* (50). Long believes that the narrator alludes to *Alice* because just as things happen to Alice "with fantastic illogicality as she passes through a series of remarkable adventures," fantastic and illogical things begin to happen to Mildred after she becomes acquainted with Rocky (50). Apparently, Long feels that Rocky brings romance and the thrill of the unexpected to Mildred's otherwise predictable and dull life. Yet, Rocky Napier is more the literary inheritor of Richardson's "seducer" as Leslie Fiedler might describe him in *Love and Death in the American Novel* (66).[13] Still, Rocky is not a seducer in the literal sense; he is more of a flirt, charming, but not in a fatal sense because he is easily seen through. Rocky makes a career of romancing lonely WRN officers during the war, but he harbors no true feelings for them. Mildred, too, finds herself in love with him, but because of her ability to be detached, she also sees through him. In one episode, when Rocky exclaims, "Ah, Mildred, what would I do without you?" Mildred thinks to herself that she knows exactly what he would do without her. In another episode which Joan Gordon discusses in "Private Space and Self-Definition in *Excellent Women*," Mildred answers Rocky's lavish praises with conventional phrases, as if she is bored with him. She has just prepared lunch for him after Helena's departure. Mildred says, "Oh, it was nothing," and feels as if "no other answer could be given" (157). She is correct that even a less attractive man than Rocky would expect a woman to prepare a meal for him.

Like some romance writers, Pym sometimes shows her heroes needing a woman's help. In a way, showing male helplessness or ineptness in some situations is another way to deflate the Byronic hero. Critic Marion Darce Frenier in *Good-bye Heathcliff* notes that romance heroes are often physically or emotionally wounded and must depend on the heroine for help (29). So, Jane must care for Rochester when he is injured and blinded in *Jane Eyre*. In Pym's world, an excellent woman is the perfect candidate to nurse the hero, physically or emotionally. Unlike the romance heroine, though, the excellent woman does not necessarily win her wounded hero at the end. Also, Pym's heroes are not that drastically wounded; like Bone, they usually just need someone to cook for them and to type their notes. A few, like Tom Mallow, need a woman to boost their self-esteem.

Pym's men are also somewhat peevish and inept. For example, Rocky Napier, that gallant paragon of Byronism, is upset with his wife for placing a hot saucepan on a good table. In any case, like many of the contemporary romance heroines Ann Rosalind Jones discusses in "Mill and Boon meets Feminism," Pym heroines are fulfilled by the hero's transformation (200). The fact, therefore, that Bone can arrange to have a meal cooked for Mildred instead of expecting her to cook is one small step in his transformation that would attract Mildred. Furthermore, as Rubinstein notes in her article on Pym, "'For the Ovaltine Had Loosened her Tongue,'" Pym women are able to use their imaginations to transform their men into the kind of heroes they want (573).

The equation for marriage in *Excellent Women* is that women receive security and a place to live while men receive a helpmeet to serve all their needs. Love does not appear to figure into the equation. In short, marriage in *Excellent Women* appears to be a very selfish business. Jane Nardin has defined marriage to a woman like Mildred as an excellent marriage that is "stable, dull, and founded on *her* self-sacrifice in *his* interest" (77). Nardin goes on to say that excellent marriage is a very different sort of marriage from the Napier's rather unstable arrangement (77). Nardin aptly writes that a union between Mildred and Everard "will be an extension of her habits of duty and self-sacrifice to a new field of endeavor" (77). Mildred would be like Esther of Sylvia Plath's story "Mothers" who, when asked what she does, replies, "I type some of my husband's work" (16-17). In Kimberly Cates's novel, *The Raider's Bride,* being an excellent woman can be fatal. The hero in *The Raider's Bride* despises marriage because excessive childbearing killed his mother. Ian Blackheath says, "My father was a selfish bastard hungry for sons and my mother was a gentle, if weak, woman, desperate to do her duty by him" (Cates 13). Blackheath claims that his mother "willingly sacrificed herself to his father's appetites" (126). Blackheath's mother thus becomes the dish that his father devours in his sexual rapacity. She is a type of sacrificial meal offered up to satisfy her husband's lust. Because she is weaker than her husband, Lady Blackheath is "edible."

In her novel, Cates also reverses the equation and writes of an "excellent man," an unselfish groom who marries a childhood friend though he does not love her. The narrator points out that the man "sacrificed himself into marriage with her" (49).

Marriage also involves self-sacrifice in Anita Brookner's *The Debut.* Brookner's style is often compared to Pym's.[14] Both Pym and Brookner often write about romantic conventions that result in selfishness in marriage. In Brookner's *The Debut,* the heroine, Ruth Weiss, is a doctoral candidate writing on Balzac. She enters into a loveless marriage with a young man named Roddy. Roddy is the nephew of her father's mistress and the proprietor of a rare book shop that Ruth's father has sold to Roddy's aunt. The narrator of *The Debut* says that Ruth married Roddy "almost as a matter of course," since her father was in favor of the marriage (187). Ruth marries Roddy without emotion and apparently without love, "but in recognition of the fact that he had paid her the compliment of asking her to be his wife" (187). Roddy at first does not even like Ruth. He becomes interested and impressed with her when she nurses him through the flu. After she helps restore him to health, Roddy begins to "collect" her from her college and Ruth begins to cook meals for him. The narrator says, "Eventually, he asked her to marry him. In this he showed sense; it is best to marry for purely selfish reasons" (187).

In *Excellent Women,* Mildred and Everard Bone may also recognize that people marry for selfish reasons. At one point, Mrs. Morris reproaches Mildred because she has not yet made a home for a man (170). Mrs. Morris is exhibiting the *Angel in the House* mentality, which says that a woman's place is to care for a man and to nurture her marriage. Charlotte M. Yonge, a nineteenth-century writer who influenced Pym, writes in "Strong-Minded Women" that it is a woman's duty to nurture her husband and to be the best wife and housekeeper she can be (589). In *Excellent Women,* Mrs. Morris warns Mildred about doing too much for Father Malory and being "left behind" by Allegra Gray who can neither cook nor sew. Mildred then agrees that it "was not the excellent women who got married but people like Allegra Gray, who was not good at sewing, and Helena Napier, who left all the washing up" (170).

In fact, the love of a "good woman" like Mildred is at best, ambiguous, at worst, something undesirable. Subconsciously, Mildred knows that this is true. At Helena's and Rocky's going away party, Helena blurts out to Mildred, "You *must* look after poor Everard Bone. . . . Oh, how he needs the love of a good woman!" (235). Rather spitefully, Rocky adds that he is glad Helena does not claim to give that sort of love. He adds, "Personally, I can't imagine anything I should like less than the love of a good woman. It would be like—oh—something very cozy and stifling and unglamorous, a large grey blanket—perhaps an Army blanket" (235). He could be comparing notes with Fabian Driver of *Jane and Prudence* who feels a net close over him when he marries Jessie Morrow. Mildred responds to Rocky with the ambiguous phrase, "Or like a white rabbit thrust suddenly into your arms" (235).

Mary Strauss-Noll has written about Pym's use of the white rabbit in "Love and Marriage in the Novels," suggesting that the white rabbit image is as ambiguous as Mildred's feelings for Rocky (76). Strauss-Noll's comment is especially accurate when one considers that white rabbits are associated with magic, Celtic myth, fertility, helplessness, the Easter Bunny, *Alice in Wonderland,* and a host of other incongruous images. Rocky's feelings for Mildred, however, are not ambiguous. He would never want to love an excellent woman because, however good a housekeeper she might be, she is tiresome and boring. Mildred may decide to marry Bone because societal attitudes like Mrs. Morris's have "worn her down," despite the fact that she enjoys her independence.

Everard clearly does not do things that he does not enjoy. For example, he wants to marry Mildred because he wants a wife who is willing to perform the more unpleasant tasks of his work, i.e., proofreading and indexing (Nardin 78). He also wants someone to tell Helena that he does not love her. Because Mildred is willing to do so, Nardin writes that Bone becomes interested in her (78). In short, Everard wants to marry a "sensible person" (*Excellent Women* 188-89). The reader can translate "sensible" to mean a woman with no romantic expectations who is willing to sacrifice herself so that Everard's work may be completed. In fact, Nardin claims Everard only makes overtures to Mildred when he wants something from her (79). As Nardin writes, Bone's "first dinner invitation is the result of his having 'some meat to cook' [*Excellent Women* 218] and no one to cook it for him" (Nardin 79). Everard later becomes jealous at the news that the Allegra and Julian engagement is off because he feels Mildred and Julian may become involved, as everyone expects. Then, Mildred would be cooking someone else's dinner, not his (Nardin 80).

Mildred herself sums up Bone's character accurately when she says that he looks for a wife as "if [he] were going to buy a saucepan or a casserole" (188). In personality, he is truly dry as a bone. As she considers what life would be like as Everard's wife, Mildred sees herself "at his sink peeling potatoes and washing up; that would be a nice change when both proofreading and indexing began to pall" (255). Mildred wonders if any man is worth the burden and decides "probably not, but one shouldered it bravely and cheerfully and in the end it might turn out not to be so heavy after all" (255). The word "burden" is often used in religious texts. Use of "burden" makes Mildred sound as if she were considering a religious duty. Still, because of Mildred's ironic wit and independence, the reader is not convinced she would be content to follow in Bone's shadow. In this one instance, she is like Cassie Miles's heroine in *Tongue Tied*, a romance from Harlequin's *Temptation* series. Miles's heroine is a speech therapist who says, "I'm a skilled person . . . I can't be happy as an adoring bystander" (qtd. in Thurston 94).

Jane Nardin in *Barbara Pym* takes a different view from Mildred and from Cassie Miles's heroine who do not enjoy being helpmates who are always used. Nardin believes the Everard and Mildred relationship is interesting because Pym refuses to romanticize it (79). In fact, Charles Burkhart writes that in Pym, only those who are elderly with "calm of mind but with yet a little passion unspent" are capable of a union "unmarred by boredom and habit" (87). Perhaps it is to this end that Mil-

dred alerts her readers that she is not at all like Jane Eyre (7). Yet, there
are similarities between how the cold St. John Rivers courts Jane Eyre
and how Everard Bone courts Mildred Lathbury. Where Everard calls
Mildred sensible and then remarks that he needs a sensible wife, St. John
tells Jane she was born to be a missionary's wife. He says, "God and
nature intended you for a missionary's wife . . . Formed for labour, not
for love" (*Jane Eyre* 354). St. John is very clear in his unromantic proposal; he wants a co-worker, perhaps more of a personal servant. He tells
Jane he wants a wife, "the sole helpmeet [he] can influence efficiently in
life and retain absolutely till death" (357). A rather shocked and angry
Jane replies "I scorn your idea of love . . . I scorn the counterfeit sentiment you offer: yes, St. John, and I scorn you when you offer it" (359).
As Jane later says, St. John does not want a wife so much as he wants a
helper.

Mildred, however, is willing to enter a marriage without love. This
is despite the fact that Mildred feels pain because she is "not really first
in anybody's life" (39). For example, because she is a single woman,
married women often treat her badly and she must suffer their often
"patronizing and sometimes cruel treatment," according to Strauss-Noll
(75). Partly because Mildred has suffered inferior status for so long,
Strauss-Noll argues that she wants to marry (75). Perhaps Mildred is
thinking in the discourse of the early 1950s Harlequin heroines. In other
words, some readers saw early Harlequins as ways for women to
reassess and reinterpret cultural messages, asserts Deborah Chapell (88).
Through the way women were portrayed in early Harlequin novels,
women could see themselves as necessary and their marriages "as motivated by love instead of a desire for financial security" (88). Certainly,
other Pym heroines like Jessie Morrow of *Crampton Hodnet* and Belinda
Bede refuse marriage proposals not motivated by love. Perhaps Mildred
would like to make herself believe she is in love with Bone so that she
won't have to acknowledge that marriage to him would bring her financial security, too.

In the same way, Everard Bone invites Mildred to open a joint ven-
ture with him, as his chief cook, bottle washer, and proofreader. Perhaps
Mildred is not like Jane Eyre because she does not harbor illusions that
love awaits her in another relationship, but like Jane she is romantic
enough to desire some love and affection from the man she may marry.
Like St. John, the rather cold Everard assures Mildred she'll be of great
help to him as a wife "because she must perceive that she can be useful"
(Rossen, "On Not Being Jane Eyre" 146).

Some betrothed romance heroines, however, do not even receive the
compliment of being called "useful" or "sensible." Anya Seton has cre-

ated such a heroine in *Katharine*. As romance critic Kristin Ramsdell writes, Seton produces "especially well-researched, well-written, and insightful historical romances" (113). *Katharine* is about the sister-in-law of Chaucer and wife of John of Gaunt. The novel is set in fourteenth-century England (113). As a romance heroine, Katharine experiences a marriage proposal that is similar to those Mildred and Jane Eyre receive. The young Katharine has become betrothed to a knight, Hugh, who is brave and rich but also ugly and uncouth. In part, Hugh says the following to Katharine, "The Queen thinks me lack-wit to take you, no doubt! They all do. I see them sniggering behind their hands" (Seton 47). Since *Katharine* is a romance, the heroine is desired for her sexual allure. Despite the fact that Hugh's proposal is insulting, Katharine is still flattered. Hugh is so captivated by her physical allure that he is willing to make the ultimate "unsuitable attachment" by marrying a woman who has no dowry.

Neither physical allure nor lack of dowry comes into play during the proposal passage in Kathleen Woodiwiss's *The Flame and the Flower*. In that novel, heroine Heather Simmons is mistaken for a prostitute while she is walking alone at night. Heather is attempting to escape the miserable home an aunt has reluctantly provided her. Heather is kidnapped and taken to a ship to please the captain, Brandon Birmingham. The wealthy captain rapes her because he believes she is "skilled in the trade," but is disconcerted to discover that Heather is a virgin and well-born. After he forces sex on the heroine, the hero forces marriage on her to cover up his crime. No direct proposal is ever made to Heather. Instead, Heather's guardian, Lord Hampton, and her aunt and uncle work out a sort of business deal with Birmingham, the hero. When Heather attempts to protest, Birmingham retorts, "Were you a man, my dear, you wouldn't be in this situation" (95). The fact that Heather has been raped, impregnated, and forced into marriage does not bring her justice. Instead, Birmingham, the rapist, gains a beautiful wife and possession. Later, before her wedding night, Heather laments her fate to Lady Hampton and regrets bringing her disgrace. Lady Hampton replies, "Sometimes a girl cannot help the things that happen to her. She's just a victim of circumstances" (99).[15]

Deborah Kaye Chapell has written in her dissertation on American romances that she discovered two premises in her writing. One is, "Romances are deeply subversive of patriarchy" (184). Another is that women who read romances are not stupid, contrary to criticism levelled at them by those who disdain romance novels and romance writers (184). According to Chapell, even feminist writers who previously scoffed at romance are beginning to make these claims (184). Chapell argues that feminism and popular romance are linked with feminine principles because "both have attracted a good deal of misogyny" (3). By the same token, Pym's novels are subversive of patriarchy and of institutions which scoff at the trivial aspects of life. Those like Michael Cotsell who note similarities between Pym's writing and William Makepeace Thackeray's might agree with the following comment, by Avrom Fleishman in *The English Historical Novel,* that history is partly meant to "sketch the manners and the life of the old world" (130). Similarly, Pym writes in "Finding a Voice" that her love of detail and triviality influenced the way she wrote novels. Moreover, one of the reasons Pym enjoyed Betjeman's poems is what she calls in "Finding a Voice" his "glorifying of ordinary things and buildings and his subtle appreciation of different kinds of churches and churchmanship." Austen and Trollope interest her because they, like her, tend to write in detail about the same type of society (383). Pym might agree with one romance reader Janice Radway interviewed for *Reading the Romance* who said, "Somehow, you *feel* more when you're reading about detail" (qtd. in Radway 111).

One sensation Pym makes her readers experience is hunger. As noted throughout the first three chapters, details about food are crucial to Pym's writing. These culinary details often comprise a character's discourse. For example, food plays an important role in defining how the characters feel about themselves and each other in *Jane and Prudence,* the story of two friends, one married, one single, who attended school together. For example, Jane Cleveland, the vicar's wife, notices what men eat and enjoys delicacies like *foie gras,* but she is indifferent to cooking and recipes do not interest her. Food for Jane is a way to express her unconscious contempt for cooking and housework. Food is also a way for Jane to criticize the role of women in her society.

Prudence's diet, on the other hand, reflects her narcissism. Her attitude is reflected in the adjectives the narrator uses to describe her food. For Prudence, who enjoys flirtation and pursuing men, food is a sort of reward for catching a "good" man, or a consolation prize for losing one. The elegant meal she has after she learns Fabian Driver will marry Jessie Morrow is one example. Like Mildred and the other female characters of *Excellent Women,* Prudence realizes that a woman alone is a curious, if unacceptable sight. So, after her breakup with Fabian, she chooses a restaurant that is "rather expensive, but frequented mainly by women, so that she felt no embarrassment at being alone" (*Jane and Prudence* 198). Her narcissism is reflected in her point of view toward her meal, for Prudence sees herself as wounded, and chooses an expensive restaurant because, unlike the self-effacing Mildred Lathbury, she feels she deserves it. As Prudence says, "[S]he must be more than usually kind to herself" (198). What the reader gleans from this line is that Prudence is kind to herself and lives well as a matter of course. Prudence is very picky about her entré. She chooses a dry martini, smoked salmon, breast of chicken, "a really ripe-yellow-fleshed peach," and the "blackest of black coffee" (198). Her meal is nothing like the solitary chop or dried-up scrap of cheese Mildred Lathbury of *Excellent Women* often eats for dinner. And Prudence drinks real coffee, not the essence of coffee Mildred must be satisfied with. When she dines alone, Prudence insists on the best ingredients, like the ripest cheese or the oiliest garlic salad dressing.

Jane Cleveland, on the other hand, is quite indifferent to food. In fact, she is rather indifferent to housework in general. Her rather disastrous dinner party illustrates this point. Jane lacks the enthusiasm of Harriet Bede of *Some Tame Gazelle* when clergymen come to her house for coffee or dinner. Jane is vague about everything her first night in the new vicarage except the fact that there will be dinner, and is quite content to open a tin (*Jane and Prudence* 16). Later, Jane mentions to her housekeeper, Mrs. Glaze, "I don't know what we are going to have for supper" (18). She allows herself to be put in the hands of the capable Mrs. Glaze who provides liver. Jane does not even notice that the garden of the vicarage is full of vegetables, and she shocks Mrs. Glaze somewhat with her indifference (18). Flora, Jane's daughter, is far more competent in household matters than Jane for she "had not inherited her mother's vagueness" (18).

Jane is more concerned with speculating about the romantic lives of the clergy than what she will feed them. When Flora reminds her they should eat before he arrives because he may not have been able to have liver himself, Jane observes Father Lomax had better not see them eating liver since he can't have any. She observes the situation would be like "meat offered to idols" (21).

Jane's alleged theories about meat seem to be played out during the meal she and Nicholas eat at the Spinning Wheel Café. Unlike Prudence, Jane does not really care about how she dresses when she goes out. Perhaps because she is married, she isn't self-conscious, either. She is just as comfortable in her old "chicken feeding" coat as she is in a silk dress. Jane does not dine out on this occasion as Prudence might because she needs consolation; she does so because Flora and Mrs. Glaze are both out and she does not know what kind of tin to open for lunch (48). Jane is so inept about planning meals that she says to Nicholas a little desperately, that she does not know what they should have (48). Their cupboard is so bare that they don't even have any Spam left from their American care packages. In the end, they decide to eat out for lunch.

Lunch at the Spinning Wheel restaurant proves to be interesting. Mrs. Crampton and Mrs. Mayhew, the two gentlewomen who run the café, decide what a person has for lunch according to his or her social standing in the parish. The everyday customers are limited to curried beef and "toad in the hole," a concoction made of sausage encased in batter. Neither is very appetizing to the Clevelands. Perhaps because he is the vicar, however, Nicholas and his wife are offered eggs and bacon, true luxuries so soon after World War II. Mrs. Crampton offers the meal by lowering her voice, thereby making the Clevelands, especially Nicholas, feel favored (50). Once the meal arrives, the narrator is very particular in noting that Jane received only one egg, a rasher of bacon and some fried potatoes cut in fancy shapes. Nicholas, however, receives two eggs and more potatoes; "Oh, a man needs eggs!" (51). Men are the pampered ones, with clergyman receiving more favor than others. Mr. Oliver, a regular at the Spinning Wheel, receives an even better meal than Nicholas. Jane, for once, is not so indifferent about food in this episode and is embarrassed that Mr. Oliver might see Nicholas's egg and feel deprived. She is shocked when Mrs. Crampton returns to Mr. Oliver with a plate "laden with roast chicken and all the proper accoutrements" which Mr. Oliver accepts "with quite as much complacency as Nicholas had accepted his eggs and bacon." Jane is so embarrassed that she turns away thinking, "man needs bird . . . Just the very best, that is what man needs" (52). She acknowledges that men need meat and eggs, "but surely not more than women did?" (51). Jane notes, with some resentment, Nicholas's complacency in accepting his larger share, as if he were used to having better meals. Jane reasons that widowhood might account for Mrs. Crampton's actions, "[P]ossibly she made up for having no man to feed at home by ministering to the needs of those who frequented her restaurant" (51).

Outspokenness at the wrong times and rebellious thoughts are not Jane's only faults as a wife or "excellent woman." Despite her desire to be a good wife and helpmate to Nicholas, Jane lacks the qualities of a competent, organized housekeeper.

Moreover, she is not capable of producing the large families so characteristic of her favorite characters. Jane only has Flora, so "she was conscious of failure, for her picture of herself as a clergyman's wife had included a large Victorian Family like those in the novels of Mrs. Humphrey Ward" (8). Jane "almost" regrets her own stillborn research "to which her early marriage had put an end" (11), but not quite. She is still willing to attempt the role of helpmate, however haphazardly, and tries to do tasks within her powers (*Jane and Prudence* 47). For example, she feels somewhat triumphant at the end of the novel because she has remembered finally to purchase confirmation books (221). Diana Benet writes in *Something to Love* that Jane had "saddled" herself with the role of helpmate, a role she adopts for the sake of a man's love (46). According to Diana Benet, "The helpmate exists, as her name indicates, to aid a man in his endeavors, to reduce herself, for love, to a pair of willing hands for the use of a more important male" (46). Benet also notes that marriage often transforms romantic heroines to wifely help-mates. Benet is accurate in this assumption. Wifely helpmates are common in the novels of Barbara Cartland and other romance writers. Also, Jane Eyre remarks at the end of Charlotte Brontë's novel that, since Mr. Rochester was now blinded, she would be his eyes. Moreover, Benet summarizes the plot of the clergyman's wife as helpmate in her book.[16] The rather disorganized Jane doesn't have a chance of fulfilling this role. As Benet writes, Jane "willingly exchanged a self-chosen role in which she was competent for the ready-made role declared by Nicholas's work, a role she can play only badly" (49). The problem for Jane is not that she is a bad vicar's wife. Rather, the problem is that Nicholas has not lived up to her imagination, either. As Jane says, "mild, kindly looks and spectacles" are the inevitable end to a story about lovers who marry for passion (53).

Other characters in *Jane and Prudence* besides Jane have ideas about what a clergyman's wife should be. For example, Mrs. Glaze, Jane's housekeeper, believes a curate's wife is often a dim, manageable sort of woman (19). Other characters criticize Jane and her household for not living up to their expectations. Prudence notices that "Jane and her family lived in an uncomfortable make-shift way," that Jane admired smoked salmon or *foie-gras* in the shops but never bought it for her own family (73). Prudence later sets Fabian Driver straight about the kind of life Jane leads. Fabian vaguely thinks that Jane leads a "useful kind of life—work in the parish and that kind of thing" (102). Prudence says though, "But she's really no good at Parish work—she's wasted in that kind of life. She has great gifts, you know. She could have written books" (102).[17] Other members of the Parish are not so kind as Prudence. Secretary Mortlake and Treasurer Whiting criticize Jane, "They say Mrs. Cleveland hardly knows how to open a tin. It isn't fair on the Vicar." Treasurer Whiting replies, "You never know, it might hold him back from promotion. . . . A man is often judged by his wife" (132). Nicholas often shares their opinions about his wife's inadequacies and is often embarrassed by his wife. In a dispute over the cover of the Parish maga-zine, Jane's outspokenness upsets Nicholas. He believes, "She would never learn when not to speak . . . Not for the first time he began to con-sider that there was, after all, something to be said for the celibacy of the clergy" (135). To Nicholas, at least, marriage, for wives, means being seen doing good works and not heard.

In fact, being seen and not heard is one way a good wife can aid her husband. Once again in *Jane and Prudence,* Pym explores the theme of woman as a nurturer who makes sacrifices for men. If women enjoyed missing meals in *Some Tame Gazelle* because it made them feel like martyrs, they enjoy feeding their men the best available food in *Jane and Prudence* because doing so fulfills their need to have "something to love." Also, a woman who serves her man takes on a subservient status; she is either the server, or the served because she is "devoured" metaphorically and literally. In "Sexism in English," Aileen Pace Nilsen writes that women are often called by food names. Nilsen comments that there is nothing more passive than a plate of food (104), so women are something to be devoured, eaten by men and others who seek to dominate them.[18] In *Jane and Prudence,* this theory is apparently played out when the lecherous Fabian Driver is served "hearts en casserole" (147).

In Jude Deveraux's *Wishes,* the plump but beautiful heroine is compared by the narrator to a peach, and one male character says that Nellie "looks like a peach, as plump and ripe as a peach" (147). Though Pym, too, uses fruit as a sexual and fertility metaphor, Deveraux is much less subtle. Like the peach, twenty-eight-year-old virgin Nellie is ripe for her first sexual experience. When Nellie is tricked into believing that Jace has betrayed her, she replaces him with food, declaring "no more men" as she grabs a pie to devour (188). Jace also attempts to seduce her in the pantry. The narrator says, "Her sleeve had been pushed up to wash dishes, and now he was kissing the inside of her elbow" (98).

Food in *Wishes* is also linked with good and bad love. Because he knows Nellie is a good cook, Jace uses food discourse to reach her. He is aware that people think of Nellie as a cook, not as a woman. She, too, thinks of herself like this. In a scene that is similar to one from *Jane and Prudence,* Nellie, wearing her old brown kitchen work dress, has tea in a teashop. She is like Jane who dines in a café wearing her old coat. Yet, the difference is that Jane is happily careless about her appearance, while Nellie has no time for hers and is constantly belittled about it. Because Nellie receives praise for her cooking but scorn for her appearance, food becomes her discourse. For example, Jace later appeals to her love of children by telling her a poor family needs her to cook for them. At one point, he asks Nellie for a biscuit recipe in order to open communications with her (121). The dialog between the two includes a list of the ingredients, in the style of Laura Esquivel's *Like Water for Chocolate.* In that novel, Esquivel uses food to discuss the role Mexican women play in creating their own national identity at the time of the Mexican Revolution in turn of the century Mexico.

Yet, Deveraux's example, which contains a discourse of food ingredients, is appropriate to Pym, too. One can almost confirm Dr. Parnell's words in *Some Tame Gazelle* that having a love of good food in common is more important than passion. Jace also puts the shy Nellie at ease by helping her snap beans. He says, "I do believe Miss Grayson, you've put a spell on me." Nellie replies, "It's the beans. They're enchanted beans. Same ones Jack used to grow his beanstalk" (*Wishes* 29). So, the beans have mythical associations just as Ricardo's vegetables do in Pym's *Some Tame Gazelle*. Also, they clue the reader that the love story will be a fairy tale with a traditional happy ending. Jace also understands Nellie's eating disorder and its cause. In an effort to empathize with her, he eats a whole bowl of apples meant for a pie. When she exclaims that he has eaten the entire pie, Jace replies, "An easy thing for a person to do" (55).

That food is tied with power in *Wishes* is indicated in the phrase "eaten alive" which Deveraux uses twice (151, 159). In the same spirit, Erica Jong writes in *Fear of Flying,* "The world is a predatory place: Eat faster!" (147). Mervyn Nicholsson expresses similar sentiments in "Food and Power." As Nicholsson writes, "Those who are weak are eaten by those who are strong, according to the survivalist outlook demonstrated in nature by Darwin. Eater and eaten modulate in hunter and quarry, the powerful and the powerless. Metaphorically, if you are weak, you are edible; if you are edible, you are weak" (39).[19]

If women fill a certain role in patriarchal society because of their relation to the food they eat and the food they serve to their men, they also fulfill a decorative role for men in relation to the clothes they wear. A well-dressed, attractive woman is a piece of art that, in a patriarchal society, exists to give men visual pleasure as a painting or statue would. In *The Blind Side of Eden,* Carol Lee writes that women who do not make the best of themselves are viewed as perverse and aggressive because "women are supposed to fit in to the image of the world that suits men" (95). Women who do not fit the image are iconoclasts, and the male image of woman shatters (95). Women like Jane Cleveland and Pym's other unfashionable women shatter the male image of the female. Women like Prudence Bates fit the image.

Clothes in romance novels indicate competition between heroines as well as their status. At times, they do so in Pym's books as well. For example, in *Jane and Prudence,* Jessie Morrow realizes she must dress at least as well as Prudence to attract Fabian Driver's attention. So, she alters the late Mrs. Driver's blue velvet dress. In Jude Deveraux's

*Wishes,* one of the heroines, Berni, recognizes the competitive nature of women's clothes. Berni is introduced to the reader after she has died. She has the opportunity to view her own funeral, too. Berni's corpse wears a $6,000 suit for the occasion. As a kind of ghost watching the funeral, Berni takes satisfaction that one of her friends has bought the same suit on sale for $4,000. Yet, because the dead Berni is wearing it, she cannot wear it (4). Like Prudence, Berni finds new and stylish clothes important to her self-esteem. When she finds herself in Purgatory, called "The Kitchen" in the novel, Berni is accused of liking clothes more than her four husbands. She answers, "The clothes gave me more pleasure" (11). She always buys expensive outfits and would never wear hand-me-downs.

In contrast, another heroine of *Wishes* could not care less about clothes. Nellie is like Jane Cleveland because she is an attractive woman who does not care how she looks. For Nellie, who is chubby but beautiful, clothes are a luxury that she does not have time for. She is an "excellent woman" of 1896, who must slavishly care for her spoiled little sister, Terel, and her cheap, tyrannical father (67). When Nellie dresses in beautiful clothes, however, her loveliness makes her Terel's rival. So, just as Jessie Morrow accidentally-on-purpose pours a drink on Prudence's expensive dress, Terel spills ink on Nellie's new blue satin ball gown (*Wishes* 141). Terel's gesture is meant to keep Nellie from attending the Harvest Ball and thus competing with Terel for male affection.

Pym's women also attempt to eliminate their female rivals from the competition for a man. For example, Jessie Morrow of *Jane and Prudence* is what Margaret Ann Jensen, author of *Loves' Sweet Return,* would call a "rival woman." Jensen's rival woman is more beautiful, older, more sophisticated, and more aggressive than the heroine (94). Pym again subverts one of the conventions of romance because Jessie acts like a rival woman, but she is not more beautiful than Prudence Bates, the woman she wishes to replace in Fabian Driver's affections. Jessie, is a drab, over-thirty paid companion. She is neither rich, nor sophisticated. She is more subversive than aggressive. Jessie's tactics are not those of the flamboyant Blanche Ingram of *Jane Eyre* or of the countless more beautiful rival women who fill the pages of Barbara Cartland's romances. Jessie is the type of woman who normally would not win the hero. The only thing Jessie may have in common with her romance sisters is that she does not use her power to attract people to establish stronger relationships with women. Jensen writes in *Love's Sweet Return* that many female characters in romances do not form friendships with women. Instead, romance heroines use their charms to undermine other women so that they can capture the man they want (95).

Jessie Morrow of *Jane and Prudence* is like these romance heroines because Jessie uses her charms to undermine Prudence Bates, and to capture a wealthy and prestigious widower, Fabian Driver.

In "Quotidian Bravery in Barbara Pym's Novels," Joan Gordon writes that Barbara Pym strives to create real people in her novels, not characters (226). Thus, like their live counterparts, Pym's heroines dwell on trivialities. Gordon notes, "In daily life, what seems trivial for literature looms into significance" (226). While, Gordon claims, we may denigrate J. Alfred Prufrock for measuring out his life in coffee spoons, we admire Pym heroines when they do the same because their mundane world is "measured out with coffee spoons of suitability and comfort" (226). Gordon singles out Prudence Bates as an example of a character described in Pym's muted style. Jane Cleveland sees her friend as someone out of a woman's magazine; she does not liken her to Helen of Troy or to a red, red rose (225). Prudence looks "lovely," not meltingly beautiful as she might in a romance novel. She is not stunning either, but "carefully groomed" (225).

Nicholas Cleveland could easily play the role of a Byronic hero, but he, too, is described in ways that make him seem real and imperfectly human. He is somewhat irritable as a husband and full of his own importance at times. Also, Nicholas is mildly eccentric. Certainly Nicholas does not hear tell-tale hearts beating, the way a character in an Edgar Allan Poe story might. But he does like to have soap animals in his bath, and the discovery of them leads to a hilarious episode in the novel when a visiting canon is shocked by the toy soaps and believes them to belong to the eccentric Jane. Moreover, the animals make Nicholas seem dependant on Jane, a sort of child who needs his toys. Yet, Jane is willing to forgive his peevish eccentricities, even if he is not prepared to forgive hers. Jane sees her husband as an heir to a great literary figure, not as a childish vicar with a liking for toy soaps.

Fabian Driver comes the closest of any of Pym's men to becoming "emasculated," for Jessie Morrow takes him in hand and puts an end to his amorous adventures when she becomes his wife. As Diana Benet notes in *Something to Love,* Fabian feels as though he has been caught in a net once he marries Jessie. For him, extra-marital affairs relieved the "ardors" of marriage (58). While, as Benet writes, romantic love may be important to women of any age, for some men it wanes, apparently. Arguably, what some men want out of marriage is to have their desires gratified (58). Robert Emmet Long believes that Fabian would have been the wrong romantic choice for Prudence (79), but they have in common the enjoyment of the pursuit of a new romance, yet do not want to be bogged down by the ardors of marriage and commitment. Long believes that Fabian is meant to be a parody of courtship and romance. His garden is really a "mock garden of romance" (83). Perhaps it is Eden after the Fall, when cynicism entered into human relationships, or a type of Rapaccini's garden where love is poisonous and destructive, the way it ultimately was for his wife Constance. For example, it is in Driver's house and garden that Constance would invite Fabian's mistresses to discuss the female arts of tapestry and cooking. It is a humorous passage for the reader, but one does not know the emotional cost to Constance.

Carol Lee has written in *The Blind Side of Eden* that man's own myths do him in. He has invented his role of sexual predator, but he devours himself as well as his intended victim (181). One could say that Fabian has set his own trap by allowing his reputation as philandering husband to grow. As a result, he has been caught in his own net by the scheming but astute Jessie. As Fabian realizes, "Life with Jessie suddenly seemed a frightening prospect, unless it could be like life with Constance all over again, with little romantic episodes here and there. But Jessie was too sharp to allow that. It was as if a net had closed round him" (*Jane and Prudence* 198). By wearing Constance's dress and rings, Jessie has deceived or tantalized Fabian into thinking life with her will be life with Constance "all over again," but it will not. Jessie, ironically, will be constant in her own way. Where his first wife was "constant" in gratifying his desires, Jessie will be a "constant" observer of his activities.

Pym spoofs the rejection scenes of romance novels with the scene where Fabian tells Prudence it is over. The narrator describes him as though he were Mr. Rochester facing Jane's rejection, or Heathcliff facing Cathy's death. His "whole bearing, hand clasped to brow, tragic eyes and ruffled hair, pointed to his taking the attitude that this would hurt him more than it hurt Prudence" (*Jane and Prudence* 192). But we know that this is Fabian's act, that he has probably performed the scene many times before. Therefore, his tragic stance is comic, akin more to *Don Juan* or *Tom Jones* than to *Jane Eyre* or *Wuthering Heights*. Robert Keily has written in *The Romantic Novel in England* that the heroes of romantic novels have nothing to learn and a great deal to tell (21). Such a statement accurately describes Fabian, for he has many war stories about his previous affairs, but he has learned nothing from them. When he marries Jessie, he does not realize that his previous infidelity was wrong; he only feels a net closing over him and he is sad that his Don Juan lifestyle must end.

Fabian, with his romantic name and amorous adventures, appears to be a Byronic hero, but like Prudence and Jane, he, too, is a realistic portrait, not a cliché. At one point, Jane is disappointed to see him carrying an overcoat and an umbrella, an ordinary man, not Lord Byron at all.

Romance heroes, however, are notorious for not carrying umbrellas or overcoats and for not caring about the effects of the weather on their bodies. For example, in Roberta Gellis's *Alinor,* the hero has been badly burned across his back, but he laughs off his wounds when the heroine tries to minister to them. Ian, the hero, says, "Oh that. A barrel of burning pitch blew apart. I was like to be a torch" (15). The tone of this voice, "normal, light and laughing" belies the serious nature of his injuries (15).

Fabian is similar to a hero created by one of Pym's favorite authors, Mrs. Humphrey Ward. In *Eleanor,* the hero, Edward Manisty, is a type of Byronic hero. Ward describes him as having an "Olympian head" that the "world likes to paint" (3). Because of his great beauty, Edward often poses for artists, and women adore him. Like Byron himself, he is also sardonic in his humor and somewhat cynical. Most odious to Edward is the notion of producing a child (71). He has no idea of what to do with either wife or son. He would rather flirt with Eleanor, the other heroine of the novel, who has survived the murder-suicide of her husband and infant son, and who, like many a Pym heroine, is on the "wrong" side of thirty, but who dresses well and is still attractive (14).

Ward's characters, though similar to Pym's, lack the touches of humor Pym gives her creations. Fabian Driver is somewhat comic because hê is so narcissistic. For example, the narrator says, "A beautiful wife would have been too much for Fabian, for one handsome person is enough in a marriage, if there is to be any beauty at all" (*Jane and Prudence* 193). Perhaps because she, too, is narcissistic, Prudence sums up Fabian correctly. In his own elegance, he "seemed to fit into the general scheme of furnishing rather too well . . . so that he might have been no more than just another 'amusing' object" (199). Fabian is more of a character in Prudence's mind, one that populates the romances she constantly reads, because he has left no part of himself in the flat nor done the things an ordinary man might do, like pottering in the kitchen or putting up a shelf (199).[20] If Fabian serves any crucial purpose at all, it is that through pursuing him, Jessie indicates to the reader that plain women are also interesting.

Other women in *Jane and Prudence* do not see marriage as escape so much as a "higher calling." Jane believed she was giving up her scholarly work and marrying Nicholas to be some sort of helpmate, the kind she read about in novels. She returns to her Oxford reunion only to discover with mild dismay that she is back where she started, just one of many Old Students who have married clergymen (8). Jane realizes that she's done nothing special with her life after all. Originally, when engaged, Jane turned her "fruitful mind" to imagining herself as a clergyman's wife. She took female characters from Victorian novelists as her models. In fact, Jane began with Trollope, worked through the Victorian novelists to stories about "present-day gallant, cheerful wives, who ran large houses and families on far too little money and sometimes wrote articles about it in the *Church Times*" (8). Jane, however, is soon disillusioned.

Jane is disillusioned because, try as she may, she cannot live up to the standards of a Charlotte M. Yonge novel. (Yonge is an author Pym read as well.) Janice Rossen writes in *The World of Barbara Pym* that Yonge's plots often involve large, Victorian families facing moral dilemmas (Rossen, *World* 8). Nicholas's first curacy is in a town "where she had found very little in common with the elderly and middle-aged women who made up the greater part of the congregation" (8). Also, Jane Cleveland's "outspokenness and fantastic turn of mind" were not appreciated (8).

For all her disillusionment and disappointment about her role as Nicholas's wife, however, Jane prefers the married state and spends a lot of her time matchmaking for Prudence. She says at one point, of Prudence and other women her friend's age, "I'm sure there is hope for them all" (10). Her comments imply marriage is certainly preferable to spinsterhood. Prudence, too, is self-conscious about being single in a group of married women. The narrator says about her: "[S]he was conscious on these occasions of being still unmarried, though women of twenty-nine or thirty or even older still could and did marry judging by other announcements in the Chronicle" (8-9).

Marriage and relations between the sexes continue to be fertile ground for Pym's subversive humor in *Excellent Women* and *Jane and Prudence*. Food serves as a means to describe the characters, but it also has a discourse of its own, which the characters borrow to express themselves. Pym continues to undermine the stock heroes and heroines of romance by using realistic portraits to fill these roles. For Pym, heroines are often spinsters on the "wrong" side of thirty who have vivid imaginations that they use to enhance their often mundane lives. Her heroes often appear to be Byronic, but have ridiculous quirks and eccentricities which deflate their Olympian status. For everyone involved, marriage does not necessarily mean a happy, romantic ending. Instead, for many of Pym's characters, it is a way to relieve boredom, and a means for defining a "full life."

# 4

# Romantic Appetites,
# or the Study of Men Embracing Women

Over the years, Pym has been known for adept studies of human character in her novels. Her novels showcase the commonplace and become a stage for the most amusing of human foibles. For example, *Excellent Women* and *Jane and Prudence* portrayed, among other characters, sardonic spinsters, femme fatales—scheming and otherwise—eccentric clergyman, and philandering widowers. Similar types, as well as anthropologists, suburban housewives, and a romance writer who studies her anthropologist boyfriend as he might study her, appear in *Less Than Angels,* which is typical of Pym's work because it involves a romance writer who gathers inspiration from everyday life.

In *Less Than Angels,* Catherine Oliphant is a romance writer for women's magazines and lives with an anthropologist named Tom Mallow. Catherine is slightly older than Tom and is "bohemian" in her appearance. She is independent and outspoken and does not make a full-time job of catering to Tom's needs. More important, Catherine loves her work and is competent and levelheaded. She defies the stereotype of the romance writer who lives her books' plots because her life is so empty. If anything, Catherine varies the patterns that appear in romance novels.

Her boyfriend, Tom, does not really see Catherine as a writer. Tom has a "wandering eye," and sees Catherine more as a cook and typist than as a lover. He soon betrays Catherine with a young anthropology student, Deirdre, who lives in the suburbs near London. Deirdre is not that interested in the academic life; she is really at school looking for a husband. Her mother is widowed and lives with her sister, Rhoda Wellcome, who has never married. Deirdre's family is conventional and has definitely traditional ideas about women being good wives and mothers. Tom, who is a son of an aristocratic family, decides to return to Africa, but is mistaken there for a native and killed. Catherine mourns briefly, but takes up with Alaric Lydgate, her next-door neighbor. Lydgate is always meaning to "write up" his notes from years of field study in anthropology, but he suffers from writer's block and writes scathing reviews of his colleague's books instead. Other characters like Digby Fox, Miss Clovis, Father Gemini, and various anthropologists and anthropology students play a role in Catherine's life as well.

In *Less Than Angels,* Pym creates a heroine in Catherine Oliphant who becomes a better observer of the human condition than the anthropologists with whom she is compared. For one thing, Catherine lives with Tom, an anthropologist, and is able to observe him firsthand. Moreover, *Less Than Angels* is a study of society's structure and the role a woman writer fulfills, or rebels against, in modern society. While Catherine follows the codes of the women's magazines and may exist in a self-made version of the muted female subculture on which these magazines thrive, she manages to create a full and independent existence for herself within the subculture and to take herself fairly seriously as a writer. It is through her independence that Catherine maintains her freedom, for, as Germaine Greer has written in *The Female Eunuch,* a woman must devise a "mode of revolt" against patriarchal society through her lifestyle and career if she is to be free (20). Moreover, Greer says, "Freedom is fragile and must be protected" (21). It is partly through achieving personal freedom that Catherine creates a satisfying life for herself. By living in an independent fashion and by not relying on Tom, Catherine is following Greer's maxim and protecting her freedom.

Catherine's written and other discourses on romance are influenced by the ideologies of her own 1950s English society and by the male editors of the magazine for which she writes. Although she is influenced by her culture, Catherine retains some originality in thought and independence by maintaining detachment in her life and work. Her stories and helpful hints are meant to help women enjoy life in their own subculture while still living within the sexual mores of their society. Also, Catherine has developed her own unique discourse by describing writing in terms of food and recipes.

Other writers besides Barbara Pym are interested in studying the language of food as a discourse. The works of Roland Barthes, for example, are particularly useful in a study of Pym's novels. In "Authors and Writers," which appears in *A Barthes Reader,* edited by Susan Sontag, Barthes writes that each author is eventually influenced by the literary ideology of the society in which she writes (189). That is, the language within which the author works is a structure, and the structure is made up of signs or symbols that are arbitrary in themselves but that become imbued with the ideology of the culture in which the language is spoken (187). Moreover, Barthes says in *Mythologies* that language consists of more than the types of written alphabet with which we are familiar.

Because "myth is a type of speech chosen by history," its alphabet consists of modes of writing, photos, and other media (94).[21]

For example, as discussed in Chapter 2, Barthes says the social ideology influencing a magazine determines how food is presented in that magazine. The recipes in the magazine provide for elaborate sauces to use with inexpensive foods so that a cheap dish might look as if it came from an expensive restaurant. Where domestic chores like cooking are glamorized, intellectual exercises like the study of literature are ignored by women's magazines.

Actually, women's magazines of the 1950s, like the ones Catherine Oliphant writes about, glamorized many aspects of the housewife's day and also gave their readers advice about how to be better wives and mothers. For example, the magazines for which Catherine writes define a certain image for their readers to follow. In *The Feminine Mystique,* Betty Friedan, in referring to American women living in the late 1950s to early 1960s, has gone so far as to say that this image shapes women's lives (34). Friedan's chapter entitled "The Happy Housewife Heroine" discusses the effect of *McCalls* magazine on American women in the early 1960s.

The discussion of *McCalls* also applies to Catherine and to other women of her time. One short story that Friedan mentions was printed in the July 1960 issue of McCalls could almost be about Deirdre taking Tom from Catherine. It is about "how a teenager who doesn't go to college steals a man away from a bright college girl" (35). Other features of this issue include a story called "Wedding Day," "glamorous pictures of models in maternity clothes" (135), a series of barbecue recipes, patterns for home sewing, and an article called "An Encyclopedic Approach to Finding a Second Husband." The magazine's main concern seems to be how to marry a woman off and how to keep her married and cooking for her husband. In fact, British writer Fay Weldon, in her story "In the Great War," has written that in the 1950s, "women were at war with women" over how to find a husband (129). As Friedan notes, *McCalls* is a big, "pretty" magazine that creates the image of a young, frivolous, almost childlike woman, "gaily content in a world of bedroom and kitchen, sex, babies, and home" (36). There are no articles dealing with ideas or the life of mind and spirit (36). Jill Tweedie, in her essay "The Experience," describes marriage in the early 1960s as playing house with the proper wife being a child. She goes so far as to call her first marriage a "romper room" where she pretended to have childlike ways when, in reality, she was squelching her own ideas and personality (3).

In England as well, modern psychologists have said that the woman of the 1960s was more childlike, and the British women's magazines reflected the same attitude and created the same frivolous image as *McCalls* (Figes 184). Germaine Greer has gone so far as to say that women tested by Masters and Johnson in their studies of human sexuality during the 1950s and 1960s were "infantile products of improper conditioning" (96). In *Patriarchal Attitudes,* Eva Figes calls the well-groomed and manicured British counterparts of the happy housewife a "highly elaborate and expensive dish" that exists to satisfy her husband's appetites (88). In this description, women are linked to cooking and kitchens; they become passive food objects, so that they turn into their own recipes. As noted in Chapter 3, there is nothing more passive than a plate of food.

Apparently, literature was an idea too abstract for a woman to understand, for the February 1949 *Ladies Home Journal* featured an article called "Poet's Kitchen," which featured Edna St. Vincent Millay cooking (Friedan 53). More recently, romance author Kathryn Falk has written *Love's Leading Ladies,* a collection of biographical sketches and favorite recipes of some of the best-known female romance writers (Jensen 68). A contemporary article about writer Jackie Collins features her meatloaf recipe. These might have been the kinds of articles that would have appealed to Pym's Catherine Oliphant, whose discourse of writing derives from domesticity and cooking. Furthermore, Hazel Holt says in *A Lot to Ask* that cooking and writing are inextricably linked for Catherine. She loves to cook and is good at it (224). Holt further writes that the same was true of Pym herself (224).

Catherine loves cooking and housework so much that she finds these activities inspire her writing. For example, the narrator of *Less Than Angels* describes Catherine as a writer for women's magazines who must "draw her inspiration from everyday life, though life itself [is] sometimes too strong and raw and must be made palatable by fancy as tough meat may be made tender by mincing" (7). In fact, Catherine has given her meat-mincing machine the literary name of "Beatrice," perhaps in honor of Dante's beloved but inaccessible Beatrice (29). The narrator describes this contraption as a "fierce little machine" (29), and one wonders whether the Beatrice Pym had in mind might not have been Beatrice Cenci, subject of many literary and artistic works, who hired assassins to kill her abusive father. In another memorable scene from *Less than Angels,* Catherine is seasoning a dish with bay leaf. She selects a bay leaf picked from a tree in the garden of Thomas Hardy's birthplace. As she cooks, Catherine ponders whether she should be cooking with the bay leaf, or whether she should have pressed it in her copy of *Jude the Obscure* (104).

In her book *Virginia Woolf and the Fictions of Psychoanalysis* (the chapter entitled "The Poetics of Hunger, The Politics of Desire"), Elizabeth Abel discusses the relationship between food and writing in a way that might appeal to Catherine, who loves to cook and to read wine lists. According to Abel, the room Woolf writes about in *A Room of One's Own* is "both a womb and a stomach" (95). She quotes the passage by Woolf that states a good dinner is important to good talk (Abel 18). Moreover, Abel points out that Woolf repeatedly discusses women's writing in terms of food. The postsuffragette female writer exists on a diet of experience that Charlotte Brontë and others wanted, but were denied (95). Abel points out that the suffragettes adopted hunger as their symbol by staging hunger strikes and so made hunger a metaphor for women's intellectual starvation as well as a symbol of their refusal of "patriarchal food" (95). Abel observes that Woolf extends this metaphor by noting that women remain spiritually unfed (96).

In the same way, one could point out that the women's magazines that do not address the life of the spirit and of ideas are not "nourishing" to their intellectual readers, or that they "starve" them by not including more thought-provoking material. This analysis would be interesting to Pym, perhaps, because she read *A Room of One's Own* (*A Very Private Eye* 159). Catherine, through her exotic recipes and bohemian lifestyle, is in a sense, rejecting the "patriarchal food" available to her. That she has a room of her own in which to write is emphasized by the fact that she has enough money to buy more exotic foods and ingredients with which to cook and that she knows to cook with wine from ethnic restaurants.

Moreover, Catherine often describes objects in terms of food, as when she says that a tulip bud looks almost like a hard-boiled egg, but with more yellow than white on it (*A Lot to Ask* 26). In yet another scene that reminds us of cooking and writing, Pym shows Catherine working on a romance story, but stopping midway through the page she is typing to cook an omelette for Tom (112). Yet these stops are not really interruptions; Catherine often works this way, typing a little, then getting up to cook or do housework.

Some romance writers do write according to a type of recipe or formula, but in "Recipes for Reading, Summer Pasta, Lobster á là Risehome and Key Lime Pie," Susan J. Leonardi writes, "Like a story a recipe needs recommendation, a context, a point, a reason to be" (340). For Leonardi, cooking and women's writing are closely linked. She calls a recipe "an embedded discourse" that has a variety of relationships "within its frame" (340). Leonardi refers to various editions of Irma S. Rombauer's and Marion Rombauer Becker's *The Joy of Cooking* frequently for examples of how telling a story as an introduction enhances a recipe. Telling the story in the introduction creates a persona for the two authors with which the reader can then relate (341). Early editions of *The Joy of Cooking* also made many references to literary texts and authors, including Austen and Fielding (342). Leonardi writes that the earlier editions of *Joy* reproduced "the social context of recipe sharing in a loose community of women that crosses the social barriers of class, race, and generation" (342). Leonardi's comments could apply to Catherine Oliphant as well. As a romance writer and advice columnist for a popular women's magazine, Catherine's writing also reproduces the custom of sharing information among women, and reaches a community of women across social boundaries.[22]

Through drawing these cooking/writing analogies, Catherine seems to subscribe to the codes of the *Elle* magazine cooking layouts that Barthes describes. She, too, is embellishing plain ingredients, the stuff of everyday life, with glacées and garnishings to make it palatable for the housewives who make up her readership. The elaborate cooking she favors reveals something about Catherine's personality, her bohemian ways, and her resistance to the status quo.

Laura Esquivel, mentioned previously, also takes the view that what she cooks reveals something about herself. In discussing her book *Like Water for Chocolate,* Esquivel says, in *People,* "Each of us has a history, either personal or national, locked inside us, and the key to unlocking that history is food. In the same way that someone explains to someone how to make a dish, one could narrate a love story" (17). Another Mexican writer, the seventeenth-century nun, Sor Juana Ines de la Cruz, has the following to say about cooking in her "Reply to Sor Philothea," [W]hat is there for us women to know, if not bits of kitchen philosophy? . . . If Aristotle had been a cook, he would have written much more" (Sor Juana 226).

In writing about food and everyday life, Catherine is like Pym herself, who used the ingredients of everyday life as inspiration for her novels. Jane Nardin notes that Pym deliberately wrote about food in great detail if for no other reason than because food, meals, and food preparation pervade daily life (20). Such an observation fits in nicely with Barthes's ideas. According to Nardin, the implication Pym wants to convey is that food is a pleasure that has not received its due in literature and, as Catherine says, "The small things of life were so much bigger than the great things" (104). E. F. Benson's, "Lucia books" are an example of how food is used to build trust through recipe sharing.[23] Even today, popular art geared to women incorporates food themes. For example, one line of greeting cards features delicate water colors of teacups and teapots. Some of the cards actually contain a teabag. Apples and strawberries appear as motifs on nearly everything, and potpourri that smells like spices and fruit is sold in almost every department store.

Pym's Catherine, however, does not limit her discourse to food. Like many other Pym heroines, Catherine uses her own work and experiences to interpret her own life. There is evidence throughout the novel that Catherine takes herself far more seriously than she lets on or than the other characters realize. For example, she is constantly writing ideas in notebooks (26), viewing passersby with detachment, describing herself in terms of the language used by the magazines for which she writes, and evaluating hers and Tom's relationship by analyzing the changes eighteen months apart had wrought in them (104). Catherine muses, "Their eighteen months apart had made them grow more like themselves, so that now they seemed almost more like strangers than when they had first met" (104). In one telling scene where she describes her own writing to Rhoda and Mabel, two nonwriters who also fit the women's audience for whom she writes, Catherine's discourse is dialogic. Catherine says that she writes "trite little stories for women, generally with happy endings" (89). Yet, the narrator tells us that Catherine's tone is misleading, for she is speaking in that "rather derogatory tone behind which writers sometimes hide from the scorn and mockery of the world" (89). In other words, Catherine cares enough about her writing to protect herself from the mockery of others. She critiques it and apparently dismisses it herself by saying it is trite and she manages to make a living, while she is really defending her work by taking the offensive and deflecting the criticism others may aim at her writing. As Tanya Modleski writes, because of the scorn for all things feminine, female novelists are defensive, to the point that some, like George Eliot, scorned other women who wrote (13).

Also, when she reads and critiques Tom's thesis, Catherine reveals that she considers the talents of novelists superior to those of anthropologists. She thinks to herself, "Oh what cowards scholars are! When you think how poets and novelists rush in with *their* analysis of the human heart . . ." (167). As Jane Nardin states in *Barbara Pym,* Catherine believes the imaginative literature usually written by women is "superior to the serious social science that is largely the property of men" (99). Dry factual discourse is not enough for her. One might see Tom's dry diction as a coroner's report, which objectifies a human being and gives all the biological data, but gives no inkling into the subject's personality. Like the coroner, Tom has difficulty conceiving of his subjects as human beings. For Catherine, an imaginative treatment of a subject is far better than a factual one. Perhaps because of her imagination, Catherine is a better, more successful writer than Tom.

Furthermore, Catherine is professional enough to hide her personal feelings when she meets with the male editor to discuss her stories. The meeting with the editor is also important because it shows that, though Catherine works within the male-created codes of her society and of the magazines, she is aware that these rules are artificial and that they are created by men for their own purposes. When Tom expresses disbelief that a man edits a woman's magazine, Catherine says men do know something about women and at least like to form women's tastes (129). This statement acknowledges that she knows women do not always form their own tastes or ideas; she would agree with Friedan on this point. Also, Catherine, because of her nontraditional physical appearance and love for literature, is an anachronism to these magazines because, though she moves within the male world, no man has formed her taste for her and she is capable of understanding literary ideas. Proof of this statement is that the other characters view her as "bohemian" and that she is brave enough to live with a man out of wedlock in the mid 1950s. Even in her "bohemianness," Catherine defies description, for, as Tom's aunt discovers, she is not at all what a woman "living in sin" is supposed to be (135). More telling is the aunt's perhaps unconsciously sympathetic comment to Catherine that she herself does not think there should be separate sexual codes for men and women, though the highest circles in society require them (135).

Catherine is also detached enough to view Tom with Deirdre in the Greek restaurant in a somewhat dispassionate manner. She does not make a scene, merely buys her wine and returns home (107). Later, she can bring the matter up to Deirdre in a noncommittal but sardonic manner. Though Tom has hurt her deeply, she is enough of a writer to use her experience and write a story about it.

The incident at the restaurant is pivotal in Catherine's writing career for she really begins to mature as a writer at this point and she ends by writing a story about the restaurant incident and about her life with Tom. The story included experiences about how Catherine viewed herself as a serious writer and as editor of Tom's manuscripts, about how Catherine dealt with a crisis, and about her expanding independence from Tom. By writing on her own experience instead of others' as she did previously, Catherine gains insight and shows maturity as a writer. Moreover, her detachment is a valuable tool in her profession and aids her in disciplining her own emotions. Catherine can lose herself in what Muriel Schulz calls, in her essay on Pym, "a writer's fascination" by listening to the conversations of the other women around her in a restaurant (110). Also, Catherine's detachment and skills of observation allow her to see more detail than others and into the hearts of people as well.

For all that the other characters misread Catherine as a sort of "excellent woman" who writes trite stories by day while typing her lover's more important thesis by night, Catherine shows that she is capable of defining herself within the male-dominated subculture she inhabits, while seriously pursuing her writing career, though in a somewhat "bohemian" manner. It is this independence, and her ability to detach herself so that she may observe others and analyze her own feelings, that help to make Catherine a more mature writer as well as one of the more interesting characters of *Less Than Angels*. By managing to live independently and by not depending emotionally on a man, Catherine has, as Germaine Greer might say (20), held on to her freedom and devised her "own mode of revolt" against male-dominated society through her lifestyle and career.

One way Catherine revolts is through her choice of clothing. Pym uses Catherine's clothes as a way of establishing her as an independent spirit. She dresses in "bohemian styles" that involve long, dangling earrings and blue espadrilles. She defies the stereotype that Angel Deverell's editors have of female writers in Elizabeth Taylor's *Angel*. Taylor's book is a novel about an aggressive romance writer who badgers editors into publishing her work. The male editors speculate on Angel's appearance and theorize that she is old and does not realize how "inflammatory," as they say, writing is. They think she wears a moleskin cape and smells of camphor, and that she wears a wig and carries an old bag stuffed with manuscripts (52).[24]

There is also, however, similarity between Catherine's appearance and Jane Eyre's. Early on, the narrator tells the reader that Catherine, whose hair is short, thinks of herself as a Victorian child, a sort of Jane Eyre who has had her hair cropped because of scarlet fever (7). The *Jane Eyre* comparisons persist in *Less than Angels,* perhaps because both novels involve a woman who has found her own way in life. At one point, Catherine compares Alaric Lydgate to Rochester. She says, "Oh, dear . . . he looks terribly Easter Island, or even like Mr. Rochester in *Jane Eyre*" (224). Also like Jane, who chooses not to follow St. John as a missionary's wife, Catherine decides not to go to Africa with Tom. Both of these characters are forerunners of the romantic heroes Catherine writes about. Lydgate apparently recognizes Catherine's strengths and realizes that she is stronger than he (242). Moreover, Catherine subverts the "romantic helpmeet-heroine" of the Regency romances. She does not help Lydgate by encouraging him to type his notes. She, instead, encourages him to burn his life's work and liberate himself. Perhaps the only way for Lydgate to reclaim his work is to destroy it. Lydgate has literally had his text appropriated because his notes have been eaten by white ants.

Furthermore, describing Catherine, a romance writer, as if she were Jane Eyre links her writing with the novel *Jane Eyre,* which is considered the true antecedent of the modern romance (Ramsdell 71). Like Jane Eyre, Catherine is in revolt and has chosen to make her own life by subverting the social mores of her society. Significantly, Catherine is one of the first Pym heroines who invites a man to dinner.

Alaric Lydgate, too, has managed to free himself from the restrictive role his society assigns him. Lydgate has been taught to believe that, as a British male, he must make some significant achievement in life. As Groner writes in her dissertation, *The Novels of Barbara Pym,* trunks of notes in the attic enslave Lydgate, not a mad wife like Mr. Rochester's (41). Lydgate rejects the role of an aging T. E. Lawrence or a Kipling character. He significantly changes roles by donning an African mask and throwing to the flames in ritual fashion the notes. Like Catherine, he allows his active imagination to free him. He has the courage to burn the notes that bind him to this role, and thus does not end up dead like Woolf's Percival and Jacob, or unable to commit like Peter of her *Mrs. Dalloway.*

Like Lydgate, Tom Mallow significantly changes roles by donning some sort of African garb. His role playing is not as successful, though, because his costume gets him killed. Tom runs to Africa to avoid responsibilities for, as he says to Catherine, "You're so much braver than I am" (109). In some ways, Tom is like Heathcliff of *Wuthering Heights* who runs away when he hears Cathy say it would degrade her to marry him. He is also a little like the young Rochester of Jean Rhys's *Wide Sargasso Sea,* who runs away from Antoinette and from his responsibilities to her by locking her in an attic and pretending he is single.

While the men of *Less Than Angels* behave irresponsibly or inadequately toward their women, Catherine, the "free spirit," stands by Lydgate and manages to maintain an independent living for herself. Catherine is not an "excellent woman" who submerges her own personality and interests to care for a man. Instead, she can serve as a sort of muse or inspiration to Lydgate and at the same time continue to live life according to her own discourse. Catherine can only care for Lydgate because they have things in common, like a love of wine lists. For her, passivity is not a discourse. She prefers to live a full life now through sharing her interests with Lydgate; she does not sit back and hope for change. And he does not marry her at the end of the book.

If *Less Than Angels* is a novel about a romance writer, *A Glass of Blessings* is a novel that deals with the plot of romances. The novel is a sort of drama of romantic errors that explores different types of love affairs between the characters. It is an interesting comparison to *Less*

*Than Angels.* In fact, the story Catherine Oliphant writes about the incident between Tom and Deirdre at the Greek restaurant appears in *A Glass of Blessings.* Also in *A Glass of Blessings,* one of the heroines is stood up at a restaurant and the narrator observes that the restaurant serves "a special kind of meal provided (at a reduced price) for women whose escorts had failed to turn up" (69).

In *The Pleasure of Miss Pym,* Charles Burkhart writes that *A Glass of Blessings* is about a "useless woman" (40). The "useless woman" in question is Wilmet Forsyth, a thirty-three-year-old woman who is spoiled and pampered and married to Rodney Forsyth. Rodney, a civil servant, is boring and predictable to his wife. Wilmet is attracted to a handsome academic, Piers Longridge, who is a homosexual. Wilmet, apparently, is the only character in the novel who does not realize that Piers is gay. Wilmet wears expensive clothes and is on good terms with her mother-in-law, Sybil. Sybil is outspoken and forthright on almost every subject. She surprises Wilmet because she eventually marries Professor Root, an archaeologist. Wilmet is surprised because Sybil, who is elderly, brusque, and unfashionable, has fallen in love and married. She is a subversion of the typically young, buxom romance heroine. Yet, it is the older woman of *A Glass of Blessings* who "gets her man."

The plot of *A Glass of Blessings* is written in first person and told from Wilmet's point of view. The story centers on Wilmet and her need to be admired and excited by the men in her life. In contrast to Wilmet and her self-centered interests, Pym has created Mary Beamish. Mary is a dowdy young woman devoted to her mother whom Wilmet tolerates but dismisses as sanctimonious and uninteresting. Mary, too, surprises Wilmet by falling in love and marrying a handsome clergyman.

Once again, food plays an important role in a Pym novel. As in *Some Tame Gazelle,* luncheon invitations extended to clergy involve elaborate meals like smoked salmon and grouse (*A Glass of Blessings* 7). Lesser clergy like Father Bode receive less elaborate fare and Wilmet, the heroine, is a little ashamed to admit that Father Bode might prefer tinned salmon because he is more common in his tastes (7).

Food is also a means of self-expression for the diner. At Wilmet's birthday meal, food is served that was specially chosen for her. The expensive gourmet meal reflects her tastes: smoked salmon, roast duckling, and gooseberry pie with cream (13). Dessert at least, is a little ironic, for once again, food symbolizes that women are prepared to go to more trouble about things. Gooseberry is a woman's fruit, the narrator tells us, because it is women who are "prepared to take trouble with sour and difficult things" (14). Given some of Pym's heroes, it doesn't take long to realize a gooseberry can stand for all things male. There are also foods women are not supposed to like and, as Sybil observes, "Women are supposed not to like port except in a rather vulgar way" (16).

In the world of romance and gothic novels that Pym briefly enters with *A Glass of Blessings,* there is apparently a "vulgar" and a "proper" way to snack as well. In Chelsea Quinn Yarbro's *Darker Jewels,* Medieval Russian aristocracy offers snacks of fancy breads, peaches covered in honey, a dish of almonds, and Hungarian wine scented with cinnamon, ginger, pepper and served in gold cups (213). The serfs in Yarbro's novel don't even have time to snack; if they did, they would most likely munch stale crusts of coarse bread.

In Pym's novels, the common people are at least entitled to a biscuit or two, but almost everyone has some sort of tea. In *A Glass of Blessings,* Wilmet, the heroine, often describes her clothes in terms that are used to define tea or coffee, so that one of her favorite outfits is dark, in "pale coffee brown with touches of black and coral jewelry" (9). For Wilmet, who is not a good cook as Catherine Oliphant is, both food and clothes are accessories that define her social class and more sophisticated personality. Moreover, Wilmet identifies herself with romance heroines, and often thinks that her one-sided love affair with Piers Longridge, the homosexual academic, contains all the elements of a romance novel. Her dark brown, coffee-colored outfit makes her seem like some Gothic heroine.

Once again in a Pym work, all that is foreign has a romantic air, so that a wine lodge becomes poetic in atmosphere and Portuguese lessons with Piers are a chance for romantic happenings. From Wilmet's point of view, even her family is or is not romantic. For example, she believes her mother-in-law's clothes have "no particular style," thus she, Sybil, could not be a heroine (12). Yet Sybil is a heroine because she attracts and keeps her Prince Charming, Professor Root, whose name befits both a loyal lover, "rooted to his beloved," and an archaeologist who roots around in the dirt of the past. Wilmet is, therefore, as surprised as everyone else when Sybil announces her marriage. When Rodney, Wilmet's husband, provides Wilmet with an "unromantic" birthday present, she compares it with the enameled Victorian box which she receives from another man that she does consider romantic (12). The box is Victorian and is heart-shaped with an inscription. Wilmet comments that when she received the secret Christmas present, she "felt like the heroine of a Victorian novel" (96).

In *The Female Imagination,* Patricia Meyer Spacks discusses how women might use romantic fantasies to critique their lives and the lives of others, even when they don't literally believe in the fantasies (441). Spack's discussion is applicable to Wilmet, who weaves romantic fantasies to fill her day. In discussing Spacks, Marlene San Miguel Groner writes in *The Novels of Barbara Pym* that Wilmet's romantic fantasies are necessary to her feelings of self-worth (68). So, the clothes Wilmet wears must be elegant and befitting her self-defined role as heroine. Even her name comes from a Charlotte M. Yonge novel (72).[25] Not many critics like Wilmet, and some see her as self-centered. Simone de Beavoir might explain Wilmet's selfishness by arguing that because she can't find a place, she gives herself supreme importance (700). To Janice Rossen, writing in *The World of Barbara Pym,* Wilmet is a little apologetic, in a style that reminds one of the self-effacing prefaces that prologue many a nineteenth-century novel (15). Like other Pym women, she, too, is a keen observer.

Because Piers stimulates her imagination, Wilmet weaves a romantic fantasy involving him. In a way, she is like Mildred Lathbury and other Pym women because, in her fantasy, she wants Piers to need her. As discussed in Chapter 3, some romance heroines fall in love with men whom they believe need their attentions or who need to be transformed. Part of the reason Wilmet is so distressed to discover that Piers has a lover is because she realizes he will never need her exclusively; there is someone else who can minister to his needs. One reason she is compelled to "cheat" on her husband Rodney, at least in her own imagination, is the fact that he seems to be completely absorbed in his world. Wilmet becomes more confirmed in this belief when she discovers that Rodney has been seeing Prudence Bates (of *Jane and Prudence* fame) behind her back.

Prudence, too, is a type of romance heroine but she is more the regency heroine of the Georgette Heyer variety. Rodney is not impressed by Prudence's decor and makes fun of her regency furniture (250). What is also interesting about Prudence's regency furniture is that such furniture is usually gilt or white wood upholstered in delicate pastel silks and satins. Prudence's decor contrasts sharply with the stark, drab nature of postwar England, where gilt and delicate wood only existed in museums, since even gracious country homes of the regency period suffered from the bombings and fire raids. The fairytale nature of her home makes Prudence even more like some character from a romance novel.

Unlike some of the other women Pym has created, Wilmet does not feel she has to fulfill some dual role as wife and career woman. In fact, the narrator parodies career women just a little bit at one point by describing a woman civil servant preparing brussels sprouts behind a filing cabinet. Other career women are spoofed as carrying baskets as well as briefcases (11). Wilmet seems to buy into the "feminine mystique" Friedan writes about. From Wilmet's point of view, a woman can be an elegant creature whose job is to remain attractive to men and to maintain an attractive home, or she can juggle two things badly and end up burning brussels sprouts behind a filing cabinet. Conversely, "career women" who work in offices should focus on their shorthand and typing, and not try to usurp the housewife's place as well. Women's magazines figure in this novel as they do in *Less Than Angels*. Even the old and tired out Miss Limpsett, who works with Piers, reads them, and Wilmet is "glad to think of her escaping into a world of romance after her dreary day at the press" (74). Despite her beliefs, however, Wilmet gets bored and yearns to go to "impossibly remote places" on the trolley bus route (20). Pym may be mocking the type of romance heroine who wants to go on a quest, but Wilmet's "quest" is far tamer than Grania O'Malley's in *Grania* by Morgan Llewellyn. In that novel, Grania becomes a pirate to fulfill her destiny.

Wilmet's friend, Mary Beamish, is sort of a Jane Eyre, a dowdy and reluctant heroine who ends up with a man to her great surprise and that of everyone else. Mary's fate is particularly interesting because she wanted to become a nun after her mother's death. Mary has been at the mercy of her mother, and is thus a type of companion, but one who is unpaid. As an unpaid companion in Pym's world, she should expect to be bullied (22). In *Daughter of Deceit,* Victoria Holt describes "excellent women" who are very much like Mary. The narrator, however, could be Wilmet, for she seems to disapprove, if ever so slightly, of "those women who know everything, can do everything, never put a foot wrong, obey all the rules and expect everyone else to do the same . . . and very likely make ordinary people's lives miserable" (Holt 25).[26]

The rogue or Byronic hero in *A Glass of Blessings* is Piers Longridge. His "aquiline features and fair hair" distinguish him, however, from the old Mr. Rochester type (6). Like Rochester, Piers is mysterious. He played a role in Wilmet's past, but the reader is not really sure what that role was. He teaches Portuguese and proofreads French, both romance languages. The narrator tells us that young women go to his class for personal and romantic reasons (65). Piers, too, thinks he is like a character from a novel, but he believes he is a character from an H. G. Wells novel (8). Pym subverts the Byronic hero in Piers, the homosexual, by giving him a harmless but eccentric hobby; he likes to memorize the numbers of license plates (11). This little game of his is very much like Nicholas Cleveland's soap animals and is a bit silly. Also, Pym makes Piers into sort of a joke as a Don Juan figure because he makes a fool of the heroine not by leaving her for another woman but for a man. Rodney, on the other hand, is more Brontësque in his personality, which is like "damp green English churchyards and intellectual walks and talks" (13).

Pym's tastes in literary husbands in *A Glass of Blessings* appear to lean toward Rodney and his Brontësque, "intellectual walks and talks." Rodney is more an ancestor of the rather sedate and severe Reverend Patrick Brontë himself than of the more mysterious and dashing Rochester. Yet Rodney fools everyone, including Wilmet, who believes she knows everything about her hitherto predictable husband, by having a flirtation with Prudence Bates. What Wilmet underestimates about her husband is the very thing she recognizes about herself; Rodney, too, has, what Diana Benet calls in *Something to Love*, a desire to be needed (77). Benet argues that this theme extends beyond romantic love into marriage.

The desire to be needed in marriage is so important to Wilmet that she becomes bored with her relationship to Rodney. If anything, he is too efficient and respectable in her eyes. He thinks of everything and even deposits a sum of money in her bank account as a birthday present. Wilmet sees this gesture as too practical; it is an example to her of the lack of romance in her life. As Benet writes in *Something to Love*, Rodney is a civil servant—stiff-looking, attractive but balding (82). To make matters worse for Wilmet, Rodney is a conventional husband as well as a predictable one. He believes that married women should not work unless they have to. As a result, Wilmet has no other interests to compensate for the romance missing in her life. In fact, Wilmet does not even have a home in which she can take an interest. She is not at all like Catherine Oliphant or Mildred Lathbury or Dulcie Mainwaring, single women in Pym's novels, who maintain their own homes and therefore their own independence. Wilmet and Rodney live in the London house belonging to Sybil, Rodney's charming but very independent mother. Thus, Benet writes that Wilmet "lives like a pampered child in another woman's domain, where she does nothing more than arrange flowers occasionally" (78). Benet notes that Wilmet lives as useless a life as Father Thames's Fabergé egg (78).

While Wilmet, however, may continue to be "useless" through a good part of the novel, Rodney is not as "romantically hopeless" as Wilmet thinks (Benet 83). In the tradition of a Harlequin romance hero, Rodney occasionally surprises Wilmet with his "little talents" and little token gifts. Pym subverts this romantic tradition, near and dear to so many romance novelists, by having Rodney "surprise" Wilmet one other way; he becomes involved in an extramarital flirtation with Prudence Bates, a beautiful career woman.

Because they are bored, married couples in *A Glass of Blessings* attempt to engage in flirtations that are often laughable because of the ineptness of the participants. Wilmet, in the style of the romance heroine, attempts to enter into a relationship with Piers because she believes he needs to be taken care of. Like Jenny of *Sweet Savage Love* and many other romance heroines, Wilmet attempts to "transform" Piers while at the same time fulfilling her desire to be needed. The irony is that Piers is gay, and already has Keith at home to cater to his needs (163). Thus, Pym subverts yet another romantic type, for the "rival woman" is really a rival man.

Piers, in his own way, is just as immature as Wilmet, for he encourages her in her flirtation by suggesting, among other things, that they drink tea like "clandestine lovers" (163). But he is not the only one of the characters to suffer from emotional immaturity. Wilmet and Rodney are not really grown up either; they still live in Sybil's house and rely on her for emotional support. It is only after Sybil surprises them with an announcement of her own engagement that Wilmet and Rodney are faced with the adult issue of finding their own home. As they begin to grow emotionally, they become more interested in each other. Thus, their marriage has the promise of becoming better as they get older; it is far more optimistic than Jane Cleveland's marriage in *Jane and Prudence* which has descended into "mild looks and spectacles," or Francis and Margaret Cleveland's marriage in *Crampton Hodnet* which is made up of codependant boredom.

To be bored is, apparently, one of the worst fates that can befall a Pym heroine. One can go beyond Diana Benet's belief that Pym women need something to love; they also need to be needed or to be purposeful. For Catherine Oliphant of *Less Than Angels,* writing fulfills her need to be purposeful. In fact, she can only minister to Alaric Lydgate because he is a frustrated writer, living a frustrating existence because he is enslaved to the idea of writing up his no longer useful notes. Catherine cannot care for a man simply because she is an "excellent woman" who needs something to love; her failed affair with Tom Mallow shows that she is too independent and creative to be only a typist or helpmate. She feels more loyalty to the readers of the women's magazines she writes for and often hopes that her writing and advice columns improve their lives somehow.

In contrast, Wilmet Forsyth could be one of Catherine's readers because she is a housewife with no home of her own who is not particularly interested in domestic matters anyway. One can almost see Wilmet leafing through the women's magazines, focusing on clothing features and articles that tell one how to choose makeup. It is indeed no accident that Catherine's story appears in *A Glass of Blessings.* Yet, what both these novels have in common is that both offer some hope of a satisfying relationship between a male and female character. Catherine appears to be building such a relationship with Lydgate, while Wilmet and Rodney grow and improve their marriage. Pym, however, is not consistent in her hopeful depictions of men and women living together and building full lives. By *No Fond Return of Love,* Pym once again creates a heroine, Dulcie Mainwaring, who trades an apparently successful life as a single woman for a man, something to love, and marriage. Now, however, Pym complicates the equations by exploring love and by elevating it above class and social status as a proper reason for marriage.

# 5

## Suitably Unsuitable Attachments

Like *Less Than Angels* and *A Glass of Blessings, No Fond Return of Love, An Unsuitable Attachment,* and *An Academic Question* explore relationships between men and women and the happy endings that often result from initially unsuitable attachments. In each novel, the heroine is an excellent woman who, unlike Mildred Lathbury, wins the somewhat subdued handsome and Byronic hero at the end of her story. What is interesting, however, is that unsuitable attachments may prove to be the best kind in these novels. Diana Benet notes in *Something to Love* that Dulcie sees suitable matches like her aunt's as both "satisfactory and depressing" (97). The so-called "unsuitable matches," like that between Bill and Viola, end up being happier. The Bill and Viola match appears to be unsuitable at first because the two share different backgrounds and interests and because Bill is a cook's brother (97). As Diana Benet writes in *Something to Love,* "Pym emphasizes the unreality on which romantic love is based, but she also insists that the imaginative recreation of others is not undertaken only by lovers" (100). Love acts as a kind of alchemy that changes suitable and unsuitable materials into the "shiny, treasured prize" of a successful relationship (97).

Creativity is definitely one of the attributes of Dulcie Mainwaring, heroine of *No Fond Return of Love.* Dulcie is a single woman who holds a well-paying, if boring, job as an indexer and proofreader. Dulcie was once engaged to Maurice, but like other Pym heroines, her engagement was broken. She meets Aylwin Forbes, the hero, after they attend the same scholarly conference. She also meets her rather prickly friend, Viola Dace, and discovers that Viola and Aylwin had some past relation-ship. Dulcie is intrigued by Forbes after he faints at the conference. Thereafter, she makes him the subject of a detective-like search.

Dulcie lives comfortably and independently in her own home, which she shares with Laurel, her niece. Dulcie learns more about Aylwin Forbes because Laurel becomes involved with him. Dulcie is disconcerted to learn that Forbes is married but legally separated. In trying to protect her niece, however, Dulcie herself becomes involved with Aylwin. The rest of the plot includes portrayals of Viola and her unsuitable marriage to a merchant, the demise of Forbes's marriage, and a look into Forbes's family life.

Food plays a major role in *No Fond Return of Love* and is a means for the characters to express their personalities. For example, Viola Dace, the untidy, eclectic acquaintance of Dulcie's, serves Dulcie an exotic supper of store-bought salads, cold meats, and croissants (141). Viola is not an "excellent woman"; no self-respecting female of that type would ever serve a guest cold, prepared foods. She would at least open and heat a tin of something and make tea. As it is, Viola is hardly equipped to entertain guests or to preside over complicated meals. She is not, in short, a perfect helpmate or server. Therefore, food, and the way it is presented, helps to define Viola as a nondomestic woman.

On the other hand, the presentation of communal meals at the academic conference Dulcie attends at the beginning of the novel accentuates the role women play as servers or helpmates to men. In mixed company, however, women are expected to serve men and to enjoy performing their "duty."

Mystery writer Jonathan Gash makes the same sort of observation in *The Grace in Older Women.* Like Pym, Gash likes to write about elderly women who run tearooms. His rogue antiques dealer hero, Lovejoy, notices when he visits the tearoom of two spinster sisters, that they love to serve him and watch him eat, but that they never seem to want to eat with him. Lovejoy does not accept being served as his due, however. When the Dewhurst sisters feed him but don't join him, he is embarrassed and comments, "They like to watch me eat. God knows why. They never have any themselves" (Gash 87).

The self-appointed woman server in *No Fond Return of Love* reminds Dulcie of a "Medieval nun" feeding the assembled poor (19). Yet, the server wears a large cameo depicting the rape of Leda (19). Dulcie later discovers she is a renowned librarian (19). Like Miss Clovis of *Less Than Angels,* the server is expected to serve the meal, perhaps as senior woman at the table. Or perhaps she is presiding as hostess at the only "home" she has, the academic conference. Note also that the Leda brooch is rich in possibilities for either humor or the more serious implications of rape by male gods. The reader may consider either possibility, depending on his or her frame of mind. Pym keeps the scene from becoming melodramatic by mentioning the racy brooch in the same breath with the renowned, older librarian and the serving of soup.

Elizabeth Taylor, friend and contemporary of Pym's, addresses the issue of women's meals in *A Wreathe of Roses.* Liz, the woman who imagines this party and who alludes to *A Room of One's Own,* is a disgruntled clergyman's wife.[27] Liz fantasizes about a literary teaparty where Charlotte (Brontë), Emily (Brontë), Jane (Austen), Ivy (Compton-Burnett), and Virginia (Woolf) are present. George Eliot and Elizabeth Barrett Browning are also guests. Apparently, the food has not lived up to the standards of the guests, for one comments, "Virginia was right to feel wounded about the food. Women are not good enough to themselves and the indifferent food is the beginning of all the other indifferent things they take for granted" (*Wreath of Roses* 36-37).

Yet, Dulcie does like a small serving of romance with her often spartan meals. For her solitary dinner, Weld notes Dulcie will "carefully prepare and romantically justify the simple fare" (Weld 141). For Dulcie, a "crusty French loaf, cheese, and lettuce and tomatoes from the garden" is one of "those classically simple meals, the sort that French peasants are said to eat and that enlightened English people sometimes enjoy rather self-consciously" (56). Dulcie does not deny herself the luxury of a good meal just because she is alone; she considers herself worth the effort. To Dulcie, preparing meals is a sort of art; she notes that "there should have been wine and a lovingly prepared dressing of oil and vinegar" (56). Still, she is resourceful and makes do with orange squash and mayonnaise. Through meal preparation, Dulcie reaffirms a trend Pym would continue to follow in *The Sweet Dove Died, Quartet in Autumn,* and *A Few Green Leaves,* where single women eat as they like, or enjoy sumptuous, tasty meals for one. In Pym's literary kitchen, women enjoy cooking good food for themselves, not for men.

It is telling that she acknowledges life for a single woman of her age is better than it used to be. She refers to an earlier society that expected unmarried women to do charity works, and as she reads "an old bound volume (*circa* 1911) of *Every Woman's Encyclopedia,*" she is "thankful that it was not in these days necessary to join 'a working party for charity,' making useful garments 'for the poor'" (57) Dulcie has an imagination as rich as her diet, and she observes that perhaps lonely women dreamed, too (57). If a solitary meal for Dulcie and other Pym women expresses self-satisfaction and imagination, dinners for two in *No Fond Return of Love* provide opportunity for romantic possibilities.

Where cooking serves as a way for a Pym heroine to express how she feels about herself, clothes in a Pym novel often draw attention to the heroine's attractiveness. Dulcie of *No Fond Return of Love* wears drab clothing, but she does not do so to emphasize her own "mousiness." Instead, Dulcie, the ultimate observer, or "spy," wears muted colors as a sort of camouflage (Nardin 72). For the women of *No Fond Return of Love,* clothing is a means of self-expression and camouflage.

Pym's World War II and postwar heroines, however, may dress drably for other reasons as well. During this time, material was scarce;

fashion itself suffered because there was little bright or quality material for clothing production. In *The Language of Clothes,* Alison Lurie writes that British clothing in general is duller in color than in other parts of Europe. She writes, "The most striking thing about British dress, both urban and rural, is its tending to follow the principle of camouflage. City clothes are often made in colors that echo the hues of stone, cement, soot, cloudy steps and wet pavements." She notes that darker shades of gray are popular colors and provincial fashion is two to ten years behind city fashion (102). Marge Piercy would agree with Lurie. She observes in *Gone to Soldiers* that all people in England during the 1940s looked "shabby and pale" (553). Georgina Howell writes in her study of *Vogue* fashion history, *In Vogue,* that by the end of World War II, clothes rationing "tightened," and all garments were hard to find. Like all other aspects of life, fashion had to be simplified (162). As Howell notes, in the 1940s, and even immediately after, people took what they could get and made what they could out of it (157).

Lurie also writes that gray is an "ambiguous, indefinite color. It suggests fog, mist, smoke and twilight—conditions that blur shapes and colors" (194). An all-gray outfit can "indicate a modest, retiring individual, someone who prefers not to be noticed, or someone who whether they wish it or not merges with their background." Lurie notes Virginia Woolf's Lily Briscoe in *To the Lighthouse* as a woman who wears gray and fades into the background (194). Still, Pym subverts one more stereotype, for her gray-clad woman of *An Unsuitable Attachment,* Ianthe, overshadows the more colorful Penelope and wins the affections of John Challow, the hero.

Dulcie wears dull colors not to hide from the world, but because the muted tones act as a sort of camouflage for her. In them, she is less obtrusive and more able to observe others. Like other Pym women, she is an artist observer, constantly watching others closely, looking up addresses and lineages in directories and cemeteries, and composing plots for romantic novels that involve her observees. The narrator wants us to know that Dulcie likes to watch others, and at one point, Dulcie actually sits by the shores of Lake Observation (Benet 89). In short, Dulcie is a snoop! Dulcie also appreciates trivia and says, about a collection of Proust's relics, that any woman's would be just as interesting (*No Fond Return of Love* 124). It is as if Dulcie has read Susan Glaspell's play *Trifles,* also known as the short story "A Jury of Her Peers." Glaspell's work is structured as a kind of murder mystery, where, by observing the trivial details of the existence of an abused wife, the friends of the wife deduce that she murdered her husband. The kitchen and sewing materials of the long-suffering Minnie Wright reveal to her friends, Mrs. Hale and Mrs.

Peters, that she killed her husband in frustration, and allow them to save her by covering up the crime. The ridicule and indifference of the male sheriff and district attorney free them to shield Minnie, even as the men make fun of their comments about Minnie's home. The irony of Glaspell's tale is brought home in the following exchange between the male county attorney and Sheriff Peters: "'You're convinced there was nothing important here?' he asked the sheriff. 'Nothing that would—point to any motive?' 'Nothing here but kitchen things,' he said, with a little laugh for the insignificance of kitchen things" (Glaspell 263). Like Dulcie, the women of *Trifles* are detectives to whom the possessions of an ordinary woman are extraordinarily interesting.

Many critics have commented on Dulcie Mainwaring in the years since Pym wrote *No Fond Return of Love*. For example, Diana Benet writes in *Something to Love* that Dulcie has glamour "thrust upon her" by the other characters but that she is a very literary heroine (100). For example, Forbes believes that Dulcie knows Austen's *Mansfield Park* very well.

Other people, however, view Dulcie as a sort of hopeless spinster who must be "taken care of." To people like Mr. Sedge and the clergyman, Neville Forbes (Aylwin's brother), Dulcie's large house and independent lifestyle are a little scandalous, a social disaster waiting to happen.[28] She needs to be put in a "nice little flat with a bit of a garden" where she can be involved in church affairs and carefully watched. This, of course, is the lifestyle Mildred Lathbury has adopted in *Excellent Women*. Dulcie, however, is slightly horrified at the idea and keeps her large home at the end of the novel. One reads a quiet defiance in her determination to do so. Neville Forbes's housekeeper suggests that Dulcie take the flat of the hapless Miss Spicer. Miss Spicer tried to "spice up" the celibate Neville's life with a bit of romance but was rebuffed. Dulcie is put into a situation where she "apologetically" explains about her large house, but has "a dreadful feeling that something was about to be arranged for her against her will." When she discovers the flat was Miss Spicer's, she is dismayed. She says, "Miss Spicer's flat—oh, the horror of it! And perhaps the same story happening all over again—[to] be herself seen by another prying stranger, running into the church in tears" (249). The fact that the male characters feel they have the right to plan Dulcie's life for her may illustrate a point Anne Wyatt-Brown makes in *Barbara Pym: A Critical Biography*. Wyatt-Brown writes that, in Dulcie's world, "men clearly have the advantage over women" (99). Still, as Penelope Lively says in "The World of Barbara Pym," Dulcie and other Pym females may have the upper hand in a "battle of the sexes."

The novel's heroes, however, do not read Dulcie as the worthy contender literary critics make her out to be. Some men see Dulcie as a spinster to be put away. They also see her, to use her own words, as a "woman manquée, who could not be expected to know what real women were" because spinsters presumably had no sexual experience with men. Both Sedge and Neville speak to her of other women's indiscretions, a topic a gentleman would not bring up with an eligible woman. Neville does not apparently consider the older, somewhat plain, Dulcie as a possible love interest for Aylwin or himself, so he tells her about Aylwin's marital strife. For example, after Neville has told her the story of Marjorie Forbes, Aylwin's young wife, who, in answer to her husband's "libertine" behavior, ran off with another man, he says "you know what women *are*" to Dulcie as if she were another man (250). Ironically, Dulcie may indeed know what flighty young women like Marjorie *are;* her niece, Laurel, also develops an infatuation for Aylwin. It is also true that both Dulcie and Viola are eager to please men, often at their own female expense, something no man would understand (Weld 144). Men like Neville and Aylwin think it is a women's duty, not prerogative, to please men. These Pym men differ from characters like Archdeacon Hoccleve of *Some Tame Gazelle,* who feels that women deprive themselves by choice because they like to please their men. This self-deprivation is not a duty in Hoccleve's opinion but a conscious decision that gives women pleasure.

Apparently, some critics of Pym and of *No Fond Return of Love* are not exactly sure what women are, either. While Anne Wyatt-Brown in *Barbara Pym: A Critical Biography* acknowledges Dulcie's spunkiness, she also reads Dulcie as a sad woman who empathizes with a beggar because "she feels some odd kinship with him, based on a sense of their mutual deprivation" (98). In fact, Wyatt-Brown alleges that an earlier manuscript for the novel was "grimmer still," with a "cranky older woman" as a heroine "who worries in a paranoid fashion about the infringement of one's civil rights" (98). Wyatt-Brown argues that "secret eating and spying . . . a kind of vicarious existence, are all that is left to many of the characters" (99). Perhaps she agrees with Marge Piercy who, in *Gone to Soldiers,* exclaims about the wounds "inflicted on women who did not meet society's standards of prettiness" (319). Wyatt-Brown also points out that Dulcie is an orphan who lives alone in suburbia with no close friends, suffering because she has recently been jilted by her fiancé, Maurice (100).

Wyatt-Brown is correct but selective in her observations. Many of Pym's most successful heroines are orphans, including Catherine Oliphant, Mildred Lathbury, and Harriet and Belinda Bede. Also, most have only one or two close friends; their social relations center on extended family and on church activities. Yet, Dulcie and these other women are not lacking in interests. Dulcie has a comfortable home and a sister who is close to her. Her niece, Laurel, comes to live with her and plays a sort of comic "other woman" who unwittingly competes for Aylwin's attention. Certainly Dulcie is not lonely or bored, especially when Viola Dace comes to live with her. It is true that Dulcie worries about being an older woman alone, but she is not a pathetic recluse, either. One must remember that Dulcie's name means "sweet," and is very similar to the name Don Quixote gives his ideal romantic heroine, Dulcinea. These clues indicate to the reader that Pym did not intend for her heroine to be a cranky and bitter old spinster. If Dulcie marries, it will be for love, not to avoid some societal stigma.

Perhaps a statement Joanne S. Frye makes in *Living Stories, Telling Lives* is an accurate assessment of women like Dulcie. In her book, Frye discusses the relationship between literature and life for women. She concerns herself with the question of "why women's novels need to subvert the conventional premises of representation in order to reveal new possibilities in women's lives" (190). Frye argues that a woman reader "learns from female characters new ways to interpret her own and other women's experiences." As a result of what she learns, a woman can reshape her own culture and its understanding of women (191). Women like Dulcie and other Pym heroines subvert their various individual cultures through a combination of sharp observation and apparent self-effacement so that they can pursue their own desires.[29] As Annette Weld points out, Dulcie is capable of clear-eyed assessment (147). Though Dulcie knows women long to be needed (*No Fond Return of Love* 103), she also knows that life can be cruel in small ways, as Weld notes (147). Thus, it pays to observe and be aware of small things.

Wyatt-Brown may choose to see Dulcie as a middle-aged heroine trapped in a "dark novel," but one can also see Dulcie as romance heroine transplanted to British suburbia. Like many romance heroines, Dulcie is orphaned and unmarried. Through an initial chance encounter, perhaps related to her job, she meets the man of her dreams. Even Wyatt-Brown acknowledges that the second half of *No Fond Return of Love* "becomes a fairy tale in which Pym gives full rein to her fantasies" (101). In fact, Dulcie travels to find out more about Aylwin's family, just as Pym did "research" on men who interested her. Romance heroines also research their potential lovers. In Jude Deveraux's novels *Sweet Liar* and *A Knight in Shining Armor,* the heroines travel and do research about their lovers' families. In *Sweet Liar,* the heroine does historical research into the 1920s to discover the link between her family and her boyfriend's family. In *Knight,* a romance involving time travel, the heroine sojourns from the twentieth century to Elizabethan England so that she can discover a secret about her lover that will save him from a traitor's death. (The heroine travels through time by touching the sarcophagus of her lover. The sarcophagus is housed in an ancient village church in England.) Even Jane Eyre is curious about Rochester, and talks about him with Mrs. Fairfax, his housekeeper and distant relation.

While Pym heroines share this curiosity about their chosen men's families, however, they are far more realistic and lighthearted about their searches than their romance counterparts. Dulcie is as much amused by the act of observing others as she is by the object of her search. Early in the book, Dulcie expresses her interest at observing everyday people. She says to Miss Foy at the conference, "Perhaps the time will come when one may be permitted to do research into the lives of ordinary people . . . people who have no claim to fame whatsoever." In response to Dulcie's comments, Miss Foy, who works at a "learned institution," laughingly replies, "Ah, that'll be the day!" (*No Fond Return of Love* 18). In her article on Pym titled "The Novelist as Anthropologist," Muriel Schulz notes that Dulcie's methods of observation are Pym's own because Pym and Dulcie are both interested in the lives and artifacts of ordinary people (107). As Dulcie notes after she hears a discussion on Proust's relics, "I think the relics of any woman could be just as interesting. . . . Particularly if she had been unhappy, and who hasn't . . . if she had kept things" (124). To show that writers do get inspiration from everyday life, the author has a Pym-like woman appear in *No Fond Return of Love* as a novelist at a dinner. The Pym-like woman observes the other diners.

Moreover, Pym gives a nod to Virginia Woolf, another great literary observer, in the dining passage where the novelist appears. Prunes and custard are served at the dinner, just as they are in *A Room of One's Own* (109). Pym writes that during dinner in a West Country hotel, the diners have stewed plums and custard with "thimble-sized" cups of coffee (*No Fond Return of Love* 176). In *A Room of One's Own* Woolf describes dinner at a woman's college, Fernham, noting that dessert is an unsatisfying dish of prunes and custard. Woolf calls the prunes "an uncharitable vegetable . . . stringy as a miser's heart" (18). Woolf's narrator often comments on literary women who perform everyday tasks, e.g., eating, cooking, and knitting. Other women writers do the same. At one point in discussing Jane, Woolf's narrator observes that Mrs. Fairfax, Rochester's housekeeper in *Jane Eyre,* makes jellies (Woolf, *Room* 72). In another passage, the narrator of *A Room of One's Own* argues that men should not argue that women confine themselves to making pudding, knitting stockings, and playing the piano (72). Where Woolf, however, would argue that women should not be condemned for seeking to do more than perform everyday tasks, Pym might say that there is a world to be studied in housework that is worthy of any scholar.

Because of her common-sensical approach to life and her interest in the mundane, Dulcie is a realistic character, a suburban "princess" in woolens who has passed her thirtieth year. As Anne Tyler writes in her review of *No Fond Return of Love*, Dulcie is amusing because she is so unself-conscious about her "snooping" (16). She is also not as helpless as many of her romance counterparts. Instead, Dulcie runs a comfortable home, cares for her niece and others, and attends professional conferences. Tyler, a writer whose style has been compared to Pym's, writes in her review that Pym's plots derive from "the daydreams of a refreshingly sensible and not obviously beautiful woman" (1). Thus, Tyler acknowledges that Pym's women like Dulcie have full lives, rich in daydreams. Dulcie and the others are firmly grounded in reality; they are not lost in escapist fantasies. As Tyler notes, character is everything in a Pym book (16). Dulcie may be mild mannered, but she is also "devilishly sharp," a skill honed perhaps by her job as an indexer-proofreader; Tyler sees Dulcie as a sharp observer who does not let the other characters get away with much (16). Dulcie is also resilient, for when Maurice, her fiancé, rejects her, she does not sulk or become reclusive. Instead, she attends an academic conference so that she can benefit from a new experience.

Not only is Dulcie independent, competent, and running her own and others' affairs, she also has opinions about love in general. Robert Smith writes that Pym's treatment of love "seems to derive from a firm emotional base" (61). Smith apparently reads into her words none of the bitterness and frustration that some critics see. For example, Dulcie says, "People blame one for dwelling on trivialities . . . but life is made up of them. And if we've had one great sorrow or one great love, then who shall blame us if we only want the trivial things?" (167). Once again, a character speaks for Pym herself, who found comfort in the commonplace.

Pym women find comfort in the ordinary because they, and others like them, are not taken as seriously as they would like by men. In Marge Piercy's *Gone to Soldiers*, Louise Kahan, a romance writer, laments that the men she works with as a war correspondent do not give her the credit she deserves as a professional. Louise notes that her male co-workers opened doors for her, gave her cigarettes, complimented her on her looks, consulted her about birthday presents for wives, and "asked her out to dine and make an occasional pro forma pass." But

Louise argues that they "also ignored any suggestions she made as if she had not spoken" (498).

Pym's heroes, however, are not ignored by reviewers or other readers. Anne Wyatt-Brown criticizes *No Fond Return of Love* in *Barbara Pym: A Critical Biography* for having a "contrived plot" (102). Wyatt-Brown also claims that Pym undermines the plot because Aylwin, the hero, is so completely discredited by the end of the story that "he hardly seems a prize worth having" (102). Aylwin Forbes is the handsome man in this novel who plays the Byronic hero. He is a bit like Fabian Driver, the philandering husband of *Jane and Prudence*. Like Fabian, Aylwin "cheats" on his wife by flirting with Viola and Laurel. Where Fabian's dalliances involve sex, however, Aylwin's flirtations are harmless and not physically consummated.

Diana Benet observes in *Something to Love* that Aylwin has come to see himself as a fictional character (99). Aylwin is a sort of Henry James character, and *Portrait of a Lady* appears in his room (*No Fond Return of Love* 214). Benet argues that Aylwin is silly because he thinks it is his destiny to love unwisely; in other words, like Fabian Driver, he sees himself as a doomed romantic (97), and doomed romantics form the ultimate unsuitable attachments. But Pym makes Aylwin look ridiculous because in the end his wife runs off and provides *him* with grounds for divorce instead of the other way around. Marjorie Forbes elopes with a man she met on a train coming from Taviscombe (243).

Arguably, both Fabian and Aylwin see themselves as descendants of Lord Byron, but a close inspection of both reveals they are hardly Byron material. Fabian is easily dominated by Jessie Morrow, and he carries a very ordinary umbrella to protect himself from the elements. Anne Tyler goes on to actually call Aylwin the "so-called" hero of the novel (1). The most serious malady that Aylwin suffers is that he faints at a conference (*No Fond Return of Love* 28). (As Weld points out; Aylwin is not the only male character to faint in fiction: Kingsley Amis's Lucky Jim does the same thing, only from drinking too much alcohol! [*Lucky Jim* 138].) Dulcie, who is at the conference, can appreciate fainting (28). Yet, the episode is an example of how Pym subverts romance novels because, in them, it is women who usually faint. Also, like many a fictional female, Dulcie carries smelling salts in her purse. The irony is that the smelling salts do not turn out to be for her benefit. They are used, instead, to revive Aylwin.

At least one critic believes Aylwin shares more qualities with women than fainting. He has been likened to Prudence Bates of *Jane and Prudence*. Diana Benet writes that Aylwin is a "male Prudence Bates," as self-conscious in his beauty as Prudence is. Benet also implies he is a Walter Mitty character; she writes, "Just as Prudence, lovely and self-dramatizing, imagined herself in strangers' eyes as a compelling figure of muted sorrow, so Aylwin, playing to an unseen audience, fears he might look ridiculous carrying a large bunch of flowers" (90). Yet, like Prudence, Aylwin creates a role for himself that shapes his life; according to Diana Benet, he considers himself an impetuous romantic whose nature dictates unsuitable choices in women. Benet writes that Aylwin's father also created roles for himself, "as if romantic impetuosity were a genetically transmitted trait" (90).

Dulcie is aware of Aylwin's faults, and she enters into a relationship with him with eyes wide open. Benet writes that Dulcie wants Aylwin despite his faults because she feels a strong sexual attraction for him (99). As Marge Piercy says, Dulcie loves Aylwin "not in the romantic way . . . [but] with a wary eye, a lack of illusion, a focused caring" (498). After all, Aylwin is not exactly a Mr. Rochester. He appears to have no dark secrets, and his wife presides over jumble sales in respectable clothing; she is not lurking, mad and forsaken, in an attic. Neither is Aylwin "maimed and wounded," as some Byronic heroes are. He does not need healing; a good "talking to" seems in order instead.[30] Other characters call him a "libertine" (80, 138), but he certainly is no Marquis de Sade, or even another Lord Byron. His infidelities to his wife are not consummated; he lusts more in his heart than in actuality. He does, however, seem to be a bit of a rake.

Marriage in *No Fond Return of Love* is portrayed more realistically than in the other novels—Aylwin's flirtations and unhappy marriage are topics of open discussion among the characters. Pym seems to take it more seriously and acknowledges that love and common interests are both important. Even Dulcie's flamboyant friend Viola Dace notes that Marjorie Forbes failed as Aylwin's wife because she was not "able to share Aylwin's interests" (227).

In *No Fond Return of Love,* Pym does not undermine the romance by deflating it with physical discomfort. In "Love and Marriage in the Novels," Mary Strauss-Noll writes that Dulcie sees marriage as a "mixed blessing" and that her attitudes fluctuate between the romantic and the cynical (80). As evidence of her ambivalence, Strauss-Noll points out that the book's title is romantic and that it refers to Dulcie's unsuccessful love affair with Maurice (80). Dulcie says Maurice is one "from whom one asks no return of love" (75). According to Dulcie, just to be allowed to love a man like Maurice is enough (75). Yet, Dulcie does not appear to be the type of woman who could occupy a subordinate position. But as Diana Benet notes in *Something to Love,* as for Mildred Lathbury of *Excellent Women,* the big question for Dulcie is whether she will merely observe or also participate in life (89). One way for Dulcie to "participate" is to marry.

Yet a "fond return of love" is not enough to ensure a happy union, either. Dulcie also worries about "dreadful marriages" where the husband is not worthy of his wife for one reason or another (54). At one point she exclaims to Aylwin, "Oh, why do you always want such unsuitable wives!" (223). Dulcie unwittingly advocates the choice of excellent women as wives and thus counters the assertion Mildred makes in *Excellent Women* that excellent women are not for marrying. She admonishes Aylwin that he needs a sensible wife, "somebody who can appreciate [his] work and help [him] with it—an older woman, perhaps" (223). Young girls like Laurel, and Deirdre of *Less Than Angels,* may seem attractive and exciting, but they will, in the end, prove disappointing.

Dulcie also realizes she is somewhat of a romance heroine, for she notes after her outburst, hot with embarrassment, that "if it had been a romantic novel . . . he would have been struck by how handsome she looked when she was angry, the sea breeze having whipped some color into her normally pale cheeks. Certainly he was looking at her more intently than before, but perhaps only because he was surprised by her outburst" (223). Like Aylwin, Dulcie "flirts" with the idea of creating a literary role for herself, according to Benet. She prefers a tragic role, the woman with the great love and great sorrow. She cannot play this role with much conviction, however, because she is too sensible (90-91).[31]

Although Dulcie is sensible, she is not against romantic marriage. As Mary Strauss-Noll writes in "Love and Marriage in the Novels," Dulcie, for all her criticism of marriage, would still like to wed (81). Strauss-Noll observes that to Dulcie, celibacy is an "unnatural state that sticks out a mile" (149). On a more serious note, Dulcie realizes that, according to her society, she is on a lower plane than other women because she is not married. Strauss-Noll attributes Dulcie's feelings, in part, to her being a woman and having a need to be needed (81).

Yet, Dulcie ironically realizes that men do not need to be needed and are often only married "in a sense," and "in a sense" marriages are common (16). Dulcie realizes that some women want more in marriage; her own sister "hankers" for romantic escape (115). It is one of the most delicious ironies of the novel that Aylwin, whom Dulcie has admonished to find a "suitable wife," ultimately proposes to Dulcie for romantic reasons (239). Perhaps she will accept him because he has come to agree with her on one point; suitable marriages are often "satisfactory and depressing" (239).[32] Diana Benet writes of the relationship between

Dulcie and Aylwin using food metaphors. She says that Dulcie is bread, and that Aylwin cannot live by bread alone (95). Still, he comes to realize Dulcie has hidden depths (224). Yet, as Benet appropriately notes, "Hidden depths are more appropriate to strudel than to bread" (95). Ironically, it appears that a woman is not quite as good if she is *not* used.

British writer Rosamund Pilcher centers on romantic stories in her books, which, in some ways, are similar to Pym novels. For example, she creates women who are "used" in much the same way Pym women are. Penelope Keeling of *The Shellseekers* is one such woman. She is far too flamboyant in dress and personality to be a true excellent woman. Even so, Penelope provides her father, husband, lover, and son with food, shelter, and support. In *September,* written after *The Shellseekers,* Penelope's spoiled, bachelor son Noel reminisces about his mother. The narrator says, "He had always been fond of her, in a detached and unsentimental manner, but basically he'd thought of her as his constant source of food, drink, clean clothes, warm beds, and when he asked for it, moral support" (11). As if to confirm that women in caretaking roles are often taken for granted, Noel's girlfriend Alexa, who is a master chef, observes that when she cooks at a director's lunch, nobody ever looks at her, as though, despite or because of her white cook's overall, she is invisible (17).

Certainly in *No Fond Return of Love,* Aylwin would like to use Dulcie as a companion and helpmate, but he finally is astonished because he comes to love her for romantic reasons. In Marge Piercy's novel *Gone to Soldiers,* a male character who is a professor, and who is in personality similar to Aylwin, falls out of love with his editorial assistant because, though she is "quick, bright, interesting and hardworking," she is not "ambitious for herself." Oscar, the professor, confides to Louise, his ex-wife, that he wanted more from a woman than just a capable assistant (556). In Pym's novel, Aylwin, too, has apparently realized that he needs more from a woman than admiration and good typing, and that Dulcie, who can bully him about unsuitable marriages, has more to offer him precisely because she is independent. Along with wanting equality, Pym women in *No Fond Return of Love, An Unsuitable Attachment,* and *An Academic Question* begin to face some of the grimmer issues in life. They come to terms with class prejudice, marital infidelity, and death, as well as jumble sales and tea parties. As Annette Weld writes, "Issues of family, shelter, food, clothing, employment, worship, and leisure will still shape the fabric of her work, but will often be edged with black. Ten years of publishing success close with *No Fond Return of Love*" (148). From there on, there seems to be a tinge of sadness to Pym's work.

One sad fact of Pym's own professional life is that after *No Fond Return of Love* was published, Pym entered an agonizing period of "silence" during which she could get nothing published. The "dry period" began with Jonathan Cape's rejection of *An Unsuitable Attachment*. Pym wrote to Robert Smith on March 19, 1963, "I had a great blow from Cape, who said they didn't want to publish my novel . . . because they feared . . . they would not sell enough copies to make a profit! And that after six novels and thirteen years and even a small amount of prestige to the house of Cape" (Holt 193). Evidently, the book was not "saleable" to its publishers. Reasons for the book's rejection are too mysterious and varied to be covered here, but Annette Weld writes in *Barbara Pym and the Novel of Manners* that though the book "lacks the fairy tale charm" of some of Pym's earlier books, its "weaknesses are not those assigned by her publisher" (164). Weld seems to agree with Pym, who felt that the book was rejected because, "After the death of Jonathan Cape, the firm set out to collect a more contemporary cadre of authors, 'mostly men and American'" (*A Very Private Eye* 213). Weld observes that in the midst of the social upheaval of 1963, a book about a woman "worried about marrying beneath her must have seemed like a refugee from Jane Austen" (167).

*An Unsuitable Attachment* details the development of a love affair between two people who ostensibly make an unlikely pair, the librarian Ianthe Broome and her slightly younger colleague, John Challow. Other characters who play a major role in the novel are Sophia Ainger and Mark Ainger, a clergyman and his wife, their cat Faustina, and Penelope Grandison, Sophia's somewhat disorganized younger sister. Rupert Stonebird is the handsome male acquaintance who appears to be a suitable match for Ianthe, but he ends by aligning himself with Penelope. For Rupert, women are "convenient" creatures who are always about to "make coffee or tea" or had "just roasted a joint in the oven" (87). Rupert is one of many Pym men who find women interesting for the useful skills they might be able to serve their men with.

Ianthe Broome, a canon's daughter, is tall with dark hair that is beginning to gray. Like most of Pym's heroines, she is somewhere in her thirties. She has led a seemingly lonely life as the only child of elderly but well-off parents. Sophia Ainger believes at the beginning of *An Unsuitable Attachment* that Ianthe will never marry. As late as the trip to her aunt's Italian villa near the end of the story when Ianthe has confided to her that she is in love, Sophia tells Ianthe that Ianthe seems destined not to marry, that she will grow into "one of those splendid spinsters . . . who are pillars of the Church" (195). With "splendid spinsters," Sophia seems to have coined a term besides "excellent women" to describe those gentlewomen who serve others selflessly but never marry.

Sophia might be thinking of her aunt, Miss Grandison, who is a tall, pale, spooky woman with "mad-looking" dark eyes (187). The aunt always wears black and seems to haunt her own villa. Sophia speaks as she does because Ianthe's near perfection and admirable qualities worry her. Sophia sees Rupert as a "catch" for her younger, beatnik sister, Penelope Grandison. Some of the other characters disagree with Sophia and believe Ianthe would be a suitable wife for Rupert Stonebird. Penelope Grandison, in particular, fears Ianthe as competition for Rupert's affections. Besides John, who marries Ianthe, Rupert himself shows an interest in her and so does Mervyn Cantrell.

One reason Sophia may not see Ianthe as marriageable is that she seems to be nearly perfect. In fact, nearly everything about Ianthe is suitable and immaculate. All of her clothes suit her in what Penelope calls boring good taste that is "chillingly virginal" (69), and her antique furniture is the envy of her effeminate male colleague, Mervyn. Actually, in spite of her sometimes unusual appearance and supposed modernity, Penelope's values are conventional. For example, she has the "right" old fashioned idea that a husband's work takes first priority over a wife's interests in a marriage (69).

Despite her plan, however, Penelope thinks she is a poor competitor next to Ianthe for Rupert's affection. Penelope is a little sloppy and does not know how to cook. And she has a knack for wearing clothes that do not suit her. Through Penelope, Pym deflates the romantic stereotype of the bodice buster heroine. Penelope, with her red hair and strange eyes, resembles the physical description of romance heroines like Marietta Danvers of *Love's Tender Fury*. Her strange eyes do not, however, tempt Rupert Stonebird. To him, they have a "bruised look" that may be the result of improperly applied eyeshadow. And Penelope's beautiful hair does not flow behind her in a fiery mane as does that of the bodice buster wench. Instead, Penelope wears her hair in a "chaotic beehive," which Rupert observes makes her look like a "Pre-Raphaelite beatnik" (39). In short, Pym deflates the romantic elements of Penelope's appearance by giving a mundane explanation, e.g., improperly applied eye makeup, for their existence.

Yet, it is not Ianthe who is ultimately paired with Rupert. Ianthe surprises everyone by falling in love with John, who is younger and of lower class than she, as well as penniless. Rupert, on the other hand, shows a growing interest in the untidy Penelope. Penelope herself finds that Rupert does not quite fit her own knowledge of men. She is used to flirting with potential suitors and being asked to "the kind of restaurants she could mention without shame next day when her colleagues at work asked 'Where did he take you?'" (83). Yet, when one night before Christmas Penelope runs into Rupert while on her way home, she finds that Rupert does not respond to her flirtatious remarks. She recognizes that his is a different discourse from hers but she reasons, "It must have something to do with being an anthropologist . . . It seemed a dark mysterious sort of profession, perhaps in a way not quite manly, or not manly in the way she was used to" (83). Instead of taking her to a nice restaurant, Rupert takes her to a pub for a drink and, as he goes to order food, asks Penelope if she would like a sandwich. She declines, believing that he could hardly eat unless she did too (83). Penelope is surprised when Rupert returns with a ham sandwich for himself and is more startled when he devours the sandwich in her presence. As the narrator says, Penelope's life in some ways had been as "narrow and sheltered as Ianthe's. Men could and did eat sandwiches while their female companions ate nothing" (83). Thus, a man's gallantry at the table is another romantic myth that Pym deflates. In Pym's books, men self-centeredly satisfy their own hunger, regardless of who else may be present.

The love stories of Ianthe and John, and Rupert and Penelope, develop while the lives of the other characters fall into place. By the end of *An Unsuitable Attachment* Ianthe and John are together, and Penelope has won over Rupert Stonebird. At first glance, the unsuitable attachment that gives the novel its title appears to be the relationship between Ianthe and John. Yet, a closer look reveals that the real "unsuitable" attachments exist in relationships between other characters. For example, Sophia is too obsessed with Faustina, her cat, and with playing matchmaker for her sister, to pay much attention to her own husband. Ianthe's aunt and uncle suffer through a dry, loveless marriage and Dr. Pettigrew, the vet, leaves a broken marriage to make a home with his eccentric sister who performs charity work for cats. Mervyn, the middle-aged "mamma's boy" of the book, criticizes John Challow, but Mervyn only wants to marry Ianthe to acquire her antiques. In this novel, Pym comments on the class system that prevailed in British society by having her "princess," Ianthe, marry a mere worker, the "frog," and live happily ever after. Pym has revised the stories of *Cinderella* and *Jane Eyre,* with John playing the role of both the charwoman who marries a prince and the governess who marries the master of the house. The word "unsuitable" or variations of it appear frequently in the novel, at least thirty times, with Rupert and Ianthe using the word most often. It is ironic that, socially, they are the two who make "unsuitable" matches in that they marry for love, not class appropriateness.

Relationships of all types are explored in *An Unsuitable Attachment*, with all the characters providing social commentary. Pym uses the familiar pattern of a "broad and mostly comic collection of humanity" living in one parish as Annette Weld notes (149). Like *Crampton Hodnet*, the novel is structured around church festivals; like *Less Than Angels*, it deals with anthropologists. Finally, as in *Jane and Prudence*, a matchmaking heroine, "married to a vague if well-meaning clergyman," tries to marry off her friends (149). By the end of the novel, Ianthe and John choose to be together, despite what society thinks. To them, their attachment is romantically suitable. In spite of its happy ending and romantic plot, *An Unsuitable Attachment* marks the beginning of its author's difficulties with publishers. Yet, though apparently cursed, *An Unsuitable Attachment* shares much with Pym's other, successful novels.

One theme *An Unsuitable Attachment* shares with Pym's other works is a keen interest in food as a metaphor for romance. At one point in the book, Ianthe and Sophia visit Sophia's aunt, Miss Grandison, who has lived for many years in a small town in the south of Italy. Among other attractions, Miss Grandison's villa features a beautiful garden and a large lemon grove. As Sophia takes a walk through the lemon grove, she thinks about the little bundle of lemon leaves that was at her place at dinner. After the evening meal, she untied the little bundle and "began to remove leaf after leaf until the fragrant raisins were revealed at the centre" (196). Sophia believes that peeling off the layers of lemon leaves has something to do with uncovering the secrets of the heart (196).

The fact that dried leaves can yield the wonderful secret of sweet fruit is a metaphor; maybe Ianthe, who is over thirty, can still have a fruitful and full life. Of the lemon leaves, Annette Weld says in *Barbara Pym and the Novel of Manners*, "Those beautifully wrapped, hidden sweets carry enough metaphorical weight for Pym that she considered both *Wrapped in Lemon Leaves* and *Among the Lemon Leaves* as titles for the book" (151). In fact, Pym writes in *A Very Private Eye*, that she loved Italy for its lemon groves. Pym mentions, in particular, the bundles of leaves that when unwrapped, reveal "a few delicious lemon-flavored raisins in the middle" (202). The sedately, but beautifully "wrapped" or dressed Ianthe is hiding or repressing hidden sexual sweets for John Challow of which she isn't aware. Sophia thinks that Ianthe needed to come to Italy to realize that she loved John, and that Sophia has helped her to admit her feelings by helping Ianthe to probe the layers of her heart as if they were dried lemon leaves (196). Later, when Sophia learns of the impending marriage between John and Ianthe, she muses, "The lemon leaves had been unwrapped and there were the fragrant raisins at the heart" (248).

The visit to Italy with its fragrant lemon leaves and delicious food has inspired some of the characters of *An Unsuitable Attachment* to imitate Italian cooking. Sophia has been cooking spaghetti enthusiastically since her visit. Penelope, after her return home, invites Mark and Sophia to dinner and attempts to cook spaghetti bolognese. Mark is surprised that the meal Penelope cooks is delicious (228). Actually, it is so good that the recipe appears in *The Barbara Pym Cookbook*. Penelope observes that the secret of her sauce is that she cooked it very slowly for hours and hours (228). Like the lemon leaves earlier, the slowly simmering sauce is a metaphor for the relationship that is "slowly cooking" between Penelope and Rupert. Suitably enough, almost every meeting between Penelope and Rupert involves food. In the last scene of the novel, Rupert approaches Penelope at a garden behind St. Paul's Cathedral. The garden is scattered with bits of broken marble. He finds Penelope with a half eaten sandwich in her hand. Like Penelope's simmering sauce, or like the slowly unwrapped lemon leaves, the half sandwich represents the unknown possibilities of a love affair between Penelope and Rupert. Without Rupert, Penelope's life is half-lived just as her sandwich is half-eaten.

While Penelope and Rupert enjoy Italian food, other characters find Italian food too rich and exotic, so that a distrust of anything foreign is manifested in a Pym story. For example, when Mervyn, John, and Ianthe discuss Italian food, Mervyn declares grated cheese on everything is too rich for his mother and that cannelloni is overrated. He laments that Italian coffee is served half a cup at a time and is not even cappucino (132). Poor Mervyn—like the cup of cappucino, his life is only half-full. He is only able to love Ianthe for her furniture and ornaments, and considers her more as a replacement for his elderly mother than a wife (202). As a humorous comment on Mervyn's Oedipal condition, Pym contrives the plot so that he and Ianthe meet Penelope and her friend "Jocasta" in the restaurant shortly after Ianthe and Mervyn have discussed marriage to each other. In this instance food and eating at a restaurant serve as props and setting for the comedic proposal of marriage from Mervyn to Ianthe. Pym is subtle, and the characters themselves are unaware of the laughable situation in which they play a role. The humor is not lost, however, on an observer, or for that matter, on the reader.

Restaurants serve as props for other romantic settings as well. For example, the last scene of the book features Rupert and Penelope in an outdoor setting behind St. Paul's where people eat lunch. The lush gardens evoke images of Adam and Eve. The pieces of broken marble give the scene a "Love Among the Ruins" flavor. Rupert himself sees a middle-aged woman sitting among the heaps of broken marble and thinks, "If only this could have been Penelope . . . what a splendid and unusual place for a love scene" (256). Pym deflates the romantic setting by having a middle-aged woman in place of Penelope. But Pym deflates the romance in another way, too. The heaps of marble behind St. Paul's bring to mind Rome, with its classical ruins, and the scene at the Spanish Steps where Rupert first realized his love for Penelope. What one must remember is that a similar romantic evening in Rome gave Henry James's heroine Daisy Miller the fever that killed her.[33]

Pym not only alludes to classical continental settings, but also to classic literary situations involving matchmakers. Sophia Ainger is a somewhat humorous matchmaker whose own marriage is bizarre, to say the least. Sophia is not one of Pym's observers, although she likes to fix her sister up with men. Despite her disinterest in observing others, Sophia does have a vivid imagination. Once, while walking home, Sophia had "seen a cluster of what she took to be exotic tropical fruits in one of the windows, only to realize that they were tomatoes put there to ripen" (*An Unsuitable Attachment* 16). Sophia looks for touches of romance in everyday life, but the reality of what she thinks she sees is often disappointingly common and everyday. Perhaps it is because her imagination has disappointed her that Sophia is not curious about others' lives. For consolation, Sophia becomes absorbed in her cat. There are even times when being a good wife means to Sophia that she rewards her husband with food the way she does her cat.

In fact, Sophia sees food as a reward for others as well. For example, Ianthe's aunt and uncle, the Burdons, pay Sophia a surprise visit while she is trying to feed liquid paraffin to Faustina with an apostle spoon (220). Because she is a vicar's wife and Ianthe's neighbor, the Burdons have come to seek her aid. They are distressed about the relationship between Ianthe and John. Though she is distracted by the visitors, Sophia can provide a decent tea of sponge cake and thin brown bread and butter. She decides on quince jelly and discovers it is Randolph Burdon's favorite, so she gives him a jar to take with him. Sophia senses that Randolph is more interested in the jelly than in Ianthe's love affairs and she gives him the jar as a prize for his patience. Sophia thinks, "At least he [Randolph] would be taking away a pot of his favorite jelly . . . which was a great deal more than one usually got out of trying to interfere in other people's business" (224).

Interfering in others' business, even when that business concerns what the characters will eat, is a pastime for other people in the novel, too. For example, Lady Selvedge, the titled but tight friend of Sophia's mother, makes a "shielding movement" around someone else's pudding at a cafeteria, then infuriates the young man by implying people of his class (lower than hers) are better off eating greens (58). Lady Selvedge does not elaborate on the type of greens, but she comments in an "audible whisper" to Mrs. Grandison, "Those sort of people eat far too much *starch*" (58). She apparently practices colonialism at the dining table because she "colonizes" the young man's meal by appropriating his dessert. When he complains, she implies that she, an upper-class, more knowledgeable woman, takes the pudding for his own good. Since he is of a lower social class, he is not savvy enough to know that simple greens are better for him than dessert.

While people dine out in Pym's novels, they also have interesting meals at home. For example, Penelope peers into Rupert's house one evening and sees Rupert and the back of a dark-haired woman as well as the "remains of a kind of a meal—a loaf of bread, a hunk of . . . cheese and two glasses—were set out on one half of the table. Altogether it was a little disturbing—the man, the woman, the Omar Khayyam-like details" (54). But Penelope is relieved and the romance is deflated because Penelope's rival is only the anthropologist Miss Clovis, that dumpy, dog-haired "excellent woman" from *Less Than Angels.*

Food is also an indicator used to define excellent women in *An Unsuitable Attachment.* For example, excellent women are kind to those less fortunate than they and bring the poor unfortunates gifts of food. Whether the excellent women like the less fortunate or not is not important. Lonely men, in particular are good candidates for gifts of food. For example, Ianthe gives the repressed homosexual Mervyn crystallized fruits for Christmas (73). Though Ianthe apparently did not consciously choose Mervyn's gifts as a comment on his sexuality, the crystallized fruit is ironically appropriate. Single, retired librarians like Miss Grimes may also be proper recipients of food baskets. Ianthe, moreover, is an excellent woman who chooses foods she believes to be appropriate as gifts. Early in the book, right before Christmas, Ianthe brings the somewhat elderly and unmarried Miss Grimes chicken breasts in aspic, shortbread, and chocolates, but brings sausage rolls to Rupert's party where men are present. Miss Grimes, however, surprises Ianthe. Miss Grimes begins the visit by grabbing out of the basket the purple violets and madeira that were Ianthe's Christmas gifts from John Challow and Mervyn, respectively (76). Ianthe is disconcerted, but too polite to point out Miss Grimes's error. Moreover, Ianthe is shocked that a supposedly genteel gentlewoman would "scrabble" for violets and be so pleased by an alcoholic beverage. The purple violets, which as intended for Ianthe symbolize the colors of passion, mourning, and frigid virginity, were a gift from John expressing his love. They look to Ianthe out of place in Miss Grimes's not too clean hands.

In short, Miss Grimes does not fit Ianthe's discourse of the distressed gentlewoman, and Miss Grimes knows this and pokes a bit of fun at the notion. Miss Grimes deflates the romanticized notion of the genteel, properly brought up woman now fallen on hard times by saying to Ianthe that she rather likes the idea of being a distressed gentlewoman because the term has a "nice old-world sound" (76). Moreover, Miss Grimes collects bits of antique china because she enjoys them and she says "people think more of you if you have nice things—as if you'd once had a 'beautiful home'" (76). Mervyn certainly thinks more of Ianthe than he does of other women because she has nice furnishings and antiques. On the other hand, Mervyn has no love for distressed gentlewomen like Miss Grimes. In the early part of the book he tries to force her out of her job. When Miss Grimes does leave, Mervyn is relieved and says of her rather cruelly that "one gets so tired of willing gentlewomen of uncertain age" (49). Mervyn also disparages the two women who run the Hummingbird restaurant, where Ianthe eats, by saying that he can't bear the two women because they are "English gentlewomen with a vengeance . . . the kind that have made England what she is" (48). Mervyn apparently means that Mrs. Harper and Miss Burge, the restaurant owners, have contributed to the downfall of Mervyn's England.

Miss Grimes is undaunted by people like Mervyn who disparage gentlewomen. Not even society can discourage her. She also gleefully plays along with visiting social workers by submitting her weekly food budget. Miss Grimes then laughs when the social worker objects to her weekly bottle of cheap burgundy and tells Miss Grimes to buy haricot beans and lentils instead. Miss Grimes says to Ianthe, "They'd got it all worked out what we ought to eat—would you believe it!" (77). Privately, Ianthe agrees with the social workers because it shocks her to think about an old woman drinking wine alone in her bed-sitting room. On learning of Miss Grimes's true personality, Ianthe, like Woolf's Orlando, loses some of her illusions. Still, Ianthe feels chicken breasts in aspic and haricot beans and lentils are more suitable (77). Thus Ianthe uses food to classify people.

Regardless of the type and quantity of food, there is an etiquette involved in delivering food to the unfortunate, and, as Sister Dew, the busybody nurse who lives in Ianthe's parish, notes, one does not take food to a lone woman as to a lone man (218). Sister Dew does not explain why this maxim is so.

Sometimes, a delivery of food implies a gift of love, just as it did in *Some Tame Gazelle*. When Penelope discovers that Ianthe has brought Rupert an oxtail she takes it to mean that Rupert is involved with Ianthe. Penelope experiences a "mixture" of scorn and jealousy, and she is momentarily angry with Ianthe for the gesture because to her, gifts of food imply gifts of love (87). Self-conscious about her actions, Ianthe takes John Challow food as a kind of gift of love when he is ill. Ostensibly, she relieves Mervyn of the duty because he is reluctant to go. Mervyn believes that women instinctively know what to do in an illness (108). In this episode, Mervyn sees Ianthe as Patmore's Angel of the House performing her assigned role. It does not occur to him that Ianthe may have feelings for John and would be genuinely distressed by news of his illness and discomfort.

Ianthe, on the other hand, is not quite sure of her feelings because she has suppressed her sexual urges for a long time. When John first comes to work in the library, Ianthe admits that there is something disturbing about him, but she does not know how to label her carnal feelings and thus does not recognize that she finds John sexually attractive. Ianthe admits that she could not share her feelings with anyone but herself (45). Ianthe does, however, have a romantic notion of what it is like to visit a sickroom. She imagines John tossing on his "bed of fever" and sees images of daffodils and lemon barley water (108). (In romance novels by Jennifer Wilde and Kathleen Woodiwiss, wounded heroes often toss on their own beds of fever. Pym borrows the term from the discourse of the romance novel.) The practical suggestion that Ianthe take John Beecham's powders, evidently a cold medication, disconcerts her somewhat. The image of Ianthe's dead mother surfaces reprovingly in Ianthe's brain at the thought that perhaps there has been a mistake and John is not ill. Then, Ianthe, an older, single woman, would be in the compromising position of visiting a single man in his bed-sitting room. It would appear as if she were throwing herself at him. Ianthe fears public censure and she does meet her old dressmaker, Miss Statham, on the way to John's residence. Ianthe is at a loss to explain her appearance, and Miss Statham assumes Ianthe is visiting a woman (110). Miss Statham's annoying presence notwithstanding, Ianthe continues on her mission of mercy to John. For the briefest moment, there is in Ianthe's psyche the twinge of the bodice buster heroine's daring streak for Ianthe realizes that "she was feeling almost excited, as if she were going on an adventurous journey into unknown country" (109).

For Ianthe in *An Unsuitable Attachment,* even bland and indifferent poached eggs can be romantic. When she has lunch with John she thinks: "There was to her something romantic about the idea of sitting with him in the place where she had so often sat alone, eating a poached egg or macaroni cheese at a shaky little oak table. . . . The eating of eggs together had not figured in the romantic picture, perhaps no actual food had suggested itself" (133). To Ianthe, it is the company that transforms even the most indifferent food to a romantic feast. The food by itself, no matter how tasty or elaborate, has no magical properties.

Digestive peculiarities also affect how romantic Ianthe feels. The elegance of a kiss is once again diminished in a Pym novel because the heroine refuses to attribute her lack of appetite to her amorous feelings. When John kisses her, Ianthe does not want supper. Then, she remembers she had an unaccustomed poached egg for tea and before John kissed her and she is glad to have found "a sensible reason for her lack of appetite" (137). For the repressed Ianthe to admit her romantic feelings might be dangerous for her; she would admit she was losing control over her life because of her love for a man. When Ianthe returns from Italy, however, she feels different. She is, by then, ready to accept John's love.

While *An Unsuitable Attachment* centers on the lives of Ianthe and Penelope, two single women, one "flamboyant," one "tiresomely good," the novel showcases other couples like the Aingers and the Burdons to explore what exactly an unsuitable attachment is. Pym also paints portraits of spouses who are bereft of their husbands and wives because of death and divorce to illustrate what the unhappy results of an unsuitable attachment might be. The literary portraits Pym paints are those of Rupert Stonebird, Lady Selvedge, and Edwin Pettigrew. By the end of *An Unsuitable Attachment,* it is not class, age, or mutual interest that make Ianthe and John a suitable couple. Instead, John and Ianthe are well-matched because they share love for each other, heavily dosed with sexual chemistry.

*An Academic Question* continues to develop the issue of what type of marital union is suitable. This novel is Pym's exploration into still another type of marriage, that of the academic wife. Pym wrote *An Academic Question* from 1970 to 1972. After Pym's death, Hazel Holt revised the novel and published it posthumously. According to Orphia Jane Allen, in her book *Barbara Pym, Writing a Life,* "*An Academic Question* sparkles with the wit and humor of Pym's earlier work" (37). Furthermore, Allen compares Caroline Grimstone (Caro), the heroine, to Mildred Lathbury of *Excellent Women.* Both women tell their stories in first person, and both are consummate observers of others' lives. Allen is correct, but Caro is far more stylish than Mildred, and she is a married woman with a small child. As Allen herself points out, *An Academic Question* is significant because it "contains Pym's most extended treatment of young children" (37). Caro is the only Pym heroine who actually has a young child, Kate the toddler. Allen further notes that Pym does not develop the child's character (37).

The story of *An Academic Question* is told from Caro's perspective as an attractive but bored academic wife. Subplots include Caro's worry that Alan, her husband, is having an affair with a beautiful divorcée, Iris Horniblow, who has two unruly children. As it turns out, Alan has had an affair with another young woman. Another underlying story in the novel concerns Alan's attempts as a professor to gain academic renown and promotion. Desperate to succeed in the often vicious academic competition, Alan has Caro steal a manuscript from the dying Dr. Stillingfleet, an ancient professor emeritus who is spending his last days at Normanhurst, the old peoples' home. Touches of irony enhance the plot, too. Caro has wanted a job to alleviate her boredom, but her husband doesn't approve. He allows her to work at Normanhurst, where she reads to old people, so that she will have an opportunity to steal Dr. Stillingfleet's manuscript.

By the end of *An Academic Question,* Caro and Alan are still together, but there is little hope that they have learned anything valuable about themselves or their relationships. The novel's theme of time passing is somewhat sad, and is, according to Orphia Allen, reflected in the treatment of Normanhurst and in the retirement of Alan's department head, Dr. Maynard. As the novel ends, Caro is still a well-dressed but bored academic wife, and Alan is still too caught up in his own career to notice his wife's needs.

Caro, for all her apparent self-absorption, is as much of a helpmeet to her man as any Pym heroine. In many ways, academic and other wives like Caro are the ultimate helpmeets and excellent women because they subordinate their own feelings and desires to those of their husbands. Where characters like Jessie Morrow of both *Crampton Hodnet* and *Jane and Prudence* and Mildred Lathbury of *Excellent Women* retain their individualism and personalities, the personalities of academic wives in Pym's work are often submerged into their husband's research. Not everyone sees Caro as a good academic wife, though. A. S. Byatt writes in "Barbara Pym" that Hazel Holt actually gave the book its title after Pym's death when she edited the novel and had it published (241). Pym actually began the novel in 1970. Byatt claims Caroline Grimstone's name is a reference to Lady Caroline Lamb (Byatt 241). She calls Caroline, who calls herself Caro, "simply horrid," and accuses her of being self-centered and of judging people on their failure to dress well (241). Throughout *An Academic Question,* Caro constantly worries about her looks and takes advice from various people about her appearance.

One person Caro listens to is Coco. Coco, a gay man, keeps trying to tell Caro how to dress. One is reminded of Catherine in *Less Than Angels* who writes that men like to form women's tastes for them (129). Still, Caro does not really need Coco's help because she is always well-dressed. For her, stylish outfits help fulfill an otherwise empty life. Caro really has nothing to do but plan her wardrobe. In contrast to Caro, the busy woman Caro's husband has an affair with is careless about her looks.

Because her life is empty, Caro, the heroine of *An Academic Question,* is possibly the most disgruntled of Pym's heroines. Caro, like other academic wives portrayed in the novel, does not really work. Instead, she helps with her husband's research and with his crime. Caro also works occasionally in the library (8). In general, Pym's academic wives are excellent housekeepers and cooks and do all their husband's typing as well (7). Caro is even more isolated than most wives; she is not a great cook and her husband, Alan, does his own typing; therefore, she is further cut off from him (7). Caro reads women's magazines, so she is aware of her failures as a wife. She sighs because the beautiful kitchens and bright bathrooms do not belong in her home (16). Alan would like Caro to get a job with the research department indexing cards because indexing is work that would help him, but she is reluctant because she sees how unhappy other wives are who index (16). The only way she can help her husband is to purloin a manuscript from a dying professor. Like Jane Cleveland, Caro has only one child, Kate, and she is even detached from Kate because she has no particular maternal feeling. Also, the other academic wives are not as expensively or stylishly dressed as Caro, so she feels estranged from them.

There is, however, more to Caro than her fine wardrobe. She is interested in the other people's lives, too. Caro, like other Pym women, is a sharp observer. She is critical of her husband's writing, just as Catherine is critical of Tom's thesis in *Less Than Angels*. Caro views scholarly writing as "no more than a ten-page article in an obscure missionary journal" (24). Caro notes people's clothes as if she were a "novelist storing useful information" (97). Caro thus takes part in an activity her creator enjoyed. She also attends social functions to observe the other guests and is prepared to enjoy herself "with detachment" at Miss Clovis's funeral (93). Perhaps Miss Clovis's funeral is more symbolic than one realizes at first glance. Miss Clovis, the ultimate dog-haired "excellent woman" who made tea at anthropological functions though she herself was a capable anthropologist, may symbolize another era. With her death, perhaps the "excellent woman" dies in Pym's fiction and becomes the disgruntled woman Caro represents.

Because Caro's husband has an affair, infidelity makes Caro distrust all other women, even excellent ones. She views single women, in particular, with suspicion. Caro suspects that her husband has been having an affair with a divorced colleague. In reality, Caro's husband, Alan, is having the affair with a younger woman named, appropriately, Cressida. Caro feels that her enemies are the unattached, but that they would be surprised to know that they were her foes (64). Caro recognizes that marriage gives her social status that single women lack.

But, though Caro may view the unattached with suspicion, at times she wishes she were one of them. The role of academic wife weighs heavily on her; she longs for the freedom to choose her own work. For example, at times, Caro indicates she would like to be a writer. Like Sophia Ainger of *An Unsuitable Attachment,* Caro possesses some of the descriptive talents of a romance writer. She wishes she were in a novel, "or even some other person's life where we could have gone back to his flat or to a hotel, sleazily romantic with heavy dingy lace curtains" (96). According to the novels Caro reads, deliciously illicit love affairs take place in rooms hung with dingy lace. Because the love affair is illicit, the lace curtains are dingy so no one can see through them. Besides, pure, clean, white lace curtains could imply the purity of marital union. In Caro's mind, sex with Alan has become boring. Like many a romance heroine, Caro craves romance and adventure when, in reality, her life is dull and predictable. In fact, Caro, Ianthe, and Dulcie do have traits in common with romance heroines. All three find themselves caught in some sort of love triangle and all three are gifted with keen powers of observation.

Talented though they are, however, Caro, Ianthe, and Dulcie often find themselves alone, contemplating their own expectations for their lives as well as those that others have for them. Part of the "happy end-ings" that evolve for these three women consists in realizing that they can have full lives without giving in to the expectations of others in their societies. For example, Ianthe is capable of choosing to marry the man she loves. Ianthe keeps her integrity in this respect although her rela-tives, and her society, find her choice unsuitable. Ianthe rebels against ideas of what is suitable for her, especially Sophia's idea that Ianthe will never marry but will instead be a splendid spinster serving the Church of England.

Dulcie, too, chooses to marry only for love. Although her fiancé has broken their engagement, Dulcie takes positive steps to take her mind off her sorrows. Life does not end for her because she is older and single. Dulcie attends conferences, maintains a large home, looks after others, and socializes. Like Ianthe, she enjoys good food and refuses to be stereotyped as a thirtysomething spinster. Caro's life is a little different from the lives of Ianthe and Dulcie, but she, too, manages to remain her-self throughout the book. Alan, her husband, wants her to be a proper academic wife who lives to proofread and index for him while wearing drab clothes. Caro, however, expresses herself through her impeccable taste in clothes and enjoys herself with more flamboyant acquaintances than Alan. For example, she is frequently in the company of Coco and his mother. Of the three, Caro's life remains somewhat unsatisfactory at the end of the novel, but she does make the best of situations that would defeat other women. Caro can even treat her husband's infidelity in a more offhand manner than is usually done in literature. The ending to Caro's story may be more pragmatic than happy because Pym was experimenting with a more realistic, in her terms, "less cozy" format. Pym wrote *An Academic Question* during the time when she could not get published. She was attempting a "more swinging" style that would appeal to a more modern audience. So, Hazel Holt indicates in *A Lot to Ask* that Caro is a transitional heroine; she is an excellent woman who was forced to behave as a 1970s academic wife (Holt 228). As an academic wife, Caro became familiar with issues like abortion, infidelity, and intellectual dishonesty. In any case, any decisions Caro, Ianthe, and Dulcie make for themselves are not tinged with regret and bitterness. They are aware that life can always hold positive changes and possibilities.

The same, however, cannot be said for the characters of *The Sweet Dove Died, Quartet in Autumn,* and *A Few Green Leaves.* In these last three novels, regret and bitterness move closer to center stage than they have ever been in a Pym novel.

# 6

# The Bittersweet Desserts of Excellent Women:
# What to Do When Mr. Rochester
# Has Left the Building

The novels discussed in Chapter 5, *No Fond Return of Love, An Unsuitable Attachment,* and *An Academic Question,* all involve attachments that may seem unsuitable to some, but that result in some type of happy relationship. *No Fond Return of Love* and *An Unsuitable Attachment* involve single, "excellent women," who also fulfill the roles of romance heroines. *An Academic Question* deals with a wife who must endure a "rival woman" and who must also steal a manuscript for her husband to prove she loves him. All three novels are love stories. In these novels, Pym treats love lightly, with humor and comic irony.

Pym's subversion of the romance genre is often lighthearted, ironic, and witty in *No Fond Return of Love, An Unsuitable Attachment,* and *An Academic Question.* Death, when it appears, is a bit player. The same is not true, though, of the three novels that will be discussed in Chapter 6. *The Sweet Dove Died, Quartet in Autumn,* and *A Few Green Leaves* also have their humorous moments, but the humor is laced with sadness; at times, the humor is laced with regret or bitterness as well.

The relationships in *The Sweet Dove Died* are often painful and humiliating for those involved. Furthermore, one of the themes in *The Sweet Dove Died* is the decay of beauty. The heroine, Leonora Eyre, struggles with loneliness and aging. Leonora also suffers pain because she twice loses to youthful rivals the younger man who is the object of her affection. *Quartet in Autumn,* on the other hand, is the least romantic of Pym's books. The older, single women who are Pym's heroines in this novel lead isolated lives; they are forgotten by society and bereft of friends and family.

Yet Pym's elderly heroines are not forgotten by everyone. They exist in the imaginations of some of Pym's younger heroines as reminders of what their fate will be if they remain unmarried. For example, the heroine of *A Few Green Leaves,* Emma Howick, acts as if she has read *The Sweet Dove Died* and *Quartet in Autumn.* In her mid-to-late thirties, she instinctively knows what her fate will be if she remains a spinster. More likely than not, she will be poor and lonely. Moreover, there are plenty of older spinsters in the novel who serve as examples of what might happen to her. In *A Few Green Leaves,* Pym undermines romance by showing its hollowness; it fails its devotees after they age and lose their first youth, as it fails one devotee, Miss Grundy, the former romance novelist. For Miss Grundy, Miss Lickerish, Miss Vereker, and Daphne Dagnall, the single women of *A Few Green Leaves,* there is no Mr. Rochester waiting for them. Instead of love and happy endings, Pym's last three novels are full of irony, pathos, grim humor, and contrasting portraits of loneliness. The books are also about solitary existence that offers no support community. Diana Benet writes in *Something to Love* that Pym's last three novels are about the "failure to recognize the need for love" (119). Yet, maybe it is not so much that the characters fail to recognize that they need love. Instead, they may recognize that they need romance and to be loved but fail to locate a love interest. In other words, love may not be an option for an aged spinster.

One way in which some of the characters of Pym's last novels fail to obtain and keep a love interest is by competing against each other for the affections of another. The thrill of rivalry and of winning become ends in themselves for some characters. For example, Lotus Snow writes in *One Little Room an Everywhere* that *The Sweet Dove Died* is a novel woven of "ironic competitions" and contrasts (16). The main characters are Leonora Eyre, Humphrey Boyce, and his apparently bisexual nephew, James. The two men run an antique shop that sells porcelain, bronzes and small objects. Snow describes James at twenty-four as beautiful but not too intelligent, and "sexually ambivalent" (16). James's uncle, a widower near sixty, is self-assured, financially successful, and pompous. The two meet Leonora after she faints at an auction of antique books, and they immediately begin to compete for her favors.

Leonora is sexually cold but is attracted to the beautiful and passive James. Both Humphrey and James love beautiful objects, and Leonora uses these to ensnare them. Also, James could be the younger version of Leonora; they often have the same thoughts and refer to themselves in the third person as "one." Leonora is also brittle, harsh, vain, and elegant. She has no compassion for anyone but herself. Her friends, Meg and Liz, provide ironic foils for her own aloof personality. Liz is divorced; Meg is a spinster. While Leonora fulfills her need for something to love with the vapid James, Liz cares for Siamese cats. Meg, however, is infatuated with a young, gay boy, Colin, much younger than Meg, who continually leaves her and returns to her.

According to Annette Weld, Pym felt that *The Sweet Dove Died* was one of the best books she had ever written (171). The story paralleled her own unrequited affection for Richard Roberts, a man younger than she, who was an antique dealer (171). Like Leonora, Pym often suffered from Roberts's indifference and in 1962 she wrote about "the middle-aged or elderly novelist and the young man who admires her and is taken in by her [though] he is cruel to her" (MS. 55 Fol.16 Qtd in Groner 5). James Boyce may not have been as emotionally cruel to Leonora as Richard Roberts was to Pym, but James did take advantage of Leonora. For example, he accepted shelter, gifts, and food from her as if it these were his due. In accepting good food and in allowing himself to be waited on, James is not so different from other Pym men.

If food for Leonora is a way of keeping James close to her, it is also a means of maintaining her own isolated existence and for emphasizing her love of perfection. The scene at the tearoom is an excellent example. Leonora prefers dainty, creme-filled *gateau* with her tea. Like her, these tiny cakes are fancy, but without much substance. When Phoebe, a younger girlfriend of James and a rival for Leonora's affections, although Leonora is not aware of this at the time, inadvertently takes the last *gateau,* Leonora is at a loss. Her perfect world is physically diminished and she must settle for another kind of cake. Perhaps the incident is a metaphor for Leonora's relationship with James. At one point, James says he feels like a creme cake, and Leonora does, at least temporarily, lose her "creme cake," James, to Phoebe. She must settle for her second-favorite cake, as she must settle for the affections of Humphrey, her second-favorite man, by the end of the novel.

Leonora, moreover, is different from other Pym women because food, drink, and clothing do not in themselves provide satisfaction for her. Instead, these simple necessities only become pleasures for Leonora when they serve to preserve her beauty and to maintain her elegant but isolated existence. For example, she dresses in extremely good taste in styles that are calculated not to reveal her age. When an outfit makes her look older, Leonora is not aware of the effect. So, only Humphrey notes that the black lace dress she wears on one occasion makes her look washed out. Furthermore, when James comments on an outfit's aging effect by calling it Leonora's "autumnal outfit," Leonora becomes flirtatious with James. She is able to flirt with James about her clothes because she is a narcissistic woman who feels "secure enough" to joke with him. When James refers to her dress as autumnal, Leonora quips, "You mean that I look old? That I'm in the autumn of life?" (*The Sweet Dove Died* 47). According to Diana Benet in *Something to Love,* that may be exactly what James means (124), but Leonora cannot accept his comment other than as a joke because she sees herself as ageless.

Perhaps because she considers herself to be ageless, Leonora is one of the most romantic of Pym's heroines. Diana Benet in *Something to Love* calls her an older Prudence Bates (119). In some ways, Leonora seems to have stepped right out of a Barbara Cartland romance novel. For example, like many Cartland heroines, she belongs in a nineteenth-century culture. In one scene, she looks into a flawed antique fruitwood mirror and is pleased to see a woman she thinks is from another century (89). The mirror is "flawed," moreover, because it hides her age lines and aging skin. Also, because of a legacy from her parents that has left her financially well-off, Leonora no longer has to work at her "unworthy occupation" of seeing textbooks through the press (17). Besides, Leonora loves perfection, romance, and antiques. Her boring occupation could not really provide her with these amenities.

Leonora loves perfection, even in her surroundings, and hides a pitcher that is chipped. Yet while she may be an incurable romantic, Leonora is not a pleasant or considerate person. She resembles the scheming Madame Merle in Henry James's *Portrait of a Lady.* In fact, Leonora herself reads Henry James (200). Moreover, the plot of *A Few Green Leaves,* which involves an affair between an older woman and a younger man, somewhat undermines the standard romance plot where the hero is often slightly older than the heroine.

In some ways, Leonora's experiments with men echo gothic romance plots. Yet, unlike the gothic heroine, Leonora has an aversion to sex. At one point, while Leonora and Humphrey are walking, she sees a giant totem pole in the park, "shattering the peaceful beauty of the landscape" (37). Leonora thinks, "What a hideous phallic symbol . . . but of course one wouldn't mention it, only hurry by with head averted" (37). Passionate kisses also revolt her (92). Ironically, *The Sweet Dove Died* is one of Pym's more sexually explicit novels. For example, Humphrey fumbles with the front of Leonora's dress as he tries to kiss her, and she recoils in panic:

He is going to kiss me, Leonora thought in sudden panic, pray heaven no more than that. She tried to protest, even to scream, but no sound came. Humphrey was larger and stronger than she was and his kiss very different from the reverent touch on lips, cheek or brow which was all James seemed to want. . . . Surely freedom from this sort of thing was among the compensations of advancing age . . . one really ought not to be having to fend people off any more. (92)

Leonora, like other extremely self-centered women, finds the physical side of love distasteful. She is, in some ways, like a character created by Elizabeth Taylor, a friend of Pym's. In Taylor's *Angel,* the heroine is a romance novelist who writes lurid tales of love, but who shrinks from sex. The narrator says, "Like many romantic narcissistic women she shied away from the final act of love-making" (155).

Furthermore, Jane Nardin writes that Leonora does not want the emotional pain she may open herself up to by loving someone else (123). Neither does she care to substitute an animal. She is totally absorbed in her self and sustained by narcissism. For her, a full life consists of a home filled with her objects, decorated to her taste, and reflecting her own solitude and independence.

Phoebe, Leonora's rival for James's affections, is the opposite of "perfect" Leonora. Though Phoebe is a would-be author, her fiction is unexceptional. Her poetry is even worse. Phoebe is not a good housekeeper, either; in fact, her housekeeping and cooking are downright disastrous. As Weld notes, Phoebe, who wears unusual clothes and is artistic, has a few traits in common with Catherine Oliphant of *Less Than Angels,* but she lacks Catherine's talent for writing and for cooking (175). In Susan Gorsky's terms, described in Chapter 1, Phoebe does not make a satisfactory rival woman. Ned, James's homosexual friend, makes a far better rival for James's affections. Ned thrives on the drama of romance and for him the climax is "the defeat of a rival, the passion of a moment, the familiar *ennui,* the infidelities and the theatrical partings" (204). In fact, Ned sees himself as a protagonist in many of these situations. Really, Ned is very much a male Prudence Bates.

If Ned is the protagonist of the novel, James is the romantic hero. James is the nephew of an antique dealer, Humphrey Boyce. Both James and Humphrey are interested in Leonora, but for different reasons. Marlene San Miguel Groner writes in her dissertation on Pym, *The Novels of Barbara Pym,* that James has no concept of reality other than what Leonora places on him (83). He does not know who he is yet, so he allows others to define his roles in life. Leonora, like the heroines discussed in Chapter 3, manages to transform James into her ideal and perfect companion. In fact, James himself feels at times that Leonora created him (*The Sweet Dove Died* 51). Groner writes that as long as James and Leonora share the same "fictive reality," James is content to play the part Leonora writes for him (83). In playing the part that Leonora writes for him, however, James has lost whatever portion of his personality is already formed. He is passive, not at all Byronic and unoriginal. He has beautiful golden hair like a cherub, but he lacks character. He does not even have the ridiculous idiosyncrasies or quirks that other

Pym heroes have, which make them interesting. James is at a loss on how to deal with the relationships in his life, particularly with the controlling Leonora. Groner writes that he identifies with neutered cats and kittens and other caged animals (84). For example, the flat Leonora prepares for him at the top of her own house has bars on its windows. When James notices the bars with some chagrin, Leonora assures him that the room was probably a nursery (129). In some ways, the room is like the one that imprisons the heroine of Charlotte Perkins Gilman's *The Yellow Wallpaper;* there seems to be no escape for James from the clutches of Leonora.

Yet the nursery motif fits the immature James, too. It is a comic way for Pym to deal with the Oedipal attraction between James and the much older Leonora. Perhaps Pym was parodying herself a bit, and her involvement with the younger Richard Roberts. Weld also notes that James is the "sweet dove" of Keats' poem for which the novel is named.[34] Pym degrades further the image of the Byronic hero in James. Though handsome, James is neither heroic nor passionate. Instead, he is petulant and childlike. James is like a child who eats too many creme cakes; he quickly sickens on Leonora.

While Pym writes of creme cakes, she hasn't much to write about wedding cake in *The Sweet Dove Died.* Yet marriage is present in the novel, if only in the way that Leonora rejects it. She considers her married acquaintances to be silly, and rejects the institution itself by refusing to be insulted by people who wonder why she has not married. Leonora also rejects suitable social roles for single women, many of which are discussed in Chapter 3. For example, she is not at all interested in church jumble sales or in charity work. Leonora reasons that she has not married because, as with everything else, she would expect perfection in marriage. Of course, no one has lived up to Leonora's inhumanly perfect expectations.

While Leonora Eyre seems to be a bit inhuman because of her love of perfection, the characters of *Quartet in Autumn* are all too human, leading solitary, imperfect lives full of pathos. *Quartet in Autumn* is the story of four office workers in late middle age. Marcia, Letty, Edwin, and Norman have seen each other every day at work for years, but they have virtually nothing to do with each other outside work. Instead, each lives a life that centers on his or her idiosyncrasies and on how to survive in a world increasingly hostile to older people who are alone. None of the four has family nearby, either. Letty has never married; she is, perhaps, what Belinda Bede might have become had she not had Harriet. Edwin is a widower, but his children live far away, so he is not close to them or to his grandchildren. As a result, the Church has become his family; his entire discourse is centered on religious affairs and he seems very contented with his lot. Norman is cantankerous and appears to be unfriendly; but he proves a capable friend to the others. Marcia is the most isolated and the most eccentric of the four. She collects and organizes tinned food and plastic bags, and is very specific about which milk bottles she will store in her shed. Marcia dresses in garments that resemble the tatters of a jester or of Harlequin, yet she is a kind of aging, romantic princess. In her mind, her surgeon is the Prince Charming she was denied in her youth.

After Marcia and Letty retire, the four have little to do with each other until Marcia dies. When she leaves her house and its effects to Norman, the remaining three come together in an effort to help Norman settle the estate. They come to a better understanding of their relationship to each other and form a kind of community in Marcia's memory. In a world that forces them to be isolated because it has no place for them, Edwin, Norman, and Letty make a place for themselves and give meaning to their lives when, perhaps, society will not. Because the social world does not hold much meaning for the characters of *Quartet in Autumn,* Annette Weld notes that, unlike other Pym novels, *Quartet in Autumn* keeps descriptions of social gatherings to a minimum (184). In contrast, the novel focuses on aging and what Weld calls its horrors and isolation (185).

Just as Pym keeps descriptions of social gatherings to a minimum in *Quartet in Autumn,* she keeps descriptions of meals to a minimum as well. Most of the characters eat sparingly from tins and prepared foods. Marcia Ivory eats less than everyone else, to the point where she starves herself to death. It is as if the narrator, or society, would have us believe that the elderly do not need much to eat. Ironically, Marcia eats less than any of the other characters, yet Pym focuses most on her use of food. Marcia may starve to express herself and to rebel against her society. Gilbert and Gubar write in *The Madwoman in the Attic* that repressed female characters sometimes use hunger as a way to "escape" from their restrictive lives by starving themselves (85).

Marcia, however, occasionally does share meals with others. For example, the meal the four share at Marcia's retirement party is, according to Jane Nardin in *Barbara Pym,* a step forward in their relationship (129). Nardin argues that for the four late-middle-aged characters the novel centers around, food is more seductive than sex (21). Still, their lives and social conditions do not allow the four to enjoy really good gourmet food and the companionship that often goes with it, even at holidays.

Holiday meals like Christmas dinner merely exacerbate the isolation the characters feel in *Quartet.* For example, Edwin's daughter lives so far away that Christmas dinner at her house is a special occasion with people he barely knows. Still, he at least has a family holiday that celebrates familiar customs. As the narrator says, "Only Edwin would be spending Christmas in the traditional and accepted way in his role as father and grandfather . . . though he would have preferred to spend the festival alone at home, with no more than a quick drink with Father G. between services, to mark the secular aspect of the occasion" (83).

There is none of the camaraderie of a Dickensian Christmas dinner for Norman. He recites the rhyme "Christmas comes but once a year,/ And when it comes it brings good cheer" with sarcasm because he realizes no one really wants his company (83). As the narrator says, no one would argue with Norman, for Christmas is a "difficult time for those who are no longer young and are without close relatives" (83). Norman is invited to spend Christmas with his brother-in-law, Ken, and his "lady friend," who would soon replace his dead sister's role of wife to Ken. Yet, there is little charity in the invitation other than that Ken and his friend realize Norman "has nobody," and they "allow" Norman to visit them from time to time (83).

Both Norman and Edwin regard Christmas dinner as more of a nuisance or necessity to be tolerated. It is Marcia and Letty who have the "real problem" with the loneliness of the celebration. Because Marcia and Letty are single, older women, they do not fulfill the traditional role of holiday cook and hostess. They have no home and tree to decorate, no family to gather at the hearth and bake cookies for. For the two women who "had no relatives they could spend Christmas with" the holiday had been for many years "an occasion to be got through as quickly as possible" (84). Marcia, who gets more and more vague as the years pass, worries less and less about Christmas. When her mother was alive, the two lone women had a "larger bird than usual," a capon their butcher recommended as suitable for two ladies dining alone (84). Traditional society in the form of the male butcher even dictates how a widow and a spinster should celebrate holidays. Too big a bird and too flamboyant a celebration won't do at all. When Marcia's mother died, Marcia marked Christmas quietly with Snowy, her cat, who filled her need for something to love. After the cat died, Marcia let Christmas merge into a "haze of other days" without noting it (85).

Marcia's neighbors, however, do not even respect her right to be alone on Christmas. The social worker, Janice, urges them to "do something" about Marcia, because society, while it usually ignores spinsters, feels it has a duty to force them to eat Christmas dinner with someone. They see Marcia as lonely and feel that "Christmas was the time for 'doing' something about old people or 'the aged'" (85). Priscilla, the neighbor, is not even sure that Marcia is lonely; it is something she "hears" about older people. Her husband points out to her that while she is eccentric, Marcia is young enough and independent enough to work and to celebrate her own holiday (85). Marcia attends their Christmas dinner but she does not fit their pattern of the grateful, elderly spinster enjoying a Christmas dinner provided by others' charity. She neither drinks nor eats much and appears to be sullen throughout the meal.

Letty, however, might have welcomed Priscilla's invitation. She, of all the characters, regrets not having a family to spend Christmas with, and she is determined to "face Christmas with courage and a kind of deliberate boldness" in order to hold loneliness at bay (85). Letty can no longer eat Christmas dinner with her friend Marjorie as she used to because Marjorie has become engaged, and Letty would be an intruder. Also, Letty does not want people to pity her because she has no invitation for Christmas dinner; she knows she would feel out of place at someone else's family celebration. At the end, Letty accepts a rough invitation from Mrs. Pope, her landlady, who spends the holiday discoursing on how people eat too much (86).

The lonely Christmas Norman and the others spend is a far cry from celebrations in other Pym novels. For example, in *An Unsuitable Attachment,* the characters visit each other and exchange gifts, and clergyman Mark Ainger worries that the Father Christmas on his Yule cake is a bit shabby. Pym deliberately takes the romance out of Christmas in *Quartet in Autumn.* A romance novelist, on the other hand, would take a lonely character and give her a festivity-filled Christmas that would lead to some kind of love connection. For example, publishers Signet Super Regency and Harlequin produce anthologies of Christmas romance stories each year entitled *A Victorian Christmas* (Signet) and *Historical Christmas Stories* (Harlequin). In "Kidnapped for Christmas" by Betina Krahn, a penniless but well-educated governess falls into the hands of a wealthy widower who gives her a fantastic Christmas and who later marries her (184). Almost all the stories involve poor and lonely but attractive women who are rescued by wealthy admirers, and who spend festive Christmases with them.

The characters of *Quartet in Autumn* do not, however, enjoy festive holidays. By the end of Pym's *Quartet in Autumn,* it is not the traditional Christmas dinner which brings the remaining characters together. Instead, Marcia's death, and the fact that she leaves her house to Norman, forces them to gather and to share her horde of tinned food. The occasion seems more like a holiday for the three because they find a bottle of sherry to open. Groner writes that Norman's invitation to share the tinned food is sort of a breakthrough in their relationship. If, as Groner points out,

Marcia has been hoarding the food as a replacement for something to love (Groner 57), then its sharing is a distribution of that love.

Sharing among the heroes and heroines is not, however, apparent in their early dealings with each other. Letty Crowe and Marcia Ivory, whose last names invoke images of black and white, might present different halves of the same female personality, so that when coupled, they harmonize the way the black and white keys of a piano come together to make music. Or, the last names "Crowe" and "Ivory" might be an indication of how opposite in personality the two women are. Their differentness may account for why they have not become close friends though they have worked together for so long. If Pym is indeed showing that Marcia and Letty are opposites, she may be pointing out that even a group—such as older, single women—about whom many generalize—is really made up of unique personalities.

Letty Crowe is sort of an aging romance heroine who never had a "knight in shining armor." She is an "unashamed reader of novels" but realizes that her own life, that of an aging, unmarried woman, is of "no interest whatever to the writer of modern fiction" (3). She does not read romantic novels any more, though, because they no longer provide what she needed in them (3). Letty once read romances for the same reason the women Janice Radway surveys in *Reading the Romance* read them: for escape and entertainment (Radway 89). Some of Radway's women comment, for example, that they read romances because they are "light reading" and because "they always seem an escape and they usually turn out the way you wish life really was" (Radway 88). Letty seems to feel disappointed with her life. Therefore, she would be happy if the novels she read ended in a way that she might have liked her life to end. When Letty read romance novels, they may have provided for her vicariously the life she wanted or expected when she was a young girl. As she grew older and the novels no longer fulfilled this need, Letty quit reading them. That happy, or at least emotionally satisfying endings provide a needed escape to some readers has been recognized by other writers, too. In her essay "Gentle Truths for Gentle Readers: The Fiction of Elizabeth Goudge," Madonna Marsden observes that Goudge, herself, labeled her novels escapist, and claimed she could not write an unhappy ending (68-69). Still, Marsden points out that several Goudge heroines find that the myths surrounding women's lives are, in truth, not that satisfying. Therefore, a reader can identify with their problems, and the happy ending coupled with the realization that even in fiction, life is not perfect, allows the reader to empathize with the character and thus enhance her own identity.

Perhaps reading romances also enhances the identity of Radway's readers. For example, the women who responded to Radway's study gave a second definition to the word "escape." The readers used the word figuratively "to give substance to the somewhat vague but nonetheless intense sense of relief they experience by identifying with a heroine whose life does not resemble their own in certain crucial aspects" (Radway 90). One of the readers, Dot, who owns a bookstore that sells romance novels, stated that when she is reading, her body is in the room, but her spirit is not (91). While she is engaged in the act of reading, her psyche meshes with that of the heroine. Therefore, her identity is enhanced by the heroine's identity.

Groner writes that Letty's desire to be a character in a novel enhances her identity (56). For example, Letty has romantic, almost Wordsworthian ideas about her own life and death when she visits Marjorie in the country. Like a suicidal romance heroine, Letty imagines lying on the "autumn carpet of beech leaves" in the wood and wondering if it "could be the kind of place to lie down in and prepare for death when life became to much to be endured" (*Quartet in Autumn* 150). The image is romantic, yet morbid. Pym deflates it and makes it humorous by asking immediately after Letty's melancholy musings,

Had an old person—a pensioner, of course—ever been found in such a situation? No doubt it would be difficult to lie undiscovered for long, for this wood was a favorite walking place for bustling women with dogs. It was not the kind of fancy she could indulge with Marjorie or even dwell on too much herself. Danger lay in that direction. (150)

Letty's fancies are dangerous, because they could lead to suicidal thoughts, but they are also "dangerous" in a comic vein, for the walking dogs could mistake her for a hidden fire hydrant, or a leafy stump!

Letty's imagination is not the only thing she has in common with romance heroines. She is also like them in the sense that she is independent. Many of Pym's heroines share this quality. Just as Dulcie Mainwaring will not be shunted off to an apartment she does not want, Letty will not allow Marjorie to place her in an old ladies' home. Letty rebels against a society that wishes to put away older spinsters. She feels indignant with Marjorie "for supposing that [Letty] would be content with this sort of existence when she herself was going to marry a handsome clergyman." Forty years ago, Letty might trail behind Marjorie, "but there was no need to follow that same pattern now" (*Quartet in Autumn* 151).

Marcia, too, is independent, and refuses to follow the pattern someone else designs for her. Yet, she shows vestiges of the romance heroine in her personality, too. Mason Cooley writes that there is an obscure thread of romance in Marcia's life, which manifests itself in ambulance rides and new nighties for Mr. Strong, her surgeon, to see (20). The young surgeon becomes for Marcia a hero, a sort of knight, who will save her from death, loneliness, and nosy social workers. His very name implies heroism and masculinity, and his handsome demeanor stirs Marcia's imagination. If Marcia were young and beautiful like a romance heroine, her eccentric personality would attract a handsome hero. As Janice Radway writes in *Reading the Romance,* a heroine's eccentricities would be "tempered and undercut" by her extraordinary beauty" (124). Therefore, Amanda Quick can create a beautiful heroine who is also a nineteenth-century paleontologist in *Ravished,* and Morgan Llewellyn can have a gorgeous heroine who is a pirate in *Grania.*

Though *Quartet in Autumn* contains touches of romance, there are no weddings in the novel. The only proposed marriage, between Marjorie and David, never takes place. The lack of bridal ceremonies is rather a grim implication that there are no possibilities for people in late middle age to marry and lead full lives. Instead, three, not two characters, come together at the end of the novel in what Annette Weld in *Barbara Pym* describes as a kind of anti-wedding feast (Weld 192). Weld writes that, in place of a wedding feast at the end of *Quartet in Autumn,* Edwin, Norman, and Letty divide among themselves Marcia's tinned food (192). There are, however, romantic associations in *Quartet.* For example, Marcia is linked with the Queen of Sheba because the sherry she owned was made from grapes that grew in vineyards that allegedly belonged to the Queen (216).

While Pym de-emphasizes romance in *Quartet in Autumn,* she resurrects it as a point of emphasis in her last novel, *A Few Green Leaves.* That novel is the story of Emma Howick, an anthropologist in her early thirties who comes to a small English village to do research on its unwitting inhabitants. As with Pym's other single women, Emma is on her own. She is somewhat dowdy in appearance and is a keen observer. She, like Mildred Lathbury and Dulcie Mainwaring, has "loved and lost," but her ex-lover, Graham Pettifer, comes back into her life after she views him on a television program. At the same time, Emma strikes up an acquaintance with Tom Dagnall, the local vicar who is a widower. Precisely because Emma remains incognito as an anthropologist, the other inhabitants of the village are curious about her. They wonder why she does not leave for work each day, why she dresses as she does, what friends and acquaintances she may have in other villages. Emma, the ultimate observer, also wonders about them, and begins classifying her neighbors almost before the pictures are hung on her new walls.

Among the customs Emma observes is the flower arranging done for the church. One type of flower arranging involves a trick of extending the life of a floral arrangement by adding a few green leaves. Hence, Pym takes the title for her final novel not from a literary quotation as is usual for her but from an ordinary household hint. Household hints notwithstanding, however, romance is a key element in *A Few Green Leaves*. Robert Cotsell says in *Barbara Pym*, "For Pym, novel writing always has a relation to the continuity of romance in life. In this, her last novel, she reaffirms this central tenet" (138).

Once again, food plays center stage in a Pym novel. Actually, other novelists use Pym's techniques, though perhaps not in such a mouthwatering manner. For example, George Bauer asserts in his study of Roland Barthes's work, "Eating Out with Barthes," that Barthes states flatly that all novels could be classified according to "the frankness of their alimentary allusion" (39). In Barthes's version of Plato's *Criton*, which details the death of Socrates, Bauer asserts that Barthes centers the action on whether or not Socrates will eat a fig (Bauer 41-42). (The friends of Socrates have attempted to take him to a place where fig trees flourish and are a staple of the diet [41].) There are similarities between Barthes's observations and Pym's work; for instance, the question of whether or not to eat becomes a vital issue for Marcia Ivory in *Quartet in Autumn*. In *A Few Green Leaves,* the issue is similar for Magdalen Raven, but the issue is more centered on whether she should eat what she wants in defiance of Dr. Shrubsole, her son-in-law, or whether she should give in to him regarding her diet.[35] In this novel, food also becomes an effective way for people to control each other. The most obvious example is young Dr. Shrubsole, who takes over his mother-in-law's diet to "preserve" her. Finally, as in Pym's other books, characters are often categorized by what they eat, and food may serve as a means of expression as well.

Pym opens *A Few Green Leaves* with a panorama of the types of Sunday suppers people might serve each other in order to introduce the various ways she will represent food in the novel. Emma considers what people will eat for Sunday dinner as part of her study. She muses that Sunday supper would, of course, be lighter than the normal daily meal. Emma thinks that the shepherd's pie, concocted from the remains of the Sunday joint, would turn up as a kind of moussaka at the rectory because the vicar's sister, Daphne, is very fond of Greece (9). Emma speculates that some village inhabitants will have meals ready-prepared from freezers or "supper dishes at the supermarket with tempting titles and bright attractive pictures on the cover" (9). Some citizens will have fish sold from the back of a van "suggesting a nobler time when fish had been eaten on Fridays" (10). Others, like Emma, prefer a simpler meal, a bit of cheese or a small tin.

Emma finally decides that, since she is a lone woman, her dinner "would have to be an omelette, the kind of thing that every woman is supposed to turn her hand to" (10). Lone women, she reasons, are not fussy like lone men. For example, her neighbor, Adam Prince, is very fussy about food; he even makes a career of it as a gourmet food inspector (10). But Emma manages to express herself through the generic omelette.

Emma is also different from other women, for instance, Mildred Lathbury of *Excellent Women,* because Emma drinks red wine and other alcoholic beverages with her meals. Emma drinks alcoholic beverages although she suspects men like Adam Prince, the gourmet critic, wouldn't approve. Emma does not care about approval, male or otherwise. She feels relaxed and at peace with her wine and often uses her leisure time to enjoy food and to watch TV. While dining alone for some women represents their failure at building a successful family, dining alone for Emma is a time to relax and enjoy herself. Moreover, like Prudence Bates, Emma prefers wine, the drink of love and romance, with a simple meal like an omelette or a salad. Like Prudence, Emma is still looking for romance in life. Both women find ways of making even a simple task like eating alone romantic.

Ironically, some of the men in the novel cannot enjoy themselves when it comes to food. For example, Dr. Shrubsole distrusts fattening foods and Adam Prince distrusts rich sauces, garnishings, and attractive pottery.[36] Prince critiques elaborate food because he feels its garnishings may hide mediocre cooking. Actually, he has a point; as discussed previously, spices and rich sauces were originally created to hide the taste of meat that was spoiling. In fact, Michelle Berriedale-Johnson gives recipes for heavily spiced potted meats in *The Victorian Cookbook.* These recipes are intended to use leftover meats about to "turn."

Still, there is something interesting in the way Pym's Adam Prince critiques food; he critiques food as other men criticize women's clothing. Like the male fashion designer who forms women's taste for them because he claims to know fashion, Prince knows all the nuances of cooking. For example, he knows the proper butter to go with spaghetti, what beverage to have with each meal, and what wine the clergy use in their rituals (27). In a way, food is Prince's discourse.

Daphne Dagnall uses food to express her love of Greece. She often incorporates Greek cooking into her own meals. For lunch, she concocts a Greek version of a "ploughman's lunch," which consists of a "hunk of stale bread, a few small hard black olives, the larger juicier kind being unobtainable . . . and something approaching a goats'-milk cheese. No butter, of course, such a decadent refinement didn't go with an attic luncheon" (29). Clearly, in this small meal, she has captured the history of an entire nation. At one point, Daphne ritualizes her meals. She forms leftover crust from a very English gooseberry tart into miniature female figures that remind her of Cycladic idols she saw in Athens (136). Also, her Hellenicized meals represent Daphne's dissatisfaction with life in England; her meals represent the kind of life in Greece she really wants.

Daphne's brother, Tom, on the other hand, is in love with all things medieval and Jacobean. So, when he spies Emma holding a bland, pudding-like dish, he immediately thinks she is holding a blanc mange, an ancient dish popular in the seventeenth century (29-30). In reality, Emma is holding a ham mousse. The ham mousse, however, is not for Tom. Emma is really expecting Graham Pettifer and his wife, Claudia, to come to lunch. What Emma expects to be a boring and maybe uncomfortable meal of fashionably cold food and salad turns out to be a potentially "dangerous liaison," for Graham comes to lunch alone and informs Emma that he and Claudia are breaking up (32-33).

Emma feels controlled by the situation once she realizes that she will be alone with Graham. But other characters use food to control events and other characters. Dr. Shrubsole uses food to control the life of his mother-in-law, Magdalen Raven. For example, he forces her to substitute saccharine for sugar, forbids her butter, and has his wife serve fresh fruit instead of puddings and cakes for dessert. Dr. Shrubsole ostensibly takes over Magdalen's diet because he is concerned about her health, but he really wants the power of life and death over her. He speculates, "If Avice's mother were not so well . . . preserved, if she were allowed all the white bread, sugar, butter, cakes and puddings that her naturally depraved taste craved . . . if she were to drop down dead, the Shrubsoles would have enough money to buy a larger house" (53). Shrubsole believes that he can regulate personally how long Magdalen lives by controlling the food she eats; when he grows weary of her once and for all, he can change her diet and be rid of her. Guilt prevents him from allowing Magdalen to eat herself to death.

Not having sugar is more of a deprivation than Magdalen may realize. She insists on having sweetener because even during World War II, she was not without sweetener for her coffee (53).[37]

The point Pym illustrates by the depiction of Magdalen and her sugar may indicate that food and drink compensate for not having something to love. For example, Tom thinks Daphne has been drinking sherry to make up for not having a dog. Magdalen only has memories of "sweeter times" during the war, perhaps when her husband was alive. For Magdalen, food takes on a risqué connotation. Furthermore, Adam Prince the gourmet critic substitutes food for sex. In fact, when he brings red wine to the "bring and buy sale," Miss Lee nearly embraces the bottle with its long, phallic shape, and is embarrassed, as are many of the other women present. It is as if Adam has introduced a sexual element by introducing the red wine into this gathering of virtuous excellent women.

If food serves as kind of code for sex, then it may also be an indicator of compatibility between men and women. For example, Tom and Emma find they first have something in common when they discuss the making of jam.[38] For Emma, the preparation of food is still an art, and she picks her own blackberries and is ashamed to serve canned rice pudding (169). Her thinking is similar to Tom's; he often laments the use of substitute, artificial materials for clothing. In fact, substitutes for food and quick preparation exist throughout the novel. Rossen notes that saccharine is substituted for sugar, margarine for butter, frozen food for fresh (Rossen, *World of Barbara Pym* 169).

Emma tends to classify people in *A Few Green Leaves* by what they wear as well as what they eat. Clothes, for example, illustrate and emphasize the generation gap apparent in the village. Young people wear jeans, the older villagers never do. Some of the villagers wear smarter, and brighter clothing than the rector and his group wear (6). In another example, Graham Pettifer pronounces that Emma is thin, dowdy, and bony, with "pitifully little 'bosom wise'" (34). Furthermore, the young academic wife, Tamsin Barraclough, is classified as the type who is able to wear Laura Ashley dresses and jumble sale clothes and get away with it (39).[39] Clothes are no longer a symbol of charity in a Pym novel. The poor "wouldn't look at cast-offs," as Daphne observes (47).

Clothes can also symbolize changes in tradition and ritual. At the jumble sale, people bring offerings to the rectory as if they were offerings to the church itself. They give their items almost reverently, in a hushed way, to Daphne. She, with her Greek name, appears to be a sort of oracle because she critiques the quality of the clothes like a goddess of fashion. For example, she hangs Adam's good suit on a hanger for all to see. She hides his "bad boy" jeans because she thinks they are unsuitable (42). The doctor's tweed coat is almost revered because it is implied it has "magical properties" (43). Emma, in a sort of defiance, brings clean but well-worn underwear and displays it, though she is embarrassed (47).

As in *Excellent Women* and her other books, Pym, through different examples, points out that once solemn rituals have been reduced to meaningless ceremonies or humorous anecdotes. In another sense, clothes, and the materials from which they are made, become historical artifacts. Tom Dagnall, who is interested in medieval and Jacobean history, reads about people being buried in wool during the month of

August 1678 (21). Pym makes Tom's observations humorous because in the same passage, Tom remembers that Miss Lickerish buries one of her hedgehogs in a woolen jumper (21). Instead of noble Jacobean subjects being interred in wool, hedgehogs are laid to rest in it. Tom also feels humanity has lost some of its solemn dignity and has estranged itself from nature by wearing artificial fibers like polyester.

For the physicians in the novel, clothes are a panacea for the ills that plague their female patients. When Daphne consults with Shrubsole, he tells her to wear more clothes, and inquires about woolen underwear (16). His prescription is a variation of the "go and buy yourself a pretty new hat mentality." In fact, his superior, old Dr. G., actually tells a depressed woman to buy a new hat (16-17). For Dr. G., women are clotheshorses, depressed when they don't have new clothes. Pym saves the hat prescription from becoming a cliché by having young Dr. Shrubsole observe in a deadpan manner that women hadn't worn hats in years (17). Shrubsole cannot understand that Daphne, who loves the warm Aegean climate, does not feel comfortable in the cold, damp English climate. After she exhibits some impatience with her brother's obsession about medieval wool, Shrubsole asks Daphne if she has always lived with Tom. When Daphne tells him that she once worked in a travel agency and shared a flat with a woman friend, his thoughts turn to sex. To Shrubsole, two unmarried women making a home together suggests some sort of frustrated lesbianism (17). When Daphne finally does leave her brother to establish a home with another woman friend, she finds the experience less than satisfactory. But she will not really be able to return home if the relationship beginning between Tom and Emma flourishes; Emma would usurp her place as the "lady of the house."

Regardless of the nature of their relationship, unmarried women who live together are not always happy in Pym's novels. For example, Daphne is not able to move to the Aegean. Instead, she must move to another place in England. She and her roommate, and old friend, do not get along as well as she had hoped, and the dog they adopt for company turns out to be more of a burden than a comfort. Also in *A Few Green Leaves,* elderly Miss Grundy has a roommate who tends to bully her. She is also sort of a prototype of what may happen to Emma. She is a romance author who has not been able to enjoy romance in her own life. The narrator calls Miss Grundy the reputed author of a romantic historical novel. Pym makes her a subject of humor, for when Miss Grundy stumbles on a rocky path, she finds herself in the "kind of situation that might have provided a fruitful plot; but it was not the son of the house who came to her assistance or a handsome stranger but Emma" (56). If this were *Jane Eyre, Wuthering Heights,* or another romance, a handsome hero would have helped Miss Grundy. Then, if it were a romance, Miss Grundy would have a romantic first name. She would be young and beguilingly helpless, as the young Cathy is in *Wuthering Heights*. When Cathy is attacked by a dog and saved by her future husband, the entire Linton family thinks she is charming. Rossen suggests in *The World of Barbara Pym* that Miss Grundy may have abandoned writing romance because the "failure of life to imitate art might have proved too disappointing for her to be able to keep writing romances" (160).

Janice Radway in *Reading the Romance* would take issue with the idea that romance writers write in an attempt to create romantic scripts for themselves, but at least one real romance writer attempts to live out her novels, or to imitate her own life when she writes. Danielle Steel lives a fairytale, romance-filled world and has carefully constructed an image for herself as a romance heroine. Moreover, she borrows heavily from her own life when she writes the plots for her stories. Ironically, Steele is about to divorce her fourth husband, a wealthy millionaire. In any case, romance is hopeless for many Pym women, and various female characters in *A Few Green Leaves* are left alone like Miss Grundy is. For example, Miss Vereker, the former governess, is the last of Pym's Jane Eyre characters, but unlike some of the others, she does not find a Rochester (Rossen, *World of Barbara Pym* 161). Instead, Miss Vereker pays homage to her former, aristocratic employers by saving mementos of her posts, including elaborately framed photos of herself posing with her former masters. Finally, Emma's friend Ianthe Potts, a museum worker is, according to Janice Rossen, "doomed to a life of loneliness; the man she loves turns out to be homosexual" (161).

Emma, however, does not have the luxury of fainting and being rescued by anyone, son of the manor or otherwise. She is too independent to fall for clichés; therefore, she is judged more harshly by society in everything, including her appearance. For example, the narrator says that Emma "is the type that the women's magazines used to make a feature of 'improving'" (1). Annette Weld describes Emma in *Barbara Pym* as a "not too young woman uneasy with her present situation" (196). Though it is the 1970s, not the 1950s, women's magazines still have influence over how women view themselves. Janice Rossen has observed about the "makeover" idea in *The World of Barbara Pym* that Emma suffers because she does not make the most of her appearance to attract a man (163). Rossen argues that this is a common failing of Pym's academic women. Actually, Rossen has a point. In fact, though he is often oblivious to fashion, Tom is actually repulsed by one of Emma's drabber dresses.

Rossen, however, writes that Emma's often nondescript clothes do not illustrate that she is at fault for not caring, but that life is difficult

(163). Others, like Graham Pettifer see her as pathetically thin and dowdy, but Tom Dagnall sees Emma "only as a sensible person in her thirties, dark-haired, thin and possibly capable of talking intelligently about local history" (1). Therefore, it is Emma's intelligence that attracts Tom, because he is passionately interested in local history and would love to have someone to discuss it with. Tom is a Pym male, however, and thus can't help but see Emma for her useful potential to him. He imagines she might be able to help in his parish as a typist, but he is more considerate than other Pym men because he realizes he would be asking an educated woman to do menial work (7). Daphne Dagnall is not so kind; she scorns Emma's research and wonders "if you can call it work" (25).

In fact, Emma, an anthropologist, is there to observe the other inhabitants of the village, just as they observe her. She, too, is a Pym artist observer, who observes her fellow citizens in time-honored manner behind the shadow of her curtains (1). One wants to know if the curtains are lace; if they are, Emma takes on some of the attributes of a romance heroine, who plans her discourse among the lacy but filmy and distortive world of romance. As Janice Rossen writes in *The World of Barbara Pym,* Emma is a heroine who has not achieved much distinction, partly because she is over thirty and unmarried. In fact, Emma is one of a series of women in the novel who represents the various stages of spinsterhood (159). Others include Daphne and Miss Grundy.

Robert Cotsell says Emma is linked to Miss Vereker, the Jane Eyre-governess figure, and that Miss Vereker is a representative of the "neglected single woman of the late nineteenth-century novels to which Emma is connected by name, if nothing else" (134). Apparently, Cotsell has read a number of nineteenth-century novels in which neglected women are named Emma. Emma's name links her with the world of romance and with Jane Austen; yet she aligns herself not with Austen but with Hardy's first wife, "a person with something unsatisfactory about her" (*A Few Green Leaves* 9). That Emma chooses her words so carefully makes the reader believe that Mrs. Hardy's "unsatisfactory" trait was something that Pym's Emma herself found positive. Emma speculates her mother named her Emma so that "some of the qualities of the heroine of [Austen's] novel might be perpetuated" (8). Emma's mother did not name her Emily. Her mother, Mrs. Howick, feared Emma would be associated with her grandmother's servants and not with the author of *Wuthering Heights.*

If Emma places herself in the plot of a romance at all, she chooses not the role of the heroine, but of the rival woman. Gorsky describes the demon and rival woman in her essay "The Gentle Doubters: Images of

Women in Englishwomen's Novels, 1840-1920." One of the rival woman's most important personality traits is that she consciously tries to achieve something (46). She may even resort to tricks or crime to achieve her goals (46). Emma does have a goal; she wants to conduct secret research in the village for a study.

If the heroine of *A Few Green Leaves* is not associated with heroines like Cathy of *Wuthering Heights,* the novel's heroes are not associated with Heathcliff, either. In fact, there is hardly anything Byronic or splendid about the two men who are interested in Emma, Tom Dagnall and Graham Pettifer. Pym does her best to deflate their romantic importance or to make them look silly. For example, Emma thinks of Dr. Graham Pettifer, "To say he had been her 'lover' was altogether too grand a way to describe what their association had been" (11). Furthermore, Graham lacks Heathcliff's dark good looks; in fact, he must not have been that handsome when he was younger because when Emma sees him on television, she notes that he had improved in looks by filling out or something (12). Janice Rossen compares Graham to Rocky Napier of *Excellent Women,* but says that he lacks Rocky's charm; still, like Rocky, Graham will use the women in his life and he accepts a "constant offering of food" as his due from Emma (164).

Besides the fact that he is an opportunist who constantly accepts food from Emma, Graham is also somewhat cold sexually. He doesn't visit Emma for the sake of romantic nostalgia; there is no indication he has missed her at all. Instead, he looks her up because he expects her to be amusing for him. He is disappointed when she does not entertain him. Of the encounter he says, "Their meeting had not been the kind of amusing romantic encounter he had imagined" (170). Though handsome, Graham is easily bored and becomes petulant. Pym undercuts Graham as a romantic hero by giving him an all too human, childish personality.[41]

Even gentle Tom Dagnall is not spared in *A Few Green Leaves.* Though Tom is tall and "austerely good-looking," he is not that attractive (1). For one thing, though he is a widower, he does not pursue single women. For another thing, he is more interested in historical trivia like what types of materials were used for seventeenth-century shrouds. Therefore, Tom's discourse is not of passion but of musty books and burial clothes. Tom's eyes are brown, like those of many a romance hero, but they are not warm and endearing; they lack the "dog-like qualities" often associated with that color, which implicitly attract a woman's sympathy. The days when the local vicar was a good catch for a romance heroine are gone. So Tom, displaced in importance by the local doctors, muddles on alone.

If she views heroes with some ambivalence in *A Few Green Leaves,* Pym views marriage with ambivalence in this novel as well. Janice Rossen correctly writes in *The World of Barbara Pym* that marriage in Pym's late 1970s seems to be more casual (157). For example, Beatrix, Emma's mother, wants her to marry, yet she herself does not set "all that much store by the status" (8). Beatrix continued to work as an academic throughout her short marriage, and when Emma's father was killed in the war, Beatrix felt comfortable resuming her life as a single woman. The narrator says that after his death, Beatrix felt she had "fulfilled herself as a woman" by marrying and having Emma and she had been able to "return to her academic studies with a clear conscience" (8). In these feelings, she is like Woolf's Orlando, who put on a wedding ring in the nineteenth century so her society would be appeased, and she would be left alone to write.

On the other hand, Graham and Claudia give a more cynical view of marriage for they are about to be divorced (33-34). Yet, their status is unclear because they later reconcile. The Shrubsoles' marriage does not appear to be equal, either. For all that he loves to control others, Dr. Shrubsole is, in turn, dominated and controlled by Avice, his wife, who carries a cudgel when she walks. For Avice, marriage is a continual process in improving one's status and in symbolizing that improvement by obtaining bigger houses. Her name is suspiciously close to "avarice." Still, the characters in *A Few Green Leaves* need something to love, just as the characters in the other novels do.

As Annette Weld notes, in *A Few Green Leaves* "Pym calls up a host of characters from earlier works for a final curtain call" (199). There is an obituary notice for Fabian Driver of *Jane and Prudence* as well as one for Miss Clovis of *Less than Angels.* Several elderly characters from *Less Than Angels* appear at her funeral. Pym finished *A Few Green Leaves* only two months before her death. Perhaps she realized it was her swan song, and she wanted to tie up the loose ends. In this last novel, Pym seems to leave the answer of whether a single woman can live a full or meaningful life of her own open. Emma and Tom move toward a serious relationship with each other, but we do not know for sure that they will marry. Emma is not bothered by her unmarried state like other women in her society. Emma is absorbed in her work as an anthropologist; she enjoys observing others and delights in giving full rein to her imagination when she thinks about the other villagers. She is not controlled by matters of fashion, either. Emma eats well and socializes with the other characters. For Emma, marriage is not an end in itself that will enhance her social status. If marriage is at all desirable to Emma, it is desirable as a new experience. And, she genuinely likes

Tom. Emma's life is already complete in many ways. Marrying Tom would be a new experience for her. For Tom, marrying Emma would be a way of alleviating his own loneliness. Emma would help Tom by aiding him in finding a lifestyle that will make him happy and a member of his community. One reason Tom is lonely is that his position in village society is being displaced by the medical profession. He is no longer the village's spiritual head. Married or not, Tom must find himself another discourse.

For that matter, the women of Pym's last three novels seek a discourse outside of marriage and romance. For example, Letty retains her romantic notions in a positive sense. For her, life holds possibilities for interesting change even at age sixty-five. Through Letty, an older literary heroine emerges from obscurity. Marcia dies, but she succeeds in defying the social system, though she may do so unconsciously. The doomed Marcia fantasizing about her Mr. Strong is Pym's parody of the romance heroine who pines away for the sake of love. Marcia is also a parody of what can go wrong for a person who falls through the cracks of the British system of social work. Finally, narcissistic Leonora Eyre does not seek marriage as an end in itself. She clearly distinguishes her idea of romance from marriage and from physical love. An artist in temperament, Leonora reshapes her surroundings to please herself. She arranges her mirrors and antiques and manipulates the lighting in her apartment to show herself in her best light. All of Pym's heroines seem to be aware of the trappings of romance, e.g., candlelight, wine, handsome heroes, but they are able to take these trappings into consideration when they expand the definition of romance to accommodate their own worlds. For Pym women, the happy endings of romances do not mean finding a handsome prince. Instead, happy endings mean living a full life. And living a full life means that a person has lived life according to her own terms.

# 7

# Trivia as a Full Life

So, can an "excellent woman" who is over thirty and alone in the world live a full life? Since more than one character has voiced the opinion that excellent women are not for marrying, one wonders if Pym meant to leave out the conventional idea of marriage constituting for women a full life when she pondered the question. In fact, can any woman in modern society live a full life? Pym borrows from the genre of the romance novel to answer this question, but also to parody the world of the romance novel with which she was familiar, but uncomfortable. Through parody, humor, and quiet subversion, Pym's women strive to live their own version of the "full life." If anything, because "excellent women" are not for marrying, Pym's women sometimes rebel through marriage or through romantic liaisons with incongruous partners. For example, Ianthe marries the "unsuitable" John Challow, Mildred Lathbury surprises even herself by accepting Everard, and Catherine Oliphant forms an attachment with Alaric Lydgate. Even in Pym's time, single women over thirty were expected to remain spinsters. Those who married at an older age were "rebels" in their society. As one of the male, titled aristocratic characters of Edith Wharton's *The Buccaneers* observes in the Masterpiece Theatre production of the novel, he can't allow his older sister to marry, even when a suitor asks for her hand. If she marries at her advanced age, her actions will "smack" of desperation.

An interesting novel written in 1901 by Florence Morse Kingsley portrays an older spinster who, like Jessie Morrow of *Jane and Prudence,* improves her physical appearance to attract a man and ends up marrying the local vicar. Because Miss Philura is well past her twenties, she has been overlooked as marriageable material. The narrator says that "more years ago than she cared to count she had grappled with her discontent, had thrust it resolutely out of sight, and on the top of it she had planted a big stone marked Resignation. Nevertheless, at times the stone heaved and trembled ominously" (Kingsley 9). Yet, Miss Philura desires marriage, and decides that it is well within her power to have that sort of happiness. Thus, she rebels, but does so through conventional means.

Her behavior is revolutionary because she scoffs at the ridicule of her contemporaries and wins the vicar's love.

Yet Pym's quietly subversive heroines carve out happy lives for themselves, and only marry when they choose to, usually for love. Pym has left a literary inheritance to other authors who have created "excellent women" who rebel in their own ways; that is, by marrying late in life, like Colleen McCullough's Missy of *The Ladies of Missalonghi*, or Angela O'Hara of Maeve Binchy's *Echoes*. There is even a touch of Pym's excellent woman in Charlotte, the outspoken, but self-sacrificing spider of E. B. White's *Charlotte's Web*. Charlotte, as all good female spiders, spins her web and lays her eggs, but she sacrifices valuable time and effort, and like a general in a war, becomes a martyr and heroine for saving the life of her friend, Wilbur. Charlotte gives of herself, and like the Angel of the House, deprives herself for the sake of her children, who will go on to spin webs, just as their mother did before them. There is nothing of the rapacious "Black Widow" who devours her mate about Charlotte. Instead, her quick wit and quiet bravery make her the first "excellent woman" of the animal literary world.

In hindsight, one wants to answer the question of whether Pym herself lived a full life with a resounding "yes." She has left her readers a legacy of novels that are increasing in literary importance and in popularity, and she has answered the critics responsible for her years of silence. What the reader learns from reading Pym's work is that for everyone, regardless of age and sex, there is always the possibility of change, for better or for worse. In the meantime, there are simple joys to be had in everyone's life. These joys include savoring and cooking good food, dining out alone and with friends, creating a comfortable home replete with good books and pleasing decor, sewing clothes and shopping at favorite stores, and socializing with others at the significant, but not always earth shattering, rituals of life, such as weddings, funerals, and church holidays.

Detectives and mystery writers have always understood that studying life's trivia is an important means of solving a crime. Everyday trivia provides clues about perpetrator, victim, and participants that enable police to dismantle the pieces of even a near-perfect crime. Pym, however, is unique because she values trivia for its intrinsic worth. For her, and for the characters she creates, living each day to its fullest is the formula for living a satisfying life. For one of Pym's women, life can be complete without a fairy tale happy ending.

In *Barbara Pym, Writing a Life,* Orphia Jane Allen notes that Pym came to distrust the often false happy endings of romance fiction to the extent that she began to lose faith in the entire genre (85). Pym rewrote the often melodramatic plots to further her philosophy that life is neither a tragic love story nor an ethical problem. Instead, most human beings are concerned with trivialities. According to Allen, Pym's fictional technique sets everyday trivia and the realities of romantic love against the context of tradition in order to "illuminate" life's comic ironies (86). Other writers share Pym's love of trivia, but their emphasis is different.

Through irony, hyperbole, and exaggeration, Pym often parodies the stock romantic plots of "potboiler" romances. Pym borrows from the discourse of romance to describe her characters, but she adds quirks to their personalities that deflate the romantic myths with which they are often associated. For instance, Pym's male characters are often dark, handsome, brooding men whose portraits are fashioned after the Byronic hero. Byronic heroes who guard some secret often appear in Pym's novels, but their secrets do not consist of buried treasure or of mad wives hidden in attics. Instead, Pym men hide the fact that they like to play with soap animals in their baths like Nicholas Cleveland, or grow prize vegetables in their gardens like Count Bianco. Characters such as Rockingham Napier and Alaric Lydgate may resemble Heathcliff, but they are peevish and inept and are often caught whining about burnt cooking pans or socks that need darning.

Pym's last novel, *A Few Green Leaves,* resembles a romance novel more than any of her other books because it appears to end with the expected marriage of Emma Howick and Tom Dagnall. At first glance, the reader might think that Pym feels she needs to marry off Emma suitably if Emma is going to have a "full life" or a life that holds possibilities for changes and excitement. But a further reading reveals that Emma already has a full life. In marrying, she would share it with the often lonely and misunderstood Tom. Emma has a clear sense of her own identity; thus, she can be happy. Tom, however, is losing his own sense of importance. Doctors have replaced him as spiritual adviser in his community and he is left to delve into the past for satisfaction by studying the trivia of the Middle Ages. Emma serves as a different kind of helpmeet for Tom. She will help him to create a new discourse for himself so that he can participate in life and not be shoved to the side because his occupation is not as popular as it once was.

Pym's heroines do not help their heroes in quite the same way as romance heroines help their lovers. Pym consciously subverts the helpful, submissive female characters of many romances by deflating the heroes' cause. For example, while the heroine of Deveraux's *The Black Lyon* helps her man by aiding him in preparation for medieval battle, Ianthe helps John in *An Unsuitable Attachment* by bringing him cold medicine and straightening his sickroom. Other romance heroines become involved in affairs of international intrigue. For these women, helping their heroes means helping their country and protecting national security. The issues in Pym's works are not so cosmic. A Pym helpmate services her man by indexing and proofreading, keeping secret his domestic eccentricities, and ministering to his loneliness.

While Pym's heroines do not succor their significant others in quite the same way as romance heroines, Pym was still familiar with romance heroines and their men. Pym read and studied many types of romance novels. Her experience taught her that the basic plot elements of a love relationship that evolve to a happy ending could be undermined, with often comic results. Pym herself has written in *A Very Private Eye* that the types of romances range from the historical to the modern. She observes further that some romances emphasize the setting, while others emphasize the love story (280). Along with other critics, Pym realizes that while the basic romance plot is similar, there are as many types of romance novels as there are readers.

Like Pym, Kristin Ramsdell is also aware of the many different types of romance novels. Her critical book, *Happily Ever After,* chronicles and describes all the varieties of romance novel. Ramsdell includes in her discussion authors like the Brontës, Barbara Cartland, Georgette Heyer, Jetta Carleton, R. F. Delderfeld, and Howard Fast. Ramsdell traces the romance novel genre to the Middle Ages (5), while Annette Townsend in an essay from Eileen Fallon's *Words of Love,* describes romance stories like Heliodorus's *Aethiopica* from Ancient Greece. Despite the comments of Pym, Ramsdell, and other critics, the sexist myth that female romance authors and their readers are somehow unbalanced and sex starved persists today in the American media.

In a recent segment of the CBS news program *48 Hours,* Dan Rather and other reporters attempted to study the romance novel industry. The attitude of CBS was that romance readers are "addicted" to their books because their own dreary lives lack adventure. Rather and company ridiculed those women who confessed to reading romances. CBS implicitly accused romance authors like Barbara Cartland and Nora Roberts of pandering to the pathetic desires of their readers and of playing out their own demented fantasies in their novels. The producers appeared to be obsessed with the sex portrayed in the novels, as if men had never written graphically about sex in their books.

Unfortunately, the *48 Hours* piece was inaccurate in that it did not define clearly the term romance and did not distinguish among the various types of novels, for example, historical, gothic, bodice ripper, and regency. Moreover, Mr. Rather and crew continually referred to the fact that they could find no men writing in the genre, yet continually featured clips from the film and book *The Bridges of Madison County,* a romance written by a man named Waller. One could almost hear Nathaniel Hawthorne muttering about that "damned mob of scribbling women" in the background. It seems that in many ways, Rumer Godden and other women writers are still correct that different types of women's fiction, including romance novels, are ridiculed because they are written by and for women.

What *48 Hours* did emphasize correctly were the conventional plots behind many romances. Pym chose to take the conventional stories and change them in some way. Indeed, for many of Pym's characters, marriage and conventional romance are not the answer. For them, life may be simple, but it is still interesting. Most of her women, for example, lead quiet and modest lives as unmarried women. Yet they manage to live in a financially independent fashion. A comment Madonna Marsden makes in her essay on Elizabeth Goudge also applies to Pym's heroines. Marsden writes that Goudge's women "find themselves pulled between the paradigm which models their happiness around their biology, and their own experiences which indicate that the paradigm may be false" (69). Society's paradigm for female happiness often fails Pym women, too. As a result, many Pym women learn to make their lives full and interesting through appreciating everyday pleasures and trivial things in their environments. Dulcie Mainwaring, in particular, leads a successful life. She has a good job and manages her own well-kept home. Ianthe Broome also supports herself successfully and has a lovely house full of antiques.

At one point or another in their discussions, each of these critics discusses one standard romance plot of the master or superior seducing or marrying the servant in her work. This plot, with varied endings, has occurred in novels that are not themselves classified as romances, but which have influenced romance writers for decades. Pym uses a milder version of this plot, as well, but her endings have comic possibilities, not tragic consequences as they often do in the other books. In Pym's novels, a paid companion like Jessie Morrow of *Jane and Prudence* may marry a man of independent means like Fabian Driver, but her husband is neither her master nor her seducer. Pym chooses to focus on class and unsuitable attachments, and her plots emphasize that it is the woman who attracts the man's attention and encourages the relationship. She is not seduced or lured into sin by her suitor. Instead, a Pym heroine may choose to refuse a proposal of marriage or a suggestive invitation.

Instead of dealing with the fears of dishonor and seduction, Pym deals with the fears of women that men will entrap them into marriage and servitude, that they will suffer isolation from other women, and that women will endure economic dependence. In this, Pym is similar to early writers of gothic romances like Anne Radcliffe. Daphne Clair, who is both a romance writer and a literary critic, has claimed that Radcliffe, with *The Mysteries of Udolpho* and other works, "changed the course of women's fiction" (63). As Clair writes, Mrs. Radcliffe wrote about women's deepest fears including the fear of being trapped and imprisoned by housework, the fear of male sexuality, and the fear of losing their identities (64). Pym allows her female characters to confront these fears in a positive manner that allows them to triumph. Therefore, Catherine Oliphant chooses to follow her own bohemian lifestyle in *Less Than Angels* and not to become Tom Mallow's wife and proofreader. The Bede sisters of *Some Tame Gazelle* prefer to remain single and independent, and Mildred Lathbury, though she eventually becomes Mrs. Everard Bone, comments aptly and sardonically on the plight of the single and married woman in post-World War II England.

Pym parodies romance to explode the unrealistic expectations it may foster in its readers, but she also wants us to know that romance can flower around a simple meal of poached eggs shared between two librarians like Ianthe and John of *An Unsuitable Attachment*. Pym's heroes and heroines are often attractive physically, but their foibles and eccentricities make them interesting as well as sexually alluring. Pym reminds the reader that love can hurt as well as titillate, and happy endings are not always satisfactory in real life. Young princes and princesses can grow to bore each other, and their passion can, as Jane Cleveland observes in *Jane and Prudence,* descend to mild looks and spectacles. Interesting, even passionate relationships can be formed between older, not-so-glamorous people of experience like Emma Howick and Tom Dagnall, or Catherine Oliphant and Alaric Lydgate, who find that they stimulate each other intellectually as well as physically.

Yet Pym does more than just parody romance novels. Pym's style is primarily realistic, and more in keeping with the techniques of writers like Ivy Compton-Burnett, Elizabeth Taylor, and Margaret Drabble. Perhaps it is because of Pym's basically realistic style that Anne Wyatt-Brown takes Pym's stories literally. Wyatt-Brown often reads Pym's novels as stories that retell Pym's own sad love affairs. Wyatt-Brown sees in Pym's characters lonely, frustrated women who live depressing, often solitary lives of quiet desperation. She portrays Pym as a frustrated woman in need of psychological help who lived a lonely, unfulfilled life.

Such a reading of Pym ignores that Pym was a great observer of people and their foibles. As an artist, she was able to weave her observations into stories that burlesqued the social manners of her time. In much the same way, Austen and Trollope parodied social conventions of the nineteenth century in their novels. A reading of *A Very Private Eye,* moreover, reveals Pym as a lively woman, Oxford educated, with many friends and an active social life. To portray Pym as a frustrated spinster reliving her lost youth and lost loves in her novels is to buy into the stereotype of the female romance writer who believes and tries to live the fantasies she writes. Authors of critical works like Janice Radway's *Reading the Romance* and Carol Thurston's *The Romance Revolution* dispel the myth that romance readers and writers are incapable of facing reality and live through the romance plots that they read and create.

In fact, the most important trait that Pym heroines share is that they are ordinary women, not the displaced princesses and aristocrats who often people romances. They inspire their common readers because they are common individuals who have made sense of their lives. While it is true, as many critics have noted, that Pym found joy in the everyday occurrences of life, she also used the seemingly trivial elements of her stories to subvert the discourse of the romance novel. While she was unable to write romances herself, she was fascinated by the stories, and often wrote of her own unhappy love affairs in her diaries, and later in her books. Romance writers and readers like Catherine Oliphant and Prudence Bates are among her most interesting characters. Catherine, whose name is an allusion to nineteenth-century writer Margaret Oliphant, is important to an understanding of Pym's work. Catherine decries the stereotype of the glamorous, lovelorn romance writer with her common sense and independent, "bohemian" ways. As we have seen earlier, Catherine illustrates Pym's own technique. That is, Catherine writes about English provincial life and about household hints and recipes in the twentieth century as Margaret Oliphant wrote about provincial life in the nineteenth century. By the end of *Less Than Angels,* other characters finally understand that Catherine is correct; the ritual and ceremony of English life also deserve study (Allen 82).

In the same way that a poet like Wordsworth could find great comfort and meaning in a daffodil or a mountain stream, Pym found inspiration in housework and cooking. Though she saw great events come and go in her own lifetime including two world wars, the Depression, the Cold War, the Chinese Cultural Revolution, the atomic bombing of Nagasaki and Hiroshima, and the coming of the space age, Pym chose as her literary subject the lives of everyday people, some taken for granted by society. By treating her often middle-aged spinster heroines as unique individuals, she painted vivid portraits, some sad, some absurd at times, but all realistic. Mildred Lathbury, for example, refuses to adopt the role of the plain spinster and insists that she is not Jane Eyre and is not actively seeking to marry Mr. Rochester, even though she does marry Everard Bone. And the Bede sisters raise female self-esteem to a high level when they refuse to marry merely for status. Belinda and Harriet prefer their independent lifestyle as single, older women even if their own society may pity or judge them for not being wives and mothers.

Though single, many of Pym's female characters manage to find objects for their affection and to establish close relationships with family and friends that give meaning to their lives. So, Mildred Lathbury is a trusted friend to Winifred and Julian Malory, and Harriet and Belinda Bede form important bonds with members of their church community. A few, like Catherine Oliphant, have careers that absorb them completely and that help them define positively their self-worth.

In all of Pym's work, food becomes a means of expression for the characters, as well as a way for them to define others in their community. Food can be a gift of love, as when Harriet Bede takes a basket to her favorite young curate in *Some Tame Gazelle*. Or food defines the class one belongs to; therefore, Ianthe Broome, the well-bred canon's daughter of *An Unsuitable Attachment*, eats a respectable dinner with coffee at 6:30 instead of making tea at that hour like the lower classes. And Mildred Lathbury of *Excellent Women* is aware of her status as a single, older woman alone on Saturday night, so that her meal is often spartan as a reflection of her lonely state. Prudence Bates of *Jane and Prudence*, on the other hand, defies convention and has a higher sense of self-esteem, so that when she dines alone, she serves herself only the freshest food made with the highest quality ingredients.

Pym's heroines do not lead the interesting and "full lives" that involve the swashbuckling, erotic adventures of many romance heroines. Yet Pym sets up her characters as if they were romance heroines, often borrowing from that genre's discourse to tell her stories. Even the seemingly most unromantic heroine of any Pym work, Marcia Ivory, is given a romantic name and has fantasies about Mr. Strong, her surgeon and knight in shining armor. She manages to weave an entire fantasy about him where he constantly saves her from death.

The characters who people Barbara Pym's work enchant us precisely because they are realistic and ordinary. Their individual peccadilloes amuse us because we see in them our neighbors, husbands, wives, lovers, children, and siblings. Her joy in trivia is infectious and is a reminder in an increasingly complex and dangerous world that life, through the mechanism of its simplicities, does go on. Often, while war was waged in the world, Pym was able to capture life at the home front in detail as intriguing as any battle plan. She chose to focus on and parody romantic love, according to her most recent biographer, Orphia

Jane Allen, because she was concerned with women being betrayed by a culture that encouraged marriage as a way to validate their lives (99). In *Barbara Pym, Writing A Life,* Allen says that Pym was dismayed by a society that advocated women's systematic search for a husband (99). Often, female characters in her novels who conduct such a search like Allegra Gray are thwarted in humorous fashion.

Perhaps, in the end, when raven tresses begin to gray, and Byronic brows become furrowed with wrinkles, a shared love of reading wine lists, an interest in history, or similar life experiences, go more toward warming a cold winter's night. And lest the reader forget, Pym reminds her or him that love wears many masks and takes many forms; having golden hair and blue eyes, or being tall and broad-shouldered is not a prerequisite. In fact, neither youth, nor even being human, are necessary elements for being loved. For instance, Sophia Ainger lavishes much of her love on their cats. Also, the elderly characters of *Quartet in Autumn* are capable of recognizing romance and the three remaining form at least a filial attachment at the end of the novel. Miss Grimes, the older gentle-woman spinster of *An Unsuitable Attachment,* finds her Prince Charming in a pub. Harriet Bede is content to flirt with her suitors and adopts young curates. Though plump and over fifty, she is well-dressed, sometimes flamboyantly, and is able to charm much younger men.

While American readers are still discovering Pym, she is well-known to contemporary British writers and their audiences who are well-acquainted with the gentlewomen types who populate Pym's novels. British television has based several dramas and comedies on English gentlewomen including *The Rector's Wife,* and *Keeping Up Appearances.* In the latter, Hyacinth Bucket (prounced Bouquet), could be the 1990s twin of Harriet Bede. From her flowered dresses and pearls to her chintz furniture and tea cups, she is a quintessential gentlewoman. Every week, Hyacinth attempts to climb the social ladder in humorous situations that involve her sisters Daisy, who has married beneath her, and Rose, who behaves like a middle-aged femme fatale. Though the physical comedy becomes slapstick at times, the plots, subtle dialogue, and settings are reminiscent of Pym.

It is Pym's humor and satiric wit that have endeared her to a whole new generation of readers and critics. Fewer critics label—or dismiss—her as a modern Jane Austen. More readers appreciate the pathos and humanity of her characters, and more women read and see themselves in the sympathetic, often triumphant characters like the Bede sisters, Mildred Lathbury, Catherine Oliphant, and Ianthe Broome. The traditional myths about a woman's life, myths regarding marriage, home, and family are being displaced. Writers as diverse as Marilyn French and

Elizabeth Jolley have continued to dismantle the idea that the only way a woman can lead a full life is to marry. Before all of them, however, stands the bemused, often sardonic figure of Barbara Pym, notebook in hand, ready to jot down material for the next installment of her vision of the human comedy.

Pym shows that there are alternative kinds of love that do not invite the reader's pity. For Pym, the real "excellent women" are those who are capable of living independently, but fully. They are able to enjoy life on their own terms, without looking over their shoulder to see if society approves.

# Notes

1. Interestingly enough, John T. Frederick notes in "Hawthorne's Scribbling Women" that Harriet Beecher Stowe's *Uncle Tom's Cabin* was one of the books Hawthorne so roundly condemned, perhaps because he was not an abolitionist (232).

2. Ramsdell also notes that medieval love and adventure stories were popular both in oral and written form (5). In fact, sixteenth-century writer Miquel de Cervantes parodies them in his masterpiece, *Don Quixote de la Mancha*, in which Don Quixote, a middle-aged nobleman, apparently loses his mind to medieval romance novels and takes after the knight heroes by riding into the countryside on an old nag to have adventures.

3. For example, Kate appears to be tamed in *The Taming of the Shrew*, but Petruchio, her husband, is also changed by his love for her. In Kate's last speech, she appears to advocate total obedience in wives, but the play is often staged with Kate winking at the audience after she talks. Her lines read "But now I see our lances are but straws,/Our strength as weak, our weaknesses past compare,/That seeming to be most which we indeed least are" (Shr.V.II.173-75).

The Wife of Bath is even more to the point; she forces her husband to burn his misogynistic book. Thereafter, they are the most loving of couples (WBT 816-25). Doubtless, she speaks for many women authors, and perhaps Pym herself was thinking of her as she wrote. When the Wife says "By God! If women hadde writen stories,/As clerkes han withinne hire oratories,/They wolde han writen of men moore wikkedness/Than al the mark of Adam may redresse," (Wife of Bath's Tale 693-96), she could be a Pym heroine.

4. According to Clair, Behn's work is a "liberationist tragedy of love, rebellion, and death that has a very good claim to be the first novel in the English language" (61).

5. In *Pamela's Daughters,* by Robert Palfrey Utter and Gwendolyn Bridges Needham, the authors point out that Pamela resists her master's initial attempts at seduction by fainting and by other means (4). After he seizes her private letters and papers, the master orders her to leave, then entreats her to return to him of her own free will (4). She does so, after her resistance to him has "tamed" him and compelled him to marry her and make an honorable woman of her. As the authors say, "If every woman in life is a daughter of Eve, so is every heroine in fiction a daughter of Pamela" (1).

6. Linn Haire-Sargent, a graduate student fascinated with Brontë, recreates Rochester as Mr. Are in her novel *Heathcliff,* a sequel to *Wuthering Heights,* which speculates that Heathcliff discovered Rochester during the years he was missing from the Moors.

7. Gorsky writes, "Between the Jilt and the classical Bad Woman lies the schemer, descendant of Milton's Eve, the wicked stepmother of fairy tales, and the conniving woman of all times." Gorsky misrepresents Eve's ancestry in this passage. Milton scholars would not agree with her portrayal. For example, Dennis Burden writes in *The Logical Epic* that Eve does not want to consciously deceive anyone for personal gain. She merely wants adventure and is curious about life outside the Garden of Eden (451).

8. Harlequin Publishers also focused on food consumption in a monthly magazine that featured recipes (Jensen 109). Besides recipes, the magazine featured a full-length novel, short stories and travel articles. The recipes were international, and some had been featured in different series of Harlequin novels (109). While Harlequin no longer publishes the magazine, recipes sometimes appear at the end of a book from the Harlequin Presents series of novels (109). For example, a common recipe for spaghetti from Patricia Lake's novel *Silver Casket* is titled "A Traditional Italian Dish" and is described as follows: "When Laura dines on spaghetti Bolognese she is treating herself to a delicious and nourishing traditional pasta dish enjoyed by lovers of Italian food everywhere. Here's a simple recipe that will feed the whole family" (qtd. in Jensen 110). Readers often write Harlequin, thanking the publishers for the recipes (109).

9. Ricardo is a distant cousin to another nobleman who inhabits one of many ruined castles of romance. Lord Saxton of Woodiwiss's *A Rose in Winter* lives in the English countryside. He rules over a great manor half-destroyed by fire. Saxton is enshrouded by a black cloak. His voice is hoarse and his arms are strong and "steel-sinewed" (123). The shadow he casts in the gloomy, cold rooms of the manor appears "twisted and misshapen," and his shadowed face appears "devoid of features" (126). To Erienne, the heroine, Lord Saxton seems to be a "great bird swooping down on her" or a "dreaded winged beast" (123). The gentle Count Bianco, on the other hand, is a mere dove in comparison. His very name recalls whiteness, openness, and purity.

10. Jennifer Wilde is the pseudonym of Mr. Tom E. Huff.

11. If eating alone is a sign of independence, preparing food for others can be a way to handle a crisis. Mildred comments several times throughout the novel that she is often called upon to make tea in a crisis (158-59). Sally Jacobs, a character in Anita Brookner's *The Debut,* also believes that any crisis can be handled through serving food and drink (Brookner 167).

12. In the same way, Julian, an unmarried clergyman, cannot do anything about his feelings. Society does not consider Julian to be a normal man, yet he has "manly feelings" (EW 5).

13. Fiedler discusses Lovelace, the seducer of Clarissa in Richardson's novel, as a figure in the tradition of Don Juan. He also notes that Lovelace differs from Don Juan because the former's opponent is "a female principle equal and opposite to the male force of Don Juan" (66). Fiedler writes that Don Juan's opponent was a father or God figure, and that the women in Don Juan's life were not strong influences, but mere two-dimensional pasteboard figures to be conquered. Clarissa, on the other hand, was a more believable personality, and therefore more of a match for Lovelace. Fiedler further discusses the figure of the seducer in works by T. S. Eliot and in romance novels like *Charlotte Temple* (1791) and *Marjorie Morningstar* (1955). Fiedler makes an interesting comment; he observes that behind the theme of seduction, popular in so many works of literature since *Clarissa,* lies the "bourgeois redefinition of all morality in terms of sexual purity" (71). Only the Pure Maiden, Fiedler writes, is the savior who can convert male sexuality, which can become animal aggression, to tenderness (72).

Furthermore, Fiedler decries the larger-than-life heroes created by some romance writers by claiming that they are remnants of the sentimental love movement that Fiedler claims attracted so many female writers during the nineteenth century. Fiedler argues that the pure, dove-like heroines, larger-than-life heroes, and evil villains have their origins in Richardson's *Clarissa.* Moreover, he writes that the same influence affected both British and American novelists, so that the English and American romance novels of today are the inheritors of the tradition Richardson established (81). According to Fiedler, the original male seducer of Richardson's books takes on a new persona, but he is still the evil-doer of the piece. Often, modern romances use the battle of the sexes theme where the seducer is finally conquered. Fiedler writes, "In popular fiction produced in America by and for females, the seduction fable comes chiefly to stand for the war between the sexes and the defeat of the seducer as a symbol of the emasculation of American men" (89). Needless to say, Fiedler's language is strong, and he has often been accused of being anti-feminist. Other critics would argue that the modern romance "transforms" the hero into a more complete, caring human being instead of emasculating him.

14. While there is no indication in *A Very Private Eye* that Pym read Brookner, some critics cite similarities between the two writers. For example Anne Wyatt-Brown writes in *Barbara Pym: A Critical Biography,* "Pym's fiction has much in common with that of a small band of contemporary novelists—Elizabeth Taylor, Penelope Mortimer, Molly Keane, Elizabeth Jolley, and Anita Brookner. They were all born in the first third of the twentieth century, and their fiction reflects slightly old-fashioned attitudes toward gender relations" (1). Wyatt-Brown says later that, like Pym, Brookner often writes about "lonely women" (8).

15. In writing about *The Flame and the Flower,* Carol Thurston notes in *The Romance Revolution* that the novel was extremely popular, drawing thousands of fan letters from readers (48). *The Flame and the Flower* was one of the three novels that served as models for other historical romances or novels of "sweet savagery" that were written in the 1970s (49). The others were Rosemary Rogers *Sweet Savage Love* and Seargeanne Golon's *Angelique and the Sheik* (49).

16. In the standard plot of the clergyman's wife, the woman is "capable and endlessly resourceful" (Benet 47). She is married to a country vicar and the entire community looks to this self-effacing woman for "cheerful help" and "quiet guidance" (47). Benet writes, the clergyman's wife "is especially helpful to her husband in dealing with the human problems presented by his flock" (47). Her "great moment" occurs when her husband is falsely accused and she "stands by her man" with great courage. While vindicating her man, she also takes care of a large family and runs a neat, perfect house on very little money (46).

George Eliot deals with this plot in *Scenes of Clerical Life* through the character of Milly Barton who literally kills herself with good works done for her vicar husband and for her family. Amos, the husband, though, is not as deserving as other vicars. Also, the pompous Mr. Collins of *Pride and Prejudice* is somewhat of a parody of the country vicar. His wife, Charlotte, clearly marries him for the sake of obtaining social status, not for any sense of calling. Finally Mollie Hardwick's Doran Fairweather stands by her vicar husband repeatedly in a series of romantic mysteries, even when he decides to leave the clergy to work at a radio station.

17. Prudence is right; Jane has other gifts, including a fruitful imagination she turns loose on almost everyone (Groner 31). Like Miss Peabody of Elizabeth Jolley's *Miss Peabody's Inheritance,* Jane can create a narrative about any situation to amuse herself. Like the metaphysical poets she studies, Jane's "differentness" is her creative discourse.

18. Margaret Atwood's *The Edible Woman* explores the theme of a woman being devoured by patriarchal society and Tama Janowitz's novel *The Cannibal in Manhattan* is about a woman who marries a supposedly reformed cannibal, only to be literally eaten by him. Furthermore, it is interesting to note that in T. S. Eliot's play *The Cocktail Party,* a female character who has an affair with a married man goes to Africa as a missionary and is crucified and eaten, implicitly because she has defied the patriarchal rules against adultery.

19. Jonathan Swift's essay "A Modest Proposal" also deals with the theme of the powerful English "devouring" the powerless Irish farmers who have more or less been colonized.

20. See Chapter 2. This description of Fabian as furniture is ironic in light of the fact that Jessie Morrow of *Crampton Hodnet* sees herself as an object, a "chair" that everyone takes for granted.

Jessie's observation, however, takes a negative assumption that people make about her and turns it into something positive because she notes that there is nothing more comforting than a good chair or one's own bed. In the same way, the narrator of Charlotte Perkin Gilman's *The Yellow Wallpaper* assigns hostile qualities to the room she is locked into. She remembers fondly furnishings in her childhood home, and like Jessie, finds them comforting. She says, "I remember what a kindly wink the knobs of our big, old bureau used to have, and there was one chair that always seemed like a strong friend" (17).

21. Barthes is especially important and appropriate for a study of Pym. Naomi Schor writes the following about Barthes in *Reading in Detail*, "The modern fascination with the trivial, the playground of fetishism, is exhibited throughout the variegated oeuvre of Roland Barthes" (6). Like Pym, Barthes is interested in writing about the trivial and commonplace; yet, Pym does not write about triviality as the "playground of fetishism."

22. Nora Ephron uses recipes in *Heartburn* to form a bond between her female narrator and her readers. *Heartburn* is the story of the narrator's breakup with her journalist husband. The narrator writes cookbooks for a living, and intersperses her story with recipes. For example, when she throws a Key lime pie in her husband's face, the narrator pauses in the story to give the recipe and directions for making the pie.

23. At least one other writer and her heroine are interested in food and in how it is presented. In Elizabeth Taylor's *Angel,* the heroine is keenly interested in good-tasting food and is highly critical of others' cooking. Angel is also narcissistic and vain, and uses food as a means to express herself. At an unveiling of her own portrait, she serves boar's head, salmon, "concoctions of lobster hung about with whispery prawns," that are "all mashed with sauces and mayonnaises, or half-mashed in aspic" (140). When Angel dines with her publisher and his wife, she finds the food to be "tasteless and unidentifiable: the fish in aspic, the chicken buries in a sauce among a confusion of mushrooms and pieces of hard-boiled egg" (61).

24. The heroine of Amanda Quick's *Seduction* is also like Catherine in that she loves reading and writing and is "untidy" about her appearance (58). Unlike the men of *Less Than Angels,* however, the hero of *Seduction* does not criticize Sophy, who is the heroine. He thinks her "sweet disarray" is sexy (58).

25. At least one critic sees Wilmet's ancestry in Austen's *Emma.* Austen writes, "I am going to take a heroine whom no one but myself will much like" (Fergus 112, n6).

26. Besides Mary, the "honorary" paid companion, there is Miss Prideaux, a former governess who had foreign adventures. With her exotic past and her foreign sounding name, Miss Prideaux is a gothic heroine grown old and her flat was "the distillation of her vivid memories of life" (28).

27. Woolf makes a comment that is relevant to Pym's style of writing in *A Room of One's Own:* "It is a curious fact that novelists have a way of making us believe that luncheon parties are invariably memorable for something very witty that was said, or for something very wise that was done. But they seldom spare a word for what was eaten" (10). Pym, on the other hand, spares more than a word for what was eaten.

28. What these men do not realize is that they help to cause the social scandals because they take advantage of single women. Men like Neville Forbes do not think twice about hiding behind their profession while they use vulnerable women whom they cause to become infatuated with them. In many ways, the Neville Forbes character, and others like him in Pym's works, play the role that the mustachioed villain who seduced young girls played in melodramas and romances a century earlier. Women alone were deemed to be weak creatures who caved in easily to fleshly desires. Men, however, did not have to curb their own aggressive behavior. Thus, single women were a "threat" to married women and to respectable single men. A man, however, was not blamed for taking advantage of single women who might be lonely and might see his advances as overtures to marriage.

29. Frye notes, "When Jane Eyre says that women need exercise for their faculties, and a field for their efforts as much as their brothers do, the woman reader is able to respond with an acknowledgement of her own needs and desires" (193).

30. In her novel *Gone to Soldiers,* Marge Piercy's romance writer character Louise Kahan contemplates the hero she will create for a new story. She rejects creating a hero maimed and wounded like Rochester (730).

31. In the same way, Angela O'Hara, a single schoolteacher in Maeve Binchy's novel *Echoes* is too sensible to play the role of embittered spinster her small Irish community writes for her. Her students see Angela as someone who does not have much to "crow about" (56). Angela teaches in tiny Castlebay in an "awful convent," stuck caring for her sick mother (57). But, Angela does not feel sorry for herself. In time, she marries and she and her husband run their own successful business, an old hotel.

32. As Muriel Schultz observes, *Some Tame Gazelle* appears on Dulcie's book shelves.

33. Scenes associated with Italy indicate romance in *An Unsuitable Attachment.* Broken marble, classical sculpture, and lemon leaves are some of the props that create romantic settings. Other vestiges of the classical setting appear early in the novel. For example, one could see the stone cherub in Ianthe's garden as a type of cupid, related to the classical marble statues, that foreshadows the romance to come for Ianthe. There is another Italian setting in the novel that is full of romantic possibilities. Pym, however, does not use it for romance. And, its appropriateness is lost on Rupert Stonebird, the anthropolo-

gist-observer. That setting is the Vatican library. Rupert goes to the Vatican library to "cool" his emotions (183), and he thinks he will be able to do "prim" and useful reading there. Ironically, if he reads long enough, Rupert's material may not be so prim. As Retha M. Warnicke points out in *The Rise and Fall of Anne Boleyn*, the papal archives house the tempestuous and often erotic love letters from Henry VIII to Anne Boleyn (76).

34. The following is the excerpted poem as quoted in Pym (6):

I had a dove, and the sweet dove died;
and what I have thought it died of grieving;
O, what could it grieve for? its feet were tied
With a single thread of my own hand's weaving

35. Note that Magdalen's name is the type of name a romance heroine might have. Her first name is associated with Mary Magdalene, and her last name, raven, with a Celtic goddess of war. But Pym undercuts the literary and romantic association by presenting her as short and dumpy. Perhaps Pym implies that this is what happens to heroines in "happily ever after" novels.

36. He probably would not agree with Barbara Cartland's preference of serving even the simplest foods in expensive china dishes, or with Barthes, who notes that women's magazines often suggest garnishing simple foods with elaborate sauces.

37. But sugar, or dessert itself, is a sign of being part of the privileged class. Irma S. Rombauer writes in *The Joy of Cooking* that desserts allow the hostess "to build a focal point for a buffet, produce a startling soufflé or confect an attractively garnished individual plate" (684). Moreover, examples of all kinds of elaborate desserts are shown in Christmas issues of magazines like *Good Housekeeping* and *Martha Stewart Living*. Thus, desserts are a chance to show one's creativity, to put a sophisticated finishing touch to meal that has already been civilized by cooking.

38. Jude Deveraux uses this technique in *Wishes* where her hero and heroine discuss baking biscuits.

39. Laura Ashley designs are viewed differently in the United States, however. The clothes are sold in speciality boutiques and are very expensive. Wearing Laura Ashley outfits is really a sign of affluence and prestige. For example, the 1994 Christmas catalog lists dresses priced at $198.00 for cotton velvet. The catalog describes a simple, button front floral dress made of cotton and wool as follows: "When elegant simplicity is called for choose this classic silhouette with gently curved waist and rounded neck" (5). Other dresses are described as having "European caché antiqued silver buttons" (5).

40. Pym herself wrote about Emma, "Once upon a time, there was an author called Austen who said of one of her heroines by the name of Emma that no one but herself would much like her. Look what happened to them both!" (Pym 165, fol.115, qtd. in Weld 197).

41. Pym is not the only author to give her heroes childish or unusual traits. Many romance authors make their heroes different from other men or vulnerable in some way. For example, Anne Rice's Ramses from *The Mummy* is an immortal man who suffers from loneliness. Heroes in Rice novels that contain elements of romance often have so-called feminine qualities or like to collect antique dolls and Christmas ornaments. Yet, Rice and other writers only paint their heroes this way to endear them to their female readers. They give them traits and interests that their female readers may want for themselves.

# Selected Bibliography

Abel, Elizabeth. *Virginia Woolf and the Fictions of Psychoanalysis*. Chicago: U of Chicago P, 1989.

Allen, Orphia Jane. *Barbara Pym: Writing A Life*. London: Scarecrow, 1994.

Amis, Kingsley. *Lucky Jim*. New York: Viking, 1958.

Atwood, Margaret. *The Edible Woman*. New York: Bantam, 1991.

Austen, Jane. *Northanger Abbey*. Philadephia: Porter and Coates, n.d.

——. *Pride and Prejudice*. Philadelphia: Porter and Coates, n.d.

Barthes, Roland. "Authors and Writers." *A Barthes Reader*. Ed. Susan Sontag. New York: Farrar, 1972. 185-93.

——. "Ornamental Cookery." *Mythologies*. Trans. Annette Lavers. New York: Hill and Wang, 1972. 78-80.

Bauer, George. "Eating Out with Barthes." *Literary Gastronomy*. Ed. David Bevan. Amsterdam: Editions Rodopi, 1988. 39-50.

Bayley, John. "Where Exactly Is the Pym World?" Salwak 50-57.

Beauvior, Simone de. *The Prime of Life*. Trans. Peter Green. 2nd ed. New York: Lancer, 1973.

Benet, Diana. *Something to Love: Barbara Pym's Novels*. Columbia: U of Missouri P, 1986.

Benson, E. F. *Make Way for Lucia*. Part 3. New York: Crowell, 1977.

Berriedale-Johnson, Michelle. *The Victorian Cook-Book*. Brooklyn: Interlink, 1989.

Betjeman, John. *The English Town in the Last Hundred Years*. Cambridge: Cambridge UP, 1956.

Bettleheim, Bruno. *The Uses of Enchantment*. New York: Vintage-Random House, 1975.

Binchy, Maeve. *Echoes*. New York: Dell, 1985.

Brontë, Charlotte. *Jane Eyre*. New York: Signet, 1960.

——. *Jane Eyre*. Ed. Richard J. Dunn. New York: Norton, 1971.

Brontë, Emily. *Wuthering Heights*. New York: Signet Classics, 1959.

Brookner, Anita. *The Debut*. New York: Linden, 1982.

Brothers, Barbara. "Women Victimized by Fiction: Living and Loving in the Novels of Barbara Pym." *Twentieth Century Women Novelists*. Ed. Thomas F. Staley. Totowa, NJ: Barnes & Noble, 1982. 61-80.

Burden, Dennis. *The Logical Epic*. Cambridge: Harvard UP, 1967.

Burkhart, Charles. *The Pleasures of Miss Pym*. Austin: Texas UP, 1987.

Butscher, Edward. *Sylvia Plath: Method and Madness.* New York: Pocket, 1976.

Byatt, A. S. "An Honorable Escape: Georgette Heyer." *Passions of the Mind.* New York: Turtle Bay, 1992. 233-40.

——. "Barbara Pym." *Passions of the Mind.* New York: Turtle Bay, 1992. 241-44.

Cameron, Stella. "Heroes of the '90s." *Romantic Times* May 1994: 12-13.

Cartland, Barbara. *The Flame Is Love.* New York: Bantam, 1975.

——. *The History of Barbara Cartland and How I Wish to Be Remembered.* Unpublished autobiographical manuscript, 1992.

——. *Look with the Heart.* New York: Jove Books-Berkley, 1994.

Cates, Kimberly. *The Raider's Bride.* New York: Pocket, 1994.

Chaucer, Geoffrey. "The Wife of Bath's Tale." *The Canterbury Tales.* Ed. F. N. Robinson. 2nd ed. Boston: Houghton Mifflin, 1957.

Chappel, Deborah K. *American Romances: Narratives of Culture and Identity.* Diss. Duke University. Ann Arbor: UMI, 1991. 9202485.

Chittenden, Margaret. "Writing the Romantic Novel You'd Like to Read." *The Writer's Handbook.* Boston: The Writer, 1990. 268-72.

Clair, Daphne. "Sweet Subversions." *Dangerous Men and Adventurous Women.* Ed. Jayne Ann Krentz. Philadelphia: U of Pennsylvania P, 1992. 61-72.

Clark, Mary Higgins. *Moonlight Becomes You.* New York: Pocket, 1997.

*Contemporary Authors, First Revision Series.* Vol. 5-8. Ed. Barbara Harte and Carolyn Riley. Detroit: Gale Research, 1969. 447-48.

Cooley, Mason. *The Comic Art of Barbara Pym.* New York: AMS, 1990.

Conrad, Peter. *The Everyman History of English Literature.* London: Dent, 1985.

Cornwell, Patricia. *The Body Farm.* New York: Berkley, 1995.

Cotsell, Michael. "Barbara Pym." *Modern Novelists.* New York: St. Martin's, 1989.

Davidson, Diane Mott. *Dying for Chocolate.* New York: Bantam, 1993.

De Sade, Marquis. "Reflections on the Novel." *120 Days of Sodom and Other Writings.* Comp. and trans. Austryn Wainhouse and Richard Seaver. New York: Grove Weidenfeld, 1966. 91-116.

Deveraux, Jude. *The Black Lyon.* New York: Avon, 1980.

——. *A Knight in Shining Armor.* New York: Pocket, 1989.

——. *Wishes.* New York: Pocket, 1989.

Donne, John. *Paradoxes and Problems.* Ed. Helen Peters. Oxford: Clarendon, 1980.

Eden, Dorothy. *The Voice of the Dolls and Listen to Danger.* Garden City: Doubleday, 1957.

Eliot, George. "Life and Opinions of Milton." *Essays of George Eliot.* Ed. Thomas Pinney. New York: Colombia UP, 1963.

——. "Silly Novels by Lady Novelists." Spender and Todd 518-34.

Fallon, Eileen. *Words of Love: A Complete Guide to Romance Fiction.* New York: Garland, 1984.

Fergus, Jan. "*A Glass of Blessings,* Jane Austen's *Emma,* and Barbara Pym's Art of Allusion." *Independent Women: The Function of Gender in the Novels of Barbara Pym.* Ed. Janice Rossen. Sussex: Harvester, 1988. 109-36.

Fiedler, Leslie. *Love and Death in the American Novel.* 1960. New York: Anchor, 1992.

Figes, Eva. *Patriarchal Attitudes.* New York: Stein and Day, 1970.

Finch, Jane. Personal Interview. 14 Mar. 1994.

Fleishman, Avrom. *The English Historical Novel; Walter Scott to Virginia Woolf.* Baltimore: Johns Hopkins P, 1971.

——. *Fiction and the Ways of Knowing: Essays on British Novels.* Austin: U of Texas P, 1978.

Fraser, Antonia. Letter to the Author. 21 Feb. 1994.

Frederick, John T. "Hawthorne's 'Scribbling Women.'" *New England Quarterly* 48 (June 1975): 231-40.

French, Marilyn. *Her Mother's Daughter.* New York: Ballantine, 1987.

Frenier, Mariam Darce. *Good-Bye Heathcliff: Changing Heroes, Heroines, Roles and Values in Women's Category Romances.* New York: Greenwood, 1988.

Friedan, Betty. *The Feminine Mystique.* New York: Dell, 1983.

Frye, Joanne S. *Living Stories, Telling Lives.* Ann Arbor: U of Michigan P, 1986.

Garland, Madge, et al., comp. *Fashion 1900-1939.* Idea Books International, 1975.

Gash, Jonathan. *The Grace in Older Women.* New York: Penguin, 1995.

Gellis, Roberta. *Alinor.* Chicago: Playboy, 1978.

Gilbert, Sandra, and Susan Gubar. *The Madwoman in the Attic.* New Haven: Yale UP, 1979.

Gilman, Charlotte Perkins. *The Yellow Wallpaper.* 1899. New York: Feminist Press, 1973.

Glaspell, Susan. "A Jury of Her Peers." *The Best Short Stories of 1917.* Ed. Edward J. O'Brien. Boston: Small, Maynard, 1918. 256-82.

Godden, Rumer. Letter to the Author. 25 June 1994.

Golon, Sergeanne. *Angelique in Barbary.* Trans. Monroe Stearns. New York: Bantam, 1963.

Gordon, Joan. "Cozy Heroines: Quotidian Bravery in Barbara Pym's Novels." *Essays in Literature* 16.2 (Fall 1989): 224-33.

Gorsky, Susan. "The Gentle Doubters." *Images of Women in Fiction.* Ed. Susan Koppelman Cornillon. Bowling Green, OH: Bowling Green State University Popular Press, 1972. 28-54.

Graham, Robert J. "Cumbered with Much Serving: Barbara Pym's Excellent Women." *Mosaic* 17 (Spring 1984): 141-60.

Greer, Germaine. *The Female Eunuch.* London: MacGibbon and Kee, 1970.

Gregory, Philippa. *Meridon.* New York: Pocket, 1990.

——. *Wide Acre.* New York: Pocket, 1987.

Groner, Marlene San Miguel. *The Novels of Barbara Pym.* Diss. St. John's U, 1988. Ann Arbor: UMI, 1988. 8900580.

Hall, Radclyffe. "Fräulein Schwartz." Spender and Todd 738-54.

Haine-Sergeant, Linn. *Heathcliff: The Return to Wuthering Heights.* New York: Pocket, 1992.

Hardwick, Mollie. *Come Away, Death.* New York: Fawcett-Crest, 1997.

Herter, Lori. Letter to the Author. 1 Mar. 1994.

——. *The Willow File.* New York: Silhouette, 1994.

Heys, Margaret. *Anne Boleyn.* New York: Beagle, 1967.

Hillier, Mary. Letter to the Author. 1 Mar. 1994.

Holt, Hazel. *A Lot to Ask: A Life of Barbara Pym.* New York: Penguin, 1990.

——. *Mrs. Mallory and the Festival Murder.* New York: Signet, 1993.

——. *Mrs. Mallory's Shortest Journey.* New York: Signet, 1995.

——. "The Novelist in the Field: 1946-74." Salwak 22-33.

——. Preface. *A Very Private Eye.* By Barbara Pym. Ed. Hazel Holt and Hilary Pym. New York: Dutton, 1984. xiii-xvi.

Holt, Victoria. *Daughter of Deceit.* New York: Fawcett-Crest, 1991.

Howell, Georgina. *In Vogue.* New York: Schocken, 1976.

Huxley, Aldous. *Crome Yellow.* New York: Carroll and Graf, 1990.

"Isn't It Romantic!" *48 Hours.* CBS Television. KFVS 12, Cape Girardeau, MO. 26 Oct. 1995.

Janowitz, Tama. *A Cannibal in Manhattan.* New York: Crown, 1987.

Jeffries, Sheila. *The Spinster and Her Enemies: Feminism and Sexuality 1880-1930.* Boston: Pandora, 1985.

Jensen, Margaret Ann. *Love's Sweet Return: The Harlequin Story.* Bowling Green, OH: Bowling Green State University Popular Press, 1984.

Jones, Anne Rosalind. *Mills and Boon Meets Feminism: The Progress of Romance.* Ed. Jean Radford. New York: Routledge, 1986.

Jong, Erica. *Fear of Flying.* New York: Signet, 1974.

Joyce, James. "The Dead." *Dubliners.* 1916. New York: Viking, 1967. 175-224.

——. "A Painful Case." *Dubliners.* 1916. New York: Viking, 1967. 107-17.

Juana Ines de la Cruz, Sor. "The Reply to Sor Philothea." *A Sor Juana Anthology.* Trans. Alan S. Trueblood. Cambridge: Harvard UP, 1988. 205-41.

Kaler, Anne K. *The Picara: From Hera to Fantasy.* Bowling Green, OH: Bowling Green State University Popular Press, 1991.

Keily, Robert. *The Romantic Novel in England.* Cambridge: Harvard UP, 1972.

Kingsley, Florence Morse. *The Transfiguration of Miss Philura.* New York: Funk, 1901.

Klein, Josephine. *Samples from English Cultures.* Vol. 1. London: Routledge, 1965.

Krahn, Bettina. "Kidnapped for Christmas." *A Victorian Christmas.* New York: Signet-NAL, 1992.

Krentz, Jayne Ann, ed. *Dangerous Men and Adventurous Women.* Philadelphia: U of Pennsylvania P, 1992.

——. Introduction. *Dangerous Men and Adventurous Women.* Ed. Jayne Ann Krentz. Philadelphia: U of Pennsylvania P, 1992. 1-10.

Lee, Carol. *The Blind Side of Eden: The Sexes in Perspective.* London: Bloomsbury, 1989.

Leonardi, Susan J. "Recipes for Reading: Summer Pasta, Lobster á là Riseholme and Key Lime Pie." *PMLA* 104 (May 1993): 340-47.

Lévi-Strauss, Claude. *The Raw and the Cooked.* Trans. Jahn and Doreen Weightman. New York: Harper, 1964.

Lewis, Jane. *Women in England: 1870-1950.* Bloomington: Indiana UP, 1984.

Liddell, Robert. *A Mind at Ease: Barbara Pym and Her Novels.* London: Owen, 1989.

——. "Two Friends: Barbara Pym and Ivy Compton-Burnett." *London Magazine* Aug./Sept. 1984: 59-69.

Rev. of *Like Water for Chocolate,* by Laura Esquivel. "Picks and Pans." *People* 16 Nov. 1992: 17.

Lively, Penelope. "The World of Barbara Pym." Salwak 45-49.

Long, Robert Emmett. *Barbara Pym.* New York: Ungar, 1986.

Lurie, Alison. *The Language of Clothes.* New York: Random, 1981.

MacLean, Jan. *White Fire.* New York: Harlequin, 1979.

Malek, Doreen Owens. "Mad, Bad, and Dangerous to Know: The Hero as Challenge." *Dangerous Men and Adventurous Women.* Ed. Jayne Ann Krentz. Philadelphia: U of Pennsylvania P, 1992. 73-80.

Marsden, Madonna. "Gentle Truths for Gentle Readers: The Fiction of Elizabeth Goudge." *Images of Women in Fiction.* Ed. Susan Koppelman Cornillon. Bowling Green, OH: Bowling Green State University Popular Press, 1972. 68-78.

McAllister, Anne. *The Eight Second Wedding.* New York: Harlequin, 1994.

McCullough, Colleen. *The Ladies of Missalonghi.* New York: Avon, 1987.

Michael, Prince of Greece. *Sultana.* Trans. Alexis Ullman. New York: Harper, 1983. 143-202.

Modleski, Tanya. *Loving with a Vengeance: Mass-Produced Fantasies for Women.* Hamden, CT: Archon, 1982.

Moore, Caroline. "Where Are the Trollies of Yesteryear?" *Spectator* 17 Nov. 1990: 45.

Mott, Frank L. *Golden Multitudes.* New York: N.p., 1957. 122.

Mussell, Kay J. "Beautiful and Damned: The Sexual Woman in Gothic Fiction." *Journal of Popular Culture* 9.1 (1975): 84-89.

Nardin, Jane. *Barbara Pym.* Boston: Twayne, 1985.

Nicholson, Mervyn. "Food and Power: Homer, Carroll, Atwood and Others." *Mosaic* 20.3 (1987): 37-55.

Nilsen, Alleen Pace. "Sexism in English: A Feminist View." *Female Studies VI: Closer to the Ground.* Ed. Nancy Hoffman, et al. Old Westbury, NY: Feminist P, 1972. 102-09.

Piercy, Marge. *Gone to Soldiers.* New York: Fawcett Crest-Ballantine, 1987.

Pilcher, Rosamunde. *September.* New York: St. Martin's, 1990.

Plath, Sylvia. *Johnny Panic and the Bible of Dreams.* New York: Harper, 1977.

Pym, Barbara. *An Academic Question.* New York: Signet Classic, 1987.

——. *Crampton Hodnet.* New York: New American Library, 1986.

——. *Excellent Women.* 1952. New York: Plume-Penguin, 1978.

——. *A Few Green Leaves.* New York: Dutton, 1989.

——. "Finding a Voice." *Civil to Strangers.* New York: Penguin, 1987. 381-88.

——. *A Glass of Blessings.* New York: Dutton, 1989.

——. "Home Front Novel." *Civil to Strangers.* New York: Penguin, 1987. 217-70.

——. *Jane and Prudence.* 1953. New York: Dutton, 1981.

——. *Less Than Angels.* New York: Dutton-Belisk, 1955.

——. *No Fond Return of Love.* 1961. New York: Dutton, 1982.

——. *Quartet in Autumn.* 1977. New York: Harper, 1980.

——. *Some Tame Gazelle.* 1950. New York: Dutton, 1978.

——. *The Sweet Dove Died.* New York: Harper, 1980.

——. *An Unsuitable Attachment.* 1982. New York: Dutton, 1982.

——. *A Very Private Eye.* New York: Vintage-Random, 1984.

Pym, Hilary, and Honor Wyatt. *The Barbara Pym Cookbook.* New York: Dutton, 1988.

Quick, Amanda. *Seduction.* New York: Bantam, 1990.

Radway, Janice A. *Reading the Romance.* Chapel Hill: U of North Carolina P, 1984.

Ramsdell, Kristin. *Happily Ever After: A Guide to Reading Interests in Romance Fiction.* Littleton, CO: Libraries Unlimited, 1987.

Rice, Anne. "The Master of Rampling Gate." *Vampire Stories.* Ed. Richard Dalby. Secaucus, NJ: Castle, 1993.

Robyns, Gwen. *Barbara Cartland.* Garden City: Doubleday, 1985.

Rombauer, Irma S., and Marion Rombauer Becker. *The Joy of Cooking.* New York: Bobbs-Merrill, 1951.

Rossen, Janice, ed. *Independent Women.* New York: St. Martin's, 1988.

——. "On Not Being Jane Eyre: The Romantic Heroine in Barbara Pym's Novels." *Independent Women.* Ed. Janice Rossen. New York: St. Martin's Press, 1988. 137-56.

Rossen, Janice. *The World of Barbara Pym.* New York: St. Martin's, 1987.

Rubinstein, Jill. "'For the Ovaltine Had Loosened her Tongue': Failures of Speech in Barbara Pym's *Less Than Angels.*" *Modern Fiction Studies* 32.4 (1986): 573-80.

Salwak, Dale, ed. *The Life and Work of Barbara Pym.* Iowa City: U of Iowa P, 1987.

Saxton, Ruth O. "Crepe Soles, Boots, and Fringed Shawls: Female Dress as Signals of Femininity." *Anne Tyler as Novelist.* Ed. Dale Salwak. Iowa City: U of Iowa P, 1994. 65-76.

Schofield, Mary Anne. "Well-Fed or Well-Loved?—Patterns of Cooking and Eating in the Novels of Barbara Pym." *University of Windsor Review* 18.2 (Spring/Summer 1985): 1-8.

Schor, Naomi. *Reading in Detail.* New York: Methuen, 1987.

Schulz, Muriel. "The Novelist as Anthropologist." Salwak 101-19.

Seton, Anya. *Katharine.* Boston: Houghton Mifflin, 1954.

Shakespeare, William. *The Taming of the Shrew. The Riverside Shakespeare.* Boston: Houghton Mifflin, 1974.

Shayne, Maggie. *Twilight Fantasies.* New York: Silhouette, 1993.

Small, Bertrice. *The Kadin.* New York: Hearst-Avon, 1978.

Smiley, Jane. "Jane Austen's Heroines, A Personal Perspective." *Victoria* May 1995: 28-29.

Smith, Robert. "How Pleasant to Know Miss Pym." *The Life and Work of Barbara Pym.* New York: Macmillan, 1987. 56-63.

Snow, Lotus. *One Little Room an Everywhere: Barbara Pym's Novels.* Orono, ME: Puckerbrush, 1987.

Spacks, Patricia Meyer. *The Female Imagination.* New York: Knopf, 1975.

Spender, Dale, and Janet Todd, eds. *British Women Writers.* New York: Bedrick, 1989.

Stevenson, Anne. *Bitter Fame.* Boston: Houghton Mifflin, 1989.

Strauss-Noll, Mary. "Love and Marriage in the Novels." Salwak 72-87.

Stuart, Anne. "Dangerous Men." *Romantic Times* Feb. 1994: 12-13.

——. "Legends of Seductive Elegance." *Dangerous Men and Adventurous Women.* Ed. Jayne Ann Krentz. Philadelphia: U of Pennsylvania P, 1992. 85-88.

Taylor, Elizabeth. *Angel.* New York: Viking, 1957.

——. *A Wreathe of Roses.* New York: Knopf, 1949.

Thurston, Carol. *The Romance Revolution.* Urbana: U of Illinois P, 1987.

Thurston, Carol, and Barbara Doscher. "Supermarket Erotica." *Progressive* Apr. 1982: 49-50.

Townsend, Annette. "Historical Overview." *Words of Love: A Complete Guide to Romance Fiction.* Ed. Eileen Fallon. New York: Garland, 1984. 3-23.

Tweedie, Jill. "The Experience." *In the Name of Love.* New York: Pantheon, 1979. 1-11.

Tyler, Anne. Rev. of *No Fond Return of Love. New York Times Book Review* 13 Feb. 1983: 1+.

Utter, Roger Palfrey, and Gwendolyn Bridges Needham. *Pamela's Daughters.* New York: Macmillan, 1936.

Visser, Margaret. *Much Depends on Dinner.* New York: Grove, 1986.

Ward, Mrs. Humphrey. *Eleanor.* New York: Harper, 1900.

——. "A Writer's Recollections." Spender and Todd 643-54.

Warnicke, Retha M. *The Rise and Fall of Anne Boleyn.* New York: Cambridge UP, 1989.

Weld, Annette. *Barbara Pym and the Novel of Manners.* New York: St. Martin's, 1992.

Weldon, Fay. "In the Great War." *Polaris and Other Stories.* Toronto: Hodder and Stoughton, 1985.

——. *The Life and Loves of a She-Devil.* New York: Pantheon, 1983.

Wells, Angela. *Golden Mistress.* Richmond, Surrey: Mills & Boon, 1993.

——. Letter to the Author. 5 Mar. 1994.

——. *Rash Contract.* New York: Harlequin, 1989.

West, Katharine. *Chapter of Governesses.* London: Cohen and West, 1949.

Woodiwiss, Kathleen. *Ashes in the Wind.* New York: Avon, 1979.

——. *The Flame and the Flower.* New York: Avon, 1972.

——. *A Rose in Winter.* New York: Avon, 1982.

——. *Shanna.* New York: Avon, 1977.

Wolfe, Elizabeth. *Boudicca.* New York: Ace, 1980.

Woolf, Virginia. "Modern Fiction." *The Common Reader.* New York: Harcourt, 1925.

——. *Orlando.* 1928. New York: Harvest-Harcourt, 1956.

——. *A Room of One's Own.* 1929. San Diego: Harvest-Harcourt, 1957.

Wyatt-Brown, Anne M. *Barbara Pym: A Critical Biography.* Columbia: U of Missouri P, 1992.

Yarbro, Chelsea Quinn. *Darker Jewels.* New York: Doherty, 1993.

Yoage, Charlotte M. "Strong-Minded Women." Spender and Todd 587-92.

# Index